Burdens of Proof

Life Writing Series

In the **Life Writing Series**, Wilfrid Laurier University Press publishes life writing and new life-writing criticism and theory in order to promote autobiographical accounts, diaries, letters, and testimonials written and/or told by women and men whose political, literary, or philosophical purposes are central to their lives. The Series features accounts written in English, or translated into English from French or the languages of the First Nations, or any of the languages of immigration to Canada.

From its inception, **Life Writing** has aimed to foreground the stories of those who may never have imagined themselves as writers or as people with lives worthy of being (re)told. Its readership has expanded to include scholars, youth, and avid general readers both in Canada and abroad. The Series hopes to continue its work as a leading publisher of life writing of all kinds, as an imprint that aims for both broad representation and scholarly excellence, and as a tool for both historical and autobiographical research.

As its mandate stipulates, the Series privileges those individuals and communities whose stories may not, under normal circumstances, find a welcoming home with a publisher. **Life Writing** also publishes original theoretical investigations about life writing, as long as they are not limited to one author or text.

Series Editor

Marlene Kadar
Humanities Division, York University

Manuscripts to be sent to

Lisa Quinn, Acquisitions Editor
Wilfrid Laurier University Press
75 University Avenue West
Waterloo, Ontario, N2L 3C5 Canada

Susanna Egan

Burdens of Proof

Faith, Doubt, and Identity in Autobiography

WILFRID LAURIER
UNIVERSITY PRESS

This book has been published with the help of a grant from the Canadian Federation for the Humanities and Social Sciences, through the Aid to Scholarly Publications Programme, using funds provided by the Social Sciences and Humanities Research Council of Canada. Wilfrid Laurier University Press acknowledges the financial support of the Government of Canada through the Canada Book Fund for our publishing activities.

Library and Archives Canada Cataloguing in Publication

Egan, Susanna, 1942–
　　Burdens of proof : faith, doubt, and identity in autobiography / Susanna Egan.

(Life writing series)
Includes bibliographical references and index.
Issued also in electronic formats.
ISBN 978-1-55458-331-1

　　1. Autobiography—Moral and ethical aspects.   2. Impostors and imposture.   3. Belief and doubt.
I. Title.   II. Series: Life writing series

CT25.E357 2011　　　　　　　　920.001　　　　　　　　C2011-902263-X

Electronic formats.
ISBN 978-1-55458-369-0 (PDF), ISBN 978-1-55458-350-8 (EPUB)

　　1. Autobiography—Moral and ethical aspects.   2. Impostors and imposture.   3. Belief and doubt.
I. Title.   II. Series: Life writing series (Online)

CT25.E357 2011a　　　　　　　　920.001　　　　　　　　C2011-902264-8

Cover design by David Drummond using image from Shutterstock. Text design by Blakeley Words+Pictures.

© 2011 Wilfrid Laurier University Press
Waterloo, Ontario, Canada
www.wlupress.wlu.ca

For Kieran, much tried, always true

Contents

Acknowledgements

Because this book is about varieties of literary fraud, I have been very keenly aware that the glamour of authorship is really a matter of borrowed plumes; readers of Chapter 5 will appreciate my need to make the following acknowledgements.

Since this small book has been a long time in the making, it has implicated many friends, students, and colleagues, who have been generous with their time, with materials, and with quite substantial criticism. Naming them here goes only a small way to acknowledging how much they have contributed to my thinking and, indeed, to the pleasure I have taken in this work.

Several research assistants over the years have found and combed through materials and responded to work in progress: Amanda Lewis produced a file that could be a book in its own right on the treatment of imposture in eighteenth-century England; Lin Khng led me through various legal rulings on individual identity; Simon Rolston was particularly helpful with documents on Grey Owl; Kate Stanley and Bettina Stumm worked on Holocaust materials. I count myself very fortunate indeed to have received so much significant help from these excellent young scholars.

Many colleagues have also been generous with suggestions and materials. Prime among these must be Courtney Booker, who emptied his history files onto my desktop and then read my second chapter, which could not have been written without his support. I am honoured that Joseph and Rebecca Hogan accepted an earlier version of this history chapter for the *a/b: Auto/biography Studies* festschrift for James Olney and John Eakin. Jack Lynch kindly enabled me to look at his fine book on deception and detection before it appeared in print. For help with work on "the Indian," I am grateful to Laura Beard, Leigh Dale, Carrie

Dawson, Margery Fee, Laura Moss, and Deanna Reder. With the final chapter on the Holocaust, I have received materials, criticism, and support from Robert Krell, Roberta Kremer, and Nina Krieger at the Vancouver Holocaust Education Centre, as well as from Jack Kuper in Toronto and Sharon Meen and Richard Menkis at the University of British Columbia. Elim Wong at the Law Library at UBC was most helpful with the unfolding legal history of Nega Mezlekia.

I have also been fortunate to speak about this work in progress at numerous conferences and to benefit from discussion and feedback. For these opportunities, I want to thank Rocio Davis at the University of Pamplona, Richard Freadman at LaTrobe University, Julia Galbus, who organized a panel on imposture at the Midwest MLA, Alfred Hornung at the University of Mainz, Craig Howes at the University of Hawaii, and Penny van Toorn at the University of Sydney.

I am afraid that more people have read this work-in-progress than will read the finished product. Most dear to me among these (and producers, also, of important leads) are Catherine Egan, David Egan, Kieran Egan, and Michael Egan. Many friends and colleagues have read some or all of this work or responded to my presentations, and many have alerted me to materials I needed to read or sent me links or cuttings: Carmen Birkle, Marlene Briggs, Miranda Burgess, Manuela Costantino, John Eakin, Carole Gerson, Janet Giltrow, Sherrill Grace, Geoff Hamilton, Margaretta Jolly, Marlene Kadar, Eva-Marie Kröller, Travis Mason, Laurie McNeill, Ann Pearson, Julie Rak, Tara Reyes, Duffy Roberts, Susan Tridgell, Mark Vessey, and Julia Watson (who also gave me the boot I needed to move into print).

I have been most fortunate in a series of research grants from the Social Sciences and Humanities Research Council of Canada that have facilitated travel and research. At Wilfrid Laurier University Press, mysterious (because anonymous) readers have made very useful suggestions. Lisa Quinn and Rob Kohlmeier have encouraged my efforts and improved my work, as has Matthew Kudelka.

For all these best efforts by so many people, a big thank you.

Doubting Thomas
The Implications of Imposture in Autobiography

Secrets, Lies, and Exposure

On 4 October 1943, Heinrich Himmler told senior SS officers assembled at Poznan that the extermination of the Jews was a proud secret, a page of German history that would never be written. They would leave no evidence, no archive. However, the speech itself served as an archive and as evidence of what it sought to hide when the judges at Nuremberg listened to the recording of it just a couple of years later. While this irony pertains to one of the major atrocities of the twentieth century, it pertains also to many aspects of autobiographical imposture: language, text, and archive both create and expose the secret lie. Just as Himmler's secret became proof of that which his regime had wanted to hide, so the impostor's story becomes proof of what it was intended to hide and serves as evidence against him. However, if secrets are vulnerable to exposure, we can find a further irony in the very danger that secrets pose to truth. When survivors of the concentration camps began to tell their stories, they were met with incredulity and revulsion; for them, the final blow—for themselves and for history—was that at some profound level, Himmler's secret remained a secret still. Today, many thousands of survivor stories exist in print and in archives around the world, bearing the burden of proof; yet the secret—that which we simply cannot know, and long to know— becomes the force behind autobiographical imposture. "I'll tell you," impostors seem to say. "I was there. I carry the scars deep in my soul." So the Swiss gentile Bruno Dösseker digs deep into his psyche (and into Holocaust archives) to create the lost child, Binjamin Wilkomirski, a Latvian Jew who somehow survived infancy in the camps and needs now to identify his parents. Or, quite recently, Monique

De Wael recreates herself as Misha Defonseca, who—she claims—walked across Europe as a small girl looking for her parents whom the Nazis had taken away. Jerzy Kosinski, who really did survive the Holocaust as a Jewish boy hiding with his family in a Polish village under an assumed identity, built fame and fortune by claiming he had survived on his own and on the run. Similarly, Herman Rosenblat's love story (*Angel at the Fence*) introduces rather implausible romantic fiction into his account of concentration camp experience. Because the apparent proof of extreme suffering in each case is in fact a lie at risk of exposure, it becomes a new secret and new kinds of proof are required to expose it or bring it to court. Court is where many of these cases end up, which is why I am using the term "burdens of proof"; but even when courts of law are not the issue, the courts of investigative journalism and public opinion invariably engage the issues and arrive at a judgment.

Imposture is not always so weighty a matter. It can even be fun—as, for example, with David Solway's creation of a mysterious Greek poet, Andreas Karavis. Or speculative, as with the autobiographical poetry of the presumed Hiroshima survivor, Araki Yasusada. Or benign, as I hope to show in the case of Grey Owl in Canada. It can draw ruthlessly on moral and political differences, as in Norma Khouri's fake memoir about the honour killing of her best friend in Jordan. Scandalous situations close to home provide vivid material, as when J.T. Leroy (a.k.a. Laura Albert) tells the story of "his" life as the abused and HIV-infected son of a truck-stop prostitute, or when Tim Barrus sets up shop as Nasdijj, an American Indian suffering from abuse. Sexuality, ethnicity, and abuse involve their own secrets, their own taboos, and therefore arouse keen interest, making fair game for the impostor with a finger on the pulse of public concerns. Exposure of imposture then runs the gamut from moral outrage to amusement, from court cases and media scandals to yesterday's news. Common to most stories of imposture are their implausibility (which may give rise to doubt) and the suffering they describe (that readers dare not doubt). They trade on experience that is normally inaccessible to their readers, piquing the attention of the voyeur. They are always to some degree sensational, and they have all been believed.

However, even when I trace the moral impact of imposture along a continuum from dangerous to harmless, specific effect is not the only question. Autobiography, whether truthful or false, does not stand alone any more than people do. It is never about only one person; it involves others, if only as minor characters. Nor does it float in space; rather, it is grounded in time and place and therefore embedded in a particular culture and history. Every imposture raises the question of what a community (of readers, for instance) believes about these people and their stories. In what do we have faith? What do we doubt? How does an imposture expose the values of the culture in which it has emerged? False representation, which we believe because it has gone to the jugular of our concerns, is also deeply disturbing because we cannot, on consideration, support it. The issue (as with extreme drug abuse in James Frey's *A Million Little Pieces*) resonates intensely, so that the false story is shocking and persuasive and escapes immediate detection as false; but exposure of the lie also causes outrage even as our own gullibility implicates us in the fraud. Could Norma Khouri have got away with *Honor Lost* if Western readers had not believed that Muslim women needed rescuing?

Because autobiography is pre-eminently a truth-telling genre (as distinct from fiction), we believe we have been told the truth. If the truth is really rather unimportant, we will not care too much; but if "the truth" takes the form of insider knowledge (as in memories of childhood in concentration camps) or a powerful secret (as in honour killing), we may care very much indeed. In fact, the impostor, like the magician, seems to be very good at knowing what people will believe and, like the comedian, very good at knowing what people will care about. I am interested in both—impostors (who know how to fool us) and the cultural climate that believes in and cares about their stories. I suspect we deserve each other. Furthermore, I suspect we can learn a lot about ourselves as readers (immersed in our culture) from the nature of the impostures that engage and then outrage us. It's a matter of truth and consequences. Why, then, does imposture matter in autobiography? Quite simply, it promises to tell the truth and then fails to do so, but it exposes the culture in which it thrives.

This book is about imposture in autobiography, which I define as a serious disconnect between the author as a person alive in the world, pre-text, before any story emerges, and the written life, what I am calling the textual identity. Imposture, in other words, is not fiction and is not even the fictionalizing of stories based on truth. Nor is it small lies such as creep into every personal story because the story sounds better that way. Nor is it lapses or distortions of memory, with which honest autobiographies are replete. Imposture is distinct from all of these because it is a pretense; impostors are frauds, fakes, plagiarists, and phonies. They claim lives they have not lived, experiences they have not had, and identities that belong to other people. They do so for many reasons and often with significant success, often, but not always, causing real damage in the real world. However, though some of the cases I examine anger me, my project is not simply a moral one; rather, it sets out to explore histories of faith and of doubt. What do we believe, and why? (Why, for instance, do we believe that regular autobiography tells the truth, or any kind of truth?) What leads us to doubt, and how do we excavate the truth that is eluding us? The impostor is like the Wizard of Oz, just a little person creating big effects from a secret hiding place. Part of my pleasure with this work has been flinging back the curtain with a triumphant "aha!" but part has also been working with the knowledge that all autobiography surely performs aspects of identity—which I understand as those partial, temporary, certainly elusive elements of self as one is perceived or as one feels oneself to be. How is imposture so different? Does it adopt the wrong posture? Does it hide the unacceptable secret?

I have always had a soft spot for Doubting Thomas. He was a faithful disciple through difficult times, prepared to die with Jesus if need be (John 11:16), but he found stories of Jesus' resurrection just over the top. His faith could not go that far: he needed proof. For Thomas, proof meant a physical body and physical wounds (John 20:24–29). Though all the gospels list Thomas as among the twelve, only John's—by far and away the least literal—develops this story of Thomas's doubt. For me, this doubt would have less impact if it appeared among the more grounded biographical narratives of Matthew, Mark, or Luke. (Indeed, who remembers Matthew's throwaway line at 28:17 that some disciples were doubtful?) The full story of Thomas's doubt appears only in John's gospel; and appears, furthermore, at a point when we as readers have given ourselves over to the impact of a story that does not depend on fact for its power. Thomas's call for factual proof is a shock. He doubts at the very point where everyone else is carried away with excitement. Their story is thrilling and astonishing (Jesus has risen from the dead), but Thomas hesitates and asks for proof. So Doubting Thomas is the patron saint of my present work because his story goes to the heart of my concerns: How and why do astonishing stories arise, and with what effects? How, and why, and with what effects, are they called into question?

Like history and biography, autobiography claims to be based on facts and to tell true stories that we may safely and reasonably believe to be neither false nor willfully invented. The information provided is often verifiable. Documents exist. Witnesses were present. This or that piece of information supports or is supported by information available from other sources. Truth is not stable or absolute, of course, because, as in a court of law, witnesses notice and remember the same events quite differently. However, as in a court of law, people promise to tell the truth as they know it, so autobiographers enter what Philippe Lejeune has famously called *le pacte autobiographique* between writer and reader, establishing that the reader may safely believe what the writer chooses to tell. Where, then, does doubt enter the equation? In metaphorical terms, I might say that Thomas was a twin and that doubt and faith are two sides of the same coin—a coin that may be quickly and easily flipped. In more practical terms, I note a plethora of false autobiographies in recent years. Some have generated national and international scandal and concern. All the ones that I know about have certainly received extensive press coverage. Clare Hitchens of Publicity and Marketing at Wilfrid Laurier University Press writes that "many of the book trade blogs have noted the latest fake memoir scandal, and more than one has posited that memoir should just be considered fiction." (She invites responses from scholars of autobiography.) So one might say that the coin has been flipped—or even, as Hitchens's e-mail suggests, that it is a false coin with no simply true face to be found.[1]

Furthermore, I have wondered whether the astonishing amount of recent imposture has been a freak storm or whether a longer perspective might not support my notion that truth telling and truth faking share a complex history. My exploration involves narrative, for sure, and to some degree also the history of text or of the book. It involves religious faith (Thomas, after all, both doubted and believed). Repeatedly it involves the law, because questions of doubt and of faith are frequently examined and sometimes resolved in law—often, however, with no absolute conviction for either side. Furthermore, law is one of the traditional bastions of social order, and its support or condemnation of particular people and particular stories goes a long way toward defining what sorts of stories may be written or received at any given time. My exploration involves people who have re-created themselves, assuming false identities whose effects are not just individual or ephemeral but also at times communal or national. In short, though false autobiography may provide an unlikely approach to true autobiography, I do not believe we should simply throw in the towel and say that autobiography is necessarily all fiction. Rather, I propose to look at matters of faith and matters of doubt for how they are constructed in various situations, what they consist of, and how they may affect each other. Finally, because these are in the end moral issues in that they do involve human choices that have social effects, I want to ask why these things matter, because I think they do.

Inevitably, when I ask why we have experienced all of these recent impostures, or how autobiography has been credible and (for the most part) has remained so despite recent impostures, the nature of textuality comes into play, with its own raft of dishonest possibilities such as false identity, false claims, false attribution of authorship, and plagiarism. Autobiographical imposture is different, after all, from bank fraud or identity theft, not only in its more amorphous consequences but also because it depends on written narrative. The very fact that it manifests as text raises questions about the (rather fraught) relations between life and language. Can a text refer precisely to an author outside the text, or does the language of the text produce the autobiographer, who as a living person has in effect been replaced by the text? Paul de Man, Philippe Lejeune, Paul John Eakin, and Sidonie Smith, among others, have worked with these questions in autobiography studies for quite some time. My brief review of some autobiography theory at the end of this chapter suggests that Doubting Thomas has been furrowing his brow from the beginning, long before we began raising questions of deliberate imposture.

My Plan for This Book

As for deliberate imposture, I have wondered what it is and, above all, why it raises so much dust. Again, unlike bank fraud or identity theft, where the gains are clear and may seem worth the risks, autobiographical imposture surely arouses much ado about relatively little. However, that little may not be so little at all if one asks a slightly different question: Just how does the text belong to or represent its writer? And that, I find, is a question with a long and troubling history. Compared with the deceptions that authors (and authorities) have practised over the centuries in textual representations that have carried serious and far-reaching burdens—such as the religious tenets of Christendom or the political power of kings and governments—autobiography is merely the survivor with contemporary heft. Historically, the problem is more extensive than autobiography and more fraught in its consequences. In Chapter 2, therefore, I ask how Western civilization (nothing timid about my questions) has produced and received writer and text in relation to each other. Who has produced texts that other people have believed in? Biblical exegesis by some of the early Church Fathers, for instance, suggests not only the political power that determined orthodoxy and heresy but also extensive association between the sacred and the "true." Faith, doubt, and political power determined the pros and cons of textual identity as well as the responsibility of its author or distributor. I also examine the evolution of doubt about textual veracity, tracing the detective work that served political masters in the old days and that depends today on investigative journalism.

While these forays into early European history may add gravitas to a contemporary phenomenon, they serve more significantly to suggest some of the emotional resonance that accompanies discovery of autobiographical imposture today. Briefly considering the proliferation of personal imposture in eighteenth-century England then enables me to consider some of the more immediate history of our contemporary experience: the inescapable kinship of fiction and autobiography; the role of print and publishing practices; and the nimble dances of deception that prefigure, in effect at least, our current experiences of text in cyberspace. Just as textual identity cannot be divorced from patterns of faith, political power, or market forces, so repeatedly, textual identity both creates and reflects the social and material culture in which it appears.

From this historical foundation, I move on to examine texts in relation to individual identity at a number of distinct and specific sites. Chapter 3 highlights the role of the media with its eagerness to support if not actually produce some of the sensational impostures of the past few years. While I do not want to suggest that the media today stand in the shoes of the Catholic Church in early Christendom, the parallel for readers is a curious one; how, if not through the media, does the reading public know what it knows or what it believes? Following in Gillian Whitlock's footsteps, I look at the marketing of the Muslim woman in the West following the American-led invasion of Iraq and the ongoing war in Afghanistan. These representations of Muslim women for Western readers rest on cultural norms informed by evangelical Christianity, Western practices of democracy, and Western capitalist enterprise. James Frey's *A Million Little Pieces* provides a completely different set of conditions but many of the same qualities of shock and opportunism. Frey's story is inescapably American—the bad boy becoming a good boy apparently by sheer strength of character. However, like Muslim women, Frey also makes for good copy by virtue of his supposed suffering and his redemption into Western ideologies. I call these identities sensational because the media create and then celebrate the circumstances that make them so. Whereras faith and doubt used to be matters of life and death, reflecting a culture immersed in the value and power of orthodoxy, they become in contemporary experience no more than opportunistic bids for celebrity. Insofar as imposture reflects its ambient culture, we may well find ours embarrassing.

Ethnic imposture, on the other hand, raises complex questions about postcolonial or settler cultures—about the shifting advantages of ethnicities in relation to one another, from the dominance of the imperial "white" to the resurgence of suppressed or marginalized peoples, and the jockeying for position among them. Ethnic imposture also highlights the physical presence and appearance (or carefully hidden absence) of the author, who must somehow look the part. No autobiographer can exist as "Anon," that prolific writer of so much fiction and poetry, because the reader of autobiography always believes in a person behind the text. For the ethnic impostor, then, personal performance can become a significant support for the textual "life." In my fourth chapter, I explore the Canadian example of "Grey Owl," whom we might call "the one that got away," both because his performance seems to have been persuasive and because his exposure as an impostor did nothing to alter the trajectory of his success. In fact, unlike his peers in the United States or in Australia, for example, Grey Owl contributed significantly to the story of his country and therefore to its national identity. Though his case is relatively benign, without extensive ethical implications, it certainly highlights the practical distinctions between personal story and fiction. In this case, too, autobiographical imposture belongs in and reflects the culture that gives it birth; it also affects what readers believe or doubt—not only about the impostor but also about themselves.

Regardless of particular focus in time or place, and regardless of the occasional physical appearance of the author, this project raises questions about "textual identity," or the autobiographer as a character in a book who claims to have this same personal identity outside the book. Chapter 5 explores false identity syndrome in literature, with particular attention to contemporary autobiographies in which the author, by one means or another, hides behind the text. Whereas the value of most personal narratives depends to a significant degree on the life of the man or woman outside the text (who would care to read Hitler's diaries if Hitler had not lived the life he did?), these works—which certainly refer to particular people—are the work of other people to whom they do not refer. In other words, textual identity emerges from some form of identity theft. Plagiarism is important here, and so is ghostwriting; both have ancient precedents (as I show in Chapter 2), which raises in turn what are very contemporary questions that situate identity predominantly, or inescapably, in text. So the mysterious Greek poet "Andreas Karavis," exists exclusively in text. More problematically, "Araki Yasusada," who also exists only in text, may (or may not) be a *jeu d'esprit* of the American Kent Johnson but escapes Detective Plod by taking off from text to hypertext, with all that that implies about elusive origins.

Finally, noticing less theoretical and more profoundly ethical implications, I turn in Chapter 6 to ways in which various texts effectively unravel both the personal and the ethnic identities of living people. I consider the comparative failures of history, law, and problematic autobiography to create a text for the identities of European Jews during the Second World War. When human life was threatened on so massive a scale, these various narratives, sanctioned by their various authorities, failed to protect or retrieve individual (or ethnic) identity; they also created the instability for Jewish identity as well as doubt about Jewish wartime experience that enabled impostors to step in. In short, the central question in this chapter pertains to the textual erasure of the Jews of Europe and the refashioning of their experiences in fraudulent texts. I turn, therefore, to Holocaust autobiography, with particular focus on imposture as an outcrop of extreme identity crisis; the frame of the story already exists, waiting for a warm body to inhabit it. The obvious danger posed by such imposture is the comfort it offers to Holocaust deniers.

Faith, Doubt, and Identity

Few of these issues involve mere truth or falsehood. The opportunist may begin from some honest or honourable starting place. The joke may get out of hand. The impostor may so need the story as to come to believe it. Readers and the media may ensure that the situation becomes inescapable. The autobiography may proceed according to acceptable methodologies only to flounder in personal animosities. Textual identity may not be seriously intended to represent personal identity. Nonetheless, several key components of autobiographical imposture recur throughout the discussions that follow. These have to do with particular times and places being so ripe for specific impostures that they seem all but inevitable. Or the story is sensational, and that sensation awakens the voyeur, blunting critical reception. Or the story is profitable and therefore irresistible. Nor does the impostor operate alone; invariably, agents and editors, publishers and reviewers, booksellers, prize adjudicators, reporters, and common readers are complicit in imposture—not merely in producing it but also in authorizing it. In short, it takes a village to raise one.

Repeatedly, factual information is a problem; investigation proves errors of fact, and lawsuits work on matters of fact pertaining both to information and to legal, ethnic, or cultural identity. (I must enter a caveat here: In the process of extensive research assistance for this book, Lin Khng took me to task for my easy assumptions about such terms as "verifiable fact" and "empirical evidence." She pointed me to Chaim Perelman's work and, most usefully, asked me to imagine even objective truth not as an item to be discovered but as an idea to be debated and, in some sense, constructed by a community, because even in scientific communities, factual truths are created and re-created all the time. Facts, she suggests, are "only ideas to which people give their greatest assent." I shall therefore be using the terms "fact" and "evidence" throughout this work as pertaining, in general parlance, to information that supports or contravenes the claims of various impostors, but with a keen awareness that my narrative, like theirs, is an act of persuasion.) In many cases, when publishers pull the fraudulent memoir in order to insert a notice or to remarket the work as fiction, they are dealing only with lawsuits or threats of lawsuits. However, like mud flung during a political skirmish, the charge of imposture sticks and affects understanding of the book. Furthermore, questions about who doubts, who investigates, and why and how they do so form a significant part of every story. After all, without detection, imposture continues to pass; to exist in its own right, it actually depends on being discovered. For autobiography, which creates its subject within the text, imposture has also raised the curious problem that verification of authenticity depends on information outside the text. For better or for worse, textual identity does not matter because it is fiction but because it depends on the men and women living in the world who create it. Facts include both information and the people who generate them.

Writing about the offence of imposture in Holocaust autobiography, Daniel Mendelsohn refers to the twenty-first century as "an era obsessed with 'identity'" and suggests: "It's useful to remember that identity is precisely that quality in a person, or group, that cannot be appropriated by others" (*New York Times*, 9 March 2008). He is right, of course. Identity has to do with sameness, or the quality of being identical, or the perfect match between claim and reality or (perhaps) between the self now and the self in other times and places. *Idem*, or "the same" (once used in footnotes to mark a previous reference), is also related to *identitem*, meaning "repeatedly," suggesting the identifiable recurrence of sameness of the person or thing, the id of identity. Writing not about Holocaust experience but about autobiography in general, Lejeune has been equally forceful: "An identity is, or is not. It is impossible to speak of degrees, and all doubt leads to a negative conclusion" (5). But that's to reckon without the opacity or the constructive power of text, which operates in many genres to serve particular social situations, and which therefore depends as much on the reader as on the writer. Textual identity is either a matter of faith (because facts and textual narration work together or because readers, deeply embedded in their culture, know how to understand this kind of text) or of doubt (because facts and narration do not match or because at least some readers recognize an appropriation of lived identity). What many impostures achieve by their very mis-taking of "identity" is renewed clarification of what particular identities mean in the world around them, what their value is, how they are read, whether they are individual or communal or national. This clarity about meaning or value has ethical implications in that it teaches us about ourselves as readers and about our world. It has always been implicit in autobiography, the personal story meeting particular needs in a public market; but autobiographical imposture creates a new situation in which what is normally relatively passive reception becomes active engagement, turning the common reader into critic of text, identity, and cultural environment.

Faith, Doubt, and Autobiography

In tandem with changing notions of what constituted an author (the problem I address in my historical survey) and what counted as secure knowledge, secular autobiography and fiction (often both scandalous and indistinguishable from each other) became increasingly popular throughout the eighteenth century, giving rise to extensive study by twentieth-century autobiography theorists. However, the problems are more extensive than autobiography and are more fraught in their consequences. Elizabeth Bruss may have been the first, some forty years ago, to argue that the "being" of autobiography is not inherent in autobiography but is shaped by external forces. So Jean-Jacques Rousseau was a man of his time and place when he celebrated his uniquely subjective life in his *Confessions* (1782). Benjamin Franklin established the self-made man in America. Slave narratives, which served the political cause of abolition, depended both on the mediation of white editors and on their own specific claims to authenticity. Frederick Douglass (the black Benjamin Franklin) needed to assert the truth of his story and the fact that he had written it himself. I return in Chapter 4 to Olaudah Equiano (1745–1797), whose journey from Africa through slavery to freedom became canonical for African American Studies. By the end of this astonishing century, of course, experience of the French and the American Revolutions had led to Thomas Paine's *Rights of Man* (1791) and indeed to Mary Wollstonecraft's *Vindication of the Rights of Woman* (1792). Whereas spiritual autobiography, grounded in religious faith, has a long history (I consider the doubts it raises in Chapter 2), this secular self, addressing a wide readership and developing languages of subjectivity, human rights, gender, and race in a literature both personal and political, was a new phenomenon in the eighteenth century and has, accordingly, received attention in a number of fields.[2]

I consider in Chapter 2 how these new opportunities for personal narrative created opportunities for narrative imposture. I turn now to questions of faith and doubt as these have been expressed in autobiography studies. Going to the heart of the matter, Bettina Stumm writes in the course of her work for me on the philosophical underpinnings of autobiography studies: "I wonder if questions of authenticity, identity, and fraud are all rooted in the way the self is conceived? ... What makes a fraud of self but our understanding of selfhood and truth? ... I'm just thinking how central a definition of self will be to your analysis."[3] Jack Lynch has demonstrated just how problematic such definition was for the autobiographer of the eighteenth century, how uncertain the self might be in its nature, qualities, or manifestations. Bettina's questions also pertain very justly to the distinctions that come into play for assessing the authorship or integrity of any text, when for instance dwarves standing quite acceptably on the shoulders of giants become simple plagiarists; or, on the other hand, when claims to personal experience or self-knowledge serve also as claims to incontrovertible truths. Connecting "the self" through both fiction and autobiography in the eighteenth century, Patricia Meyer Spacks notes the role that memory plays, overriding philosophical doubt about "the self" and providing an area of continuity and therefore confidence for the autobiographer. Dealing as it does with fictions (Spacks 4), autobiography is nonetheless rhetorically distinct from fiction in its imagination of a self. For James Treadwell, the emergence of autobiographical confidence has produced "a sense of genre" (ix), which has dogged believers and doubters alike ever since.

After the historicizing that I find crucial to situating particular conditions for imposture, it is here, in the genres of self, that the study of autobiography, and therefore of autobiographical imposture, begins. Here, furthermore, in autobiographical texts and in the theorizing that follows from them, I note pervasive and keen anxiety. Invariably, the autobiographer worries about self-examination, exoneration, glorification, and exposure. How naked is this self? Laura Marcus describes the truth about the self as conventionally imaged through the body, especially as clothed or naked, private or public, decent or indecent, and refers to W.A. Gill's very early foray in this field in an article titled "The Nude in Autobiography" in *The Atlantic Monthly* in 1907. More recently, identity politics has located the self firmly in the body as the site at which specific difference authenticates differing needs and stories. For the impostor, this embodied self is called into performance as proof for the storied self, or must be concealed because it cannot provide such proof (as when a man writes as a woman or a white as an Aboriginal). Surely attention to the embodied self (often enough in conflict with some anterior sense of a more authentic self) gives rise to illness narratives or revelations of sexual abuse. The "victim self" is another subject but also supports my sense that genres of the self are fraught with anxiety.

This same anxiety drives theorists of autobiography. Why else, so many decades after Gill's article, or Anna Robeson Burr's monograph in 1909, did autobiography studies emerge slowly (with Georges Gusdorf in 1956, Roy Pascal in 1960, Philippe Lejeune from 1971, James Olney in 1972, and Elizabeth Bruss in 1976) to become rather suddenly an intense area of study—and an intense area of production by the 1990s? One clear answer comes from the various developments in theory that undermined and overruled the humanist self, complicating autobiography practice and theory and challenging us to rethink narratives of the self. Another, surely, has been accelerating developments in technology that have realized Walter Benjamin's anxiety about mass production, led to Baudrillard's articulation of "simulacra" and the "hyperreal," and called both the individuality and the very human selfness of self into question (as in the case, for instance, of cyborgs or clones). Early work in autobiography studies had been content to classify the text with straightforward reference to the life outside the text (that of the butcher, baker, or candlestick maker) or to read autobiography as a flowering of the great humanist tradition in which the value of the self was consistent and assured. Such categories might have provided a comfortable place to rest but would not have given rise to much posture or imposture. (Who wants to be a candlestick maker? Why would being a candlestick maker matter?) Recognizing the potential of autobiography to spread like a fungus, affecting all works of literature (as emanating from the self), Lejeune and Bruss, along with others who sought loose classification and categories, suggested boundaries for autobiography, describing what it looked like and how it worked.[4] Even so, the genres of autobiography have refused to stay still because they serve particular social situations and evolve with the cultures that produce them (see Marcus, Chapter 6). We see them as unstable through the eighteenth century and then again, to an astonishing degree, in the twentieth; in 1994, Leigh Gilmore titled her introduction to *Autobiographics* "A Map for Getting Lost." Relatively recent and rapid generic developments travel from the never to be repeated prose of Rousseau to the "rumpled bed" that Sidonie Smith and Julia Watson examine, to work on photographs, film, comics, reality TV, blogs, death notices, and the merest traces. Given that none of these possibilities displaces any of the others, but that each identifies new locations and expressions for whoever the self may be, the multiple genres of self create excitement but cannot allay anxiety. Who, after all, do we think we are?

Prefiguring some of this sea change, in "Autobiography and the Cultural Moment," James Olney was concerned with the consciousness of self and self-knowledge. For him, the "I" in autobiography, situated in history as well as in literature, half discovers and half creates itself in writing. Working as he does on memory and metaphor, Olney wonders whether autobiography does not also half discover and half create "a deeper design and truth than adherence to historical and factual truth could ever make claim to" (11). Though Olney's work belongs in the humanist tradition, he indicates here some of the central issues of the theory wars that have followed. Not least, he recognizes the demographic shift that was taking place in autobiography toward the end of the twentieth century, suggesting that autobiography may reveal the experience and vision of very different peoples, thereby informing "all the literature of that people" (13). He points, in other words, to identity politics and the value of autobiographical genres for identity politics. Here, as with the traumatized or suffering victim who has taken such a prominent place in the recent literature, we find not only serious personal and community concerns but also opportunities tailor-made for the impostor. From the margins of societies that have been dominant come stories that destabilize hierarchies of class and race, demoting those in particular who have controlled the story so far.

Finally, but not least, I think of the power surge in autobiographical practice and theory of the past forty years as a phenomenon of post-faith cultures. Just as Psalmanazar was able to manipulate anti-Catholic sentiment in eighteenth-century England, so I note the intensity of imposture when religion is an issue. Religion defines both self and community. Like race and ethnicity, religion creates its own comprehensible boundaries between self and other. To claim religious faith is to have access to all these privileges of self-definition. Socially if not always spiritually, people of faith do in fact know who they are. However, in a post-religious age, when so many lack profound or agreed-upon religious paradigms, the self is up for grabs, open to doubt, available for reconstruction. I have tended to assume that imposture would not be possible in spiritual autobiography, but Bettina suggests that such rewards as canonization could make imposture tempting, and my friend Ann Pearson, responding to an early draft of this chapter, wondered whether we might not find "a Tartuffe of spiritual autobiography deserving exposure." Nonetheless, I confine myself here merely to observing some of the social conditions for imposture in general when agnosticism pertains not only to the divine but also to the sources of self.

If we can only roughly and inadequately determine what genres of the self actually are at any given point, and how or why they may be useful, and if they may escape the precinct of the canon we try to establish by virtue of their relevance to different kinds of people and their evident appeal to readers, theorists have good reasons to be anxious. Where feminism threw open the doors of autobiography to whole new constructions,[5] deconstruction demobbed the self outside the text. Just as minority voices discovered their forum in autobiography, that forum was devalued in terms of its reference to real-life experience. So we have been asking for decades now whether the self can be originary to writing (as in "I have a story to tell" or "we need to hear his story, or hers, or theirs"), with the origin mattering for the attention that the story deserves regardless of its intrinsic merits as story; or whether the self is written into existence, the text effectively displacing the originating life. Is the self ontological or textual? Or how can it be both?

Philosophical questions about what constitutes a self are complicated by these distinct forms that a self might take. So I note the moral responsibilities of the physical, social, and legal self that is supported by such accessible proofs as a birth certificate, voter registration, social Insurance number, passport, and so on. The behaviour of this self affects other selves at work and play in a civil society. Nonetheless, the (significantly) recognizable self of the text may lack these anchors to the world outside the text and may be recognizable simply by virtue of existing within the recognizable tropes of recognizable genres of self. In short, the textual self may not have authenticating life support. Ironically, regardless of all of these complications, one distinctive problem for autobiography in all its many forms is the common tendency for both writer and reader to conflate the text with the life. Even the fairly sophisticated reader may assume as much in ordinary parlance, referring to the man or woman in the world when they mean the character in the text. Lejeune has remarked that despite all he understands about the disappearing acts induced by deconstruction or the inability of text to constitute the self as a complete subject, "in spite of the fact that autobiography is impossible, this in no way prevents it from existing" (131–32). In this moment of surprise, between impossibility and fait accompli, the impostor slips through, pulling the cloak of invisibility around him, managing, in this minimally charted terrain, to "pass."

However, for honest broker and impostor alike, even if the life is not the origin for the text, the text is the origin for some kind of life. The text is a new life, narrated, readable, apparently separate from the world outside it,but, like Friday's footprint, it provides a trace, or evidence, of the lived life. The quasi-judicial nature of this relationship between text and life, the one being evidence for the other, and all that the term "quasi-judicial" implies for possible effects on the real world, emerges in the language used to describe it. Lejeune's *pacte autobiographique* is a prime example, his insistence on a contract between writer and reader, the writer pledging in his proper name to be telling his reader the truth. So deeply engrained is belief among readers in general that this is so that the recent spate of impostures has given rise to a further spate of lawsuits and threatened lawsuits when the *pacte* has been perceived to be broken. Lejeune himself may revisit and revise this concept, but it has remained memorable and influential in its original form, a measure of our general desire to know some things for sure. This pact not only defines and justifies reader expectations of a truthful narrative, but also situates the life story quasi-judicially, again, among all the other quasi-judicial records or transactions of a life that pertain both to the life and to its story, such as records of family, business, possessions, and civic or professional experience.

Anxiety, of course, has very little to do with faith and a lot to do with doubt (which is not a bad starting place for the scholar). So I cannot say for sure what a "self" is, or what genres of the self tend to look like, only that wiser people than I in autobiography studies have been proposing thoughtful but always tentative options for several decades. If the self resides in life (undoubtedly shape shifting with time and circumstances) as well as in the text (which claims, at least, to be true to the life), what about the role of the story, oral or written? Paul John Eakin's work suggests both how intimately connected life and story are but also how problematic this concept may be. If the autobiographer "invents" and narrates the self—perhaps even in some deeply neurophysiological way—what then to make of dysfunctional identity and "dysnarrativia" or failure of story due, for example, to neural disorders (Eakin 1999)? In keeping with the anxiety I find prevalent throughout contemporary theories of self-narration, Eakin joins Oliver Sacks and G. Thomas Couser in his concern that a storied self seems to exclude from selfhood those who, for whatever psychic, physical, or neurological reason, cannot in fact produce stories for themselves. If creating and rehearsing and developing one's own story is so crucial to self or identity, then must we assume that such people have no selves? Furthermore, what about the self-narrative that, as Eakin puts it, "breaks the rules," offending by virtue of trespass on other people's lives or because it "fail[s] to display an appropriately normal model of narrative identity" (2001, 120)? In this instance, too, I need to remember that, whether as life or as text, genres of the self are subject to the culture in which they find themselves. For these reasons, too, a culture determines what is normal and determines, also, what kind of narrative is extreme.

Causes for anxiety increase and multiply apparently in proportion to theorists' efforts to allay them. Believing devoutly in story, Gusdorf wrote: "We may call it fiction or fraud, but its artistic value is real: there is a truth affirmed beyond the fraudulent itinerary and chronology, *a truth of the man* ... who, for his own enchantment and that of his readers, realizes himself in the unreal" (43, my italics). Some twenty years later, John Sturrock insisted that "whatever an autobiographer writes, however wild or deceitful, cannot but count as testimony. It is impossible ... for an autobiographer not to be autobiographical" (52). At some point, in some fashion, the life is the bullion on which the value of the printed page depends. I think we know and perhaps sympathize with what both of them mean, recognizing self-expression as one component of autobiography; but carelessness with fact or chronology is not the full issue. Eakin's problem is surely not that people do not create themselves in narrative; it is, rather, that he takes self and self-story to be so inevitably and inextricably combined that he could not pry them apart if he wanted to. For Eakin, then, the self is life and text together. What happens, I now ask, if readers do indeed pry them apart?

Crucially, they do so not only, as Bettina suggests, because our fraud of self depends on our understanding of self and of truth, but also because the reader must provide the recognition without which all autobiography withers on the vine. Roland Barthes ceded this authority to the reader even as he described the death of the author. The impostor knows what game s/he is playing but cannot possibly play it alone. Although we know that Virginia Stephen may dress as a man and claim to be an Abyssinian prince, she only succeeds (as she did) if people receive her as one. The reader is the one (sometimes aided and abetted by the storyteller) who must pry the story and the self apart and recognize that the two do not match each other. (A large part of the discussion that follows focuses on this process.) As H. Porter Abbott wrote twenty years ago: "To read fictively is to ask 'how is this story complete?' To read factually is to ask: 'how is this story true?' And to read autographically is to ask: 'how does this story reveal the author?'" (613). (At which point both Olney and Sturrock may relax.)

When the reader doubts, as David Stoll doubted Rigoberta Menchú, the autobiographer is either defrocked, as in many of the situations that follow, or the situation serves to revise yet again what autobiographical means and how it works. What happens in this case is that the text educates and thereby creates its audience (as Holocaust survivors had to and, Rocio Davis argues, as migrants have had to). Nonetheless, Stoll comes closer to the heart of my problem than those who argue for narrative as some form of truth regardless of the facts. What if, indeed, the outlandish story that claims to be true has simply no grounding at all in fact, if life and story separate? And furthermore, what if they do so to the benefit of the writer, who receives money and prizes and fame and glory? (This notion of intent and benefit matters to the writer and to assessment of the writer, but not at all to the text, further suggesting how fraught the relationship between the two inevitably remains.) I suspect this question has haunted all the other grounds for anxiety in autobiography studies. Barrett J. Mandel wrote in 1980 about this "borderland" or "horizon" of assumptions that the author and his reader share ensuring that the reader "project[s] truthfulness" from his own collection of assumptions onto the text (68). Shirley Neuman wonders, in her discussion of Hal Porter, how we know "that the autobiographer's protestations of sincerity are made in good faith" (319). G. Thomas Couser's article on "Making, Taking, and Faking Lives" recognizes this constant undercurrent of anxiety in autobiography studies. After all, he notes, "autobiographers … are generally not viewed as obliged to research their own lives; the presumed subjectivity of the genre gains them a degree of latitude" (217). Symbiosis between writer and reader, or between impostors and the cultures in which they perform, remains a constant issue that may provide reassurance or, then again, not.

Timothy Dow Adams has written at length on lying in American autobiography, using particular examples to examine ways in which memory, narrative, traditions of the tall tale, and so on, all inform the muddied accounts we receive as autobiography. He concludes that "little difference exists between deliberately playing with readers' expectations in a genre such as the eighteenth-century novel, which gained its power by pretending to be nonfiction, or in modern American autobiography, which uses its indeterminate generic position as a rhetorical strategy" (*Telling Lies* 172). These men and women, he contends, are autobiographers, not liars, and "are not telling lies but telling their lives" (173). Having identified a range of rhetorical strategies within a specific literature, Adams is less anxious than many of his colleagues about accepting mendacity. Nonetheless, with the turn to ethics that has emerged since Adams was writing,[6] and with the inescapably political work that autobiography is counted on to perform (Menchú's case being just one dramatic instance),[7] I think that questions not just about lapses of memory or strategic manoeuvres with chronology but also about the integrity of life and story and the effects of fraudulent autobiography are gathering weight and urgency. So, for instance, Couser examines the ethics of Lauren Slater's treatment of "her epilepsy" in her memoir, *Lying: A Metaphorical Memoir* (2000), and suggests, among other things, that this work "does for the memoir what post-modernism has done for the novel" ("Disability as Metaphor" 2). For Couser, as for Smith and Watson, autobiographical narrative is distinct from fiction in its effects on the world outside the text. Smith and Watson take the discussion to the narrative theorists with their 2005 essay, "The Trouble with Autobiography." Citing "four problematics of autobiographical practice," they complicate understanding of situation and narrative possibilities. They are not dealing here with amusing peccadilloes but with fraught issues of life, text, and reception. To readers accustomed to dealing with narrative in emphatically literary terms, Smith and Watson provide the useful distinction that autobiography is not so much a genre as a practice (or set of practices) that one may safely assume has non-literary effects.

What autobiographers say, how they say it, and to whom; how readers receive their stories; and whether or how we understand them—these can all be life-and-death issues. In the chapters that follow, I certainly address some of the amusing shenanigans that impostors get up to, but I also find the effects of some imposture deeply disturbing. Faith has been a long habit that we might do well to shake. But justified doubt causes harm beyond the text and beyond the single life. As I examine various sites and characteristics of imposture, my questions invariably pertain to the intersections between text and life but also—as I have tried to establish here at the outset—to the bigger cultural questions that disturb autobiographers and theorists alike: Just who gets to tell what story, when, and to whom, why, and with what effects?

2
Faith, Doubt, and Textual Identity

I have suggested in my invocation of Doubting Thomas that faith and doubt are Janus-faced, two sides of the same experience. Anne Sexton knew this; as epigraph for her poem sequence *The Jesus Papers*, she asks, "And would you mock God," and then responds, "God is not mocked, except by believers." This line of thinking informs my exploration of faith and doubt in early European textual history. Even though my examples are not always specific to individual identity in a formally autobiographical sense, I look at the tropes and signs that ascribe texts to particular writers and at the kinds of authority that writers can claim—that they are who they say they are and that they themselves have written what they say they have written. When Pontius Pilate was asked not to mark the cross of Jesus with the sign "Jesus of Nazareth King of the Jews," no one seems to have challenged his authority that he had, as he said, written what he had written. A credible claim ensures acceptance that this man wrote these words and that these words express the intent and meaning of this man. Acceptance connects or aligns the man with his words and acknowledges that they belong to and define each other. Doubt or rejection is problematic.

In many ways, such claims to specific authority have not changed in two thousand years; both religious faith and secular power have been grounded on many of the same kinds of specious evidence that support contemporary imposture. I propose here to look at what these kinds of evidence are. I ask, in each situation, as one does for autobiographical imposture today, just how writers claim their texts or claim the identity that their texts present. I associate the making of texts with textual fraud and with the processes for detecting fraud. I note that claims to authenticity depend on a cultural climate that is liable to accept them, but also on such evidence as the signature or face of the author. The name and the physical presence of the person seem to provide incontrovertible authority. Even where the texts themselves are not personal, but require faith or invite doubt, their claims to validity depend on aspects of the personal. Significantly, punishment for the unacceptable text is visited on the body of the person who seems to be responsible. While I am in no way suggesting that everything is, in the end, autobiographical, I am surveying a very long history in which (as in autobiography) the person, the name, and the text either authenticate one another—or fail to do so. If we can recognize how problematic this liaison is between author and text, and how readily textual identity can fly free from the person it is supposed to represent, then perhaps we can understand how fraught a genre autobiography has always been and how little we can trust any of it.

Grounding contemporary questions about faith, doubt, and textual identity in this long history not only suggests very complicated relations among author and text and reception of text but may also suggest why—if only at a subliminal level—readers react to imposture as they do. So I begin with a conundrum: What does autobiography have in common with organized religion, political institutions, and the media? My conundrum suffers from the chicken-and-egg syndrome. I may as well ask which comes first historically: a sense of personal identity or a sense of self in a community of faith? Which comes first, the individual or the tribe, city, or nation that claims and protects the individual? Which is more influential, one's own perspective or the court of public opinion? The "faith" and "doubt" of my title do not, after all, describe religious lives or religious life writing but, rather, the activities of faith and of doubt that underpin the written life or "textual identity"—that is, the self as it is written. I look at works of religion and history as these define that which is to be believed (or doubted), because these constitute the chicken part of the conundrum: only if the chicken exists can the egg get laid; only in the context of texts defining the community can the individual make sense of his life. (Historically, these questions are emphatically male oriented.) Furthermore, I focus on Western history, religion, and literature, the stuff both of my own identity and of possible coherence for my inquiry. Finally (and firstly—that chicken and egg again), I focus on fraud or imposture; because, working backwards now, fraud and imposture, to my mind, describe what exactly matters in any given time or place. Clearly, the fraud or imposture that escapes detection has blended with its context and become invisible. However, doubt, detection, and exposure define not merely the fraud but also the community that rejects it. I note that Natalie Zemon Davis examines "Martin Guerre," both the original and the copy, in order to make sense of sixteenth-century peasant communities in Languedoc. My project in this chapter is shallower and broader than hers, but my questions are the same: What happens in any given case of imposture, and why, exactly, does it matter?

Through the early months of 2006, for example, the media kept running all the ingredients of "faith, doubt, and textual identity." Michael Baigent and Richard Leigh, co-authors of *The Holy Blood and the Holy Grail*, sued Dan Brown, author of *The Da Vinci Code*, for plagiarism and copyright infringement. How are these texts related, and to whom does the later text belong? At the heart of the scandal is a story about the secret identity of Jesus, who (this account supposes) survived or escaped crucifixion and raised a family in France. If Jesus lived beyond the end of his official history, then either he ceases to be a human link to the divine or one must trace the origins of Christian faith through a new history that doubts and therefore alters old faith. Either way, this particular story calls the official story into question: How and why did the official story gain credence in the first place, and whose interests does it serve? At the heart of the scandal is also conspiracy theory: the Church has known but hidden or destroyed the evidence of this ancient bloodline. Doubt is the prerequisite for recognizing such a massive cover-up, doubt and the sleuthing skills required to crack the codes of mysterious texts. The stakes are high, though Baigent claims that money had never been an issue, merely recognition.[1] Legal challenges, mystery and intrigue, subversion of wealth and power, all make for plenty of media attention. Furthermore, media coverage can be more significant these days than courts of law for determining, in the end, what kind of thinking is acceptable or viable, what people may care about or believe, how, in larger terms, culture may be shaped.

In pursuit of this recognition, Baigent produced a new book, *The Jesus Papers*, which competed on the bestseller list with *The Holy Blood and the Holy Grail* and *The Da Vinci Code*. Subtitled *The Greatest Cover-Up in History*, *The Jesus Papers* replays the theme of secret knowledge and a conspiracy of silence. In an interview, Baigent talked about documents dating to approximately 34 CE, which he admits he cannot read, owned by a man whom he will not name, and which he knows are letters from Jesus to the Sanhedrin, the highest court of justice and the supreme council in ancient Jerusalem—an early court of appeal, one might say, for examining questions of identity.[2] These claims put into play what Anthony Grafton (*Forgers and Critics*) calls "one of the great topoi of Western forgery, the motif of the object found in an inaccessible place, then copied, and now lost" (9). They do not, of course, meet the burden of proof. Rather, they foreground the claim that all impostors eventually make: that they themselves believe what they are reporting and that their personal integrity is beyond dispute; unfortunately, they cannot prove their point because they are working with secrets that they must continue to protect. Those who doubt the experience being presented also know that it resonates for some reason with the reading public and may therefore affect the experience or reality of others.

Why, I wonder, did we enjoy this game of trivial pursuits at this point in time in Western culture? Did it begin with Samuel Johnson's "common reader," invested these days in popular culture, from which media stars emerge, the elite, the untouchables, apparently addressing the value of the intimate and personal in a mass-produced age? Walter Benjamin has written about "the desire of contemporary masses to bring things 'closer' spatially and humanly, which is as ardent as their tendency to overcoming the uniqueness of every reality by accepting its reproduction" (223). For Benjamin, "The presence of the original is the prerequisite to the concept of authenticity" (220). Uniqueness (which he calls "aura") and authenticity (or authority) defy replication. Grieving for the ways in which technology, artifice, "the common reader," and "the cult of the movie star" or "the phony spell of a commodity" (231) have devalued the work of art (by replacing the original with copies) Benjamin seems to be describing, back in 1935, and in defiance of fascism, the phenomenon that concerns me here: the meaning and value of "truth" and the likely mismatch between original and copy, reality and reproduction, life and text. However, I suspect that Benjamin's desire for authenticity, topical as it was for him and as it remains for us, is in fact as old as the alignment of the written word with the man who wrote it.

What, We May Ask, Is an Author?

The text provides information and becomes, by virtue of its relative permanence, a proof in itself that the information is true. Justifiably or not, it becomes the source of reliable knowledge, the crucial point of reference. However, texts do not emerge *ex nihilo* but originate with the communities or individuals who produce them. Even when the authors are unknown, or unknowable, or anonymous, or when texts are incorrectly attributed to particular authors, some alignment between text and author can be found to authenticate (or discredit) the value of the text and therefore of its information. Obviously some kinds of information are more important than others, having direct implications for how individuals and communities conduct themselves in the real world outside the text. Texts that establish religious or political realities fall into this category; they need to be true and credible beyond all doubt if the earth is to keep turning (or remain flat), if God's to be in his heaven and all's to be well with the world. How more effectively to provide the authority of these texts than to attribute them to their writers? So, for example, Allah, with the help of Mohammed, is responsible for the Qu'ran, God for the Bible. They are source and subject of their own texts. With profound effects on whole civilizations, Allah and God created these texts and exist in them. More precisely, their texts provide them with a textual identity that readers, in the language of Thomas Cranmer, may "read, mark, learn, and easily digest." More accessible to burdens of proof, the human scribe stands before the judgment of his readers and is doubted or believed not on the merits of his physical reality in the world but, precisely, on the merits of this textual identity, the self he has established in his text. For autobiography, I have suggested, the space between the living, breathing human being who writes and this verbal construct, this textual identity, provides room for the impostor.

For scholars who focus on the book itself, the term "textual identity" refers to the provenance of the text, or the consistent features that make a text somehow the same despite varieties of presentation (as in multiple editions of one work). These aspects of textual identity concern me only insofar as the text represents or refers to the identity of its maker; I am, for example, less concerned with the age or condition of Baigent's papyrus than with the signature of Jesus. I am particularly interested in the metonymic relation between writer and the text that somehow represents him. Furthermore, though I try to understand the less-than-true representations of real-world people, alive or dead, textual identity will not specifically concern characters in fiction. Textual identity, for example, does not include "Jane Eyre" (though clearly, in a different discussion it could do so), but it may involve the autobiographical elements of Charlotte Brontë's story as manifested in *Jane Eyre*. I have argued elsewhere for the centrality of fiction to truthful autobiography, and I appreciate novels and stories that borrow the tropes of autobiography and that depend on first-person narration, but my argument here focuses on the role of autobiography in culture. Within this focus, I am concerned about what we believe to be true, and whether or how it matters if autobiographers, trusted as purveyors of their own truth, are impostors or liars, if this textual identity, this presentation of text and self in the text, comes unstuck.

In short, for this discussion, textual identity exists only in the text; but because my subject is autobiography, fraudulent or true, textual identity certainly depends on its connections with its author, with that lived identity outside the text. Doubtful as it is that the man Jesus wrote letters to the Sanhedrin in 34 CE, these papyrus documents have no dramatic value whatsoever if people do not even believe that Jesus lived among family and friends in that time and place. Textual identity also represents the author of the text in the text; what Jesus has to say to the Sanhedrin (if Baigent could read the document) would manifest his textual identity, his wishes or opinions or desires as the text made these known. Furthermore, because textual identity relates text and author to each other, this relationship determines the source, origin, or authority of the text, its claim to credibility. How much more likely we would be to believe in these letters if they were signed? Or if in some other way they seemed to prove their authenticity as written by Jesus? Conversely, the text that breaks or loses its human connection loses credibility. If textual and other analyses could show that these pieces of papyrus were signed by Herod the Great, or by Michael Baigent himself, then their value and meaning, the role they would play in the popular imagination, would change dramatically. Finally, textual identity is the identity that is constructed in the text, that of the man or woman who held the pen, the saint or sinner, the scholar or humble scribe, the impostor or the sleuth. Textual identity has a role to play both in the text and in its effects on its readers; it creates its particular take or perspective on reality, inserting the personal element into the larger web of history.

Because autobiography depends so crucially on this combination of alignments between author and text, this chapter focuses on how these alignments work and why they matter or, rather, what we inherit in terms of how these functions and effects have shifted and evolved over time. (A few hundred years ago, Baigent and Brown would both have been burned at the stake.) Each situation represents a crisis in its own time, with orthodoxy and heresy embattled and orthodoxy either reasserted or significantly refurbished by a merger with its opponent. For the early Church, orthodoxy meant establishing and adhering to one true doctrine. For the political regimes of young states or nations (now as well as then), orthodoxy means absolute loyalty to the ideology and ruler in power. In Western democracies, orthodoxy is more likely to mean accepted opinion or shared values, which may be as readily established in the media as in the law. Each situation also calls upon burdens of proof. So I must ask, what constitutes proof? How is it achieved? What processes of doubt, what decoding or distrusting, or what new science produces certainty beyond a reasonable doubt? How, in short, do authorship and scholarship emerge, establishing their claims to knowledge, asserting their textual identities, aligning writers and texts in ways that make the one responsible to the other and thus responsible to their readers?

Beginning with the Bible

I begin with the Bible because it has been foundational to all the orthodoxies of Jewish and Christian faith; and with early Christian writing, which has been important to early formations of the Western body politic and conceptions of individual identity.[3] The art historian E.H. Gombrich describes a manuscript illustration of St. Matthew at work on his gospel as evidence of the artist's concern to go beyond what he knew or saw to what he felt—the excitement of the writer involved in "writing" the Bible.[4] With early production of the Bible, I suggest, we can identify more substantial questions of faith, doubt, and textual identity than Baigent and Brown can provide. Certainly, the history of these early documents makes clear both the claims to faith and the causes for doubt that pertain to textual identity. I note their repeated claims on tradition or continuity even for the new story, the invention to meet the need, the opportune or serviceable fraud that the author cannot claim but must discover or attribute to someone else. Orthodoxy is crucial, but it is also precarious and may be established by the first-person singular only when that singular life is demonstrably modelled on biblical precedents. (St. Paul's conversion on the road to Damascus is a case in point for biblical precedent: it became a foundational narrative for religious conversion because it first appeared so early in the history of the Christian faith; because it was told and repeated by an identifiable hero of the early Church; because its form was so easily recognizable, an attribute equivalent to authenticity; and because it could be made to serve numerous other lives and situations.) Because the Church itself was actually founded on problematic texts, it developed methodologies to authenticate texts and "authors" and these remain in effect, less the critical element of religious faith, in contemporary thinking about an "author" or an autobiographer. On what internal evidence do we accept a text, and what are the external configurations, including our own culturally determined reading practices, that support or undermine that text?

The Bible has been foundational for Western cultures in part because it has also been—as Elizabeth A. Clark points out—literary, rhetorical, and ideological in nature.[5] Thus, hand in hand with invitations to faith go all the appurtenances of doubt. Quite apart from the questions that arise because of the inevitable corruption of texts over time, choices involved in translation, preservation, commentary, and extensive forgery have, from the earliest times, served particular purposes, vitiating textual integrity. However, the New Testament provides a flashpoint with profound historical consequences. So much of it is biographical or autobiographical that early Christians were able to insert spurious texts into the mix. (*The Jesus Papers* and the gospel according to Judas claim an ancient heritage.) Early Christians not only added pastoral letters to Timothy and Titus but also produced Apostolic Constitutions, which "tried to settle disputes about doctrines and practices by invoking the authority of the earliest and truest Christians"—that is, of course, the authentic, original kind, "speaking in the first person" (Grafton, *Forgers and Critics*, 17)—thus vouching for the indisputable authority of autobiography. In these cases, autobiographical or presumably autobiographical writings have the further effect of providing "origins" for later attempts at self-construction, as in seventeenth-century spiritual autobiography in England and America. In the time of the early Church, these writings served the construction of a Christianity on its way to becoming truly catholic.

Naming the presumed author, the source or origin of the information in the text, also establishes textual credibility and thereby invites false attributions (which are usually more effective than Baigent's Jesus). Foucault cites Hippocrates (for science) and Pliny (for history) as examples of such useful attributions of authorship (126). If these respected authorities produced the texts in question, then the texts must surely be true. Clark refers to apocryphal Acts of the Apostles composed in the second century CE, as well as to work by supposed heretics mistakenly attributed to such authorities as Jerome and Augustine. These latter similarly derive their authority from association with well-respected authors. "Here," she observes, "the 'author-function' served not just to bolster the prestige of texts, but contributed to their presentation" (170). Like the name dropping of a social climber, the text assumes authority in a hypothetical context that deflects scrutiny—common enough practices that serve impostors well.[6]

What Foucault has called the author-function could also, in this case, be editorial, introducing into the text the scholar, the code breaker, the sleuth. Even if so many scholars had not been involved in the creation and detection of inauthentic texts, I could not overlook the risks and temptations of scholarly work; what do "we" know, and when do we know it? What choices do we make, and why do we make them? To ask with what effects we distort information is not to dignify our influence but to recognize the cumulative power of knowledge repeatedly shaped in particular ways. Jerome himself, exemplifying an early exercise of stylistics, questioned the authenticity of Paul's letter to the Hebrews because the style and diction of this letter did not match those of Paul's other letters. Mark Vessey reads Foucault's construction of the modern idea of the author in terms of such "authentication of doctrinally normative texts" (551). In other words, this text (whether by Paul as letter writer or by Jerome as literary critic, depending on the moment and the reader) is foundational to accepted beliefs: the named author, who can be trusted, says that this material is true; and furthermore, the author can be trusted because of his known holiness. Vessey, again, describes how clearly Jerome understood the correlation of authority, in his time, with sanctity; and how he constructed his textual identity accordingly. However, orthodoxy is always fragile, hence its need for powerful buttressing. It would seem that no authority is so established in its time and place as to be unassailable; or, one might say, maintaining orthodox credibility in tandem with critical acumen may be a hard balancing act.

In effect, both truth and claims to truth can be seriously problematic because doubt goes to and fro upon the earth like the devil himself, seeking whom it may devour. For example, Gnostic heresy was troubling the Church after Paul's death, and as "Paul had never written against this ... a third letter to the Corinthians was written in his name to provide ... ammunition." The spurious writer confessed to forgery and repented, "but the letter was so useful that one party in the church refused to accept the denial and argued that the letter was authentic" (Morton 9). The lie or the fraud is often useful and is also often necessary in practical terms. Morton cites the Epistles of Paul as unique in the history of stylometry (the measurement of word and sentence length for stylistic consistency), in part because the Christian community has refused to doubt Paul's authority. Some truths are so established, or carry so much baggage, that doubt incurs repercussions beyond the immediate question. Because St. Paul—surely the patron saint of autobiography as of Protestant churches—has been a constant source of worry, textual scholars who have doubted Paul's authorship have been constrained by concerns for religious orthodoxy and have therefore shored up this problematic source and authority against the ruin of doubt.

The writings of St. Jerome provide another instance in which the authority of the name serves to establish orthodox faith (that is, the particulars of faith that the Catholic Church will sanction and on which it will build its strength). With Jerome, however, we can read the dialogues of doubt as they have been built into the text itself and, therefore, the claims to an authenticity that has taken doubt into account. Jerome's text becomes not merely authentic or authorized—a text in which he as writer can make particular claims—but also a palimpsest whose multiple layers provide protective covering. Such issues of problematic dogma and questionable sources significantly determine the text as well as the writer's ability to align himself with that text, to own it under his own name. Benjamin would have appreciated this dilemma. Scholars for whom criticism, faith, personal identity, and reputation were closely aligned signalled in the pages of their work the positions and relationships they wished (or needed) to claim.

Since Foucault traces his own understanding of the author-function to writers whose independence and capacity for self-presentation were limited, one must also note that the autobiographical giant among the Church Fathers, Augustine of Hippo, followed Jerome in his control of his own writing, his "textually constituted persona" (or textual identity), his "auto-authentication" (Vessey 76–78). Significantly for my present purposes, he also followed St. Paul's model for the Christian "life" as a cataclysmic conversion after emphatic delinquency. I question in these cases whether readers today may with confidence align Jerome, Erasmus, or Augustine with their literary production, as authors and, in varying degrees, autobiographers, and whether the narrative model, established by Pauline example and confirmed in Augustine's *Confessions*, allowed of any variation in the early Church. In other words, questions about authenticity must take into account the prevailing orthodoxies of the given time as well as the capacity of writers embedded in time and place to imagine their lives and their beliefs outside those norms. To do so may be to introduce heresy (with its attendant risks), or to bewilder and therefore lose one's readers and have no impact at all. On one hand, conformity to God's will is the only desirable end. On the other, nothing beside remains. Boundless and bare, one might say, alternative ways of being or living exist outside the scope of the imagination—and of narrative.[7] In the more diffuse Western cultures of the twenty-first century, which Benjamin would have found shallower and more evanescent than these ancient absolutes, I suggest that imagination for cultural choices remains similarly determined, just more loosely so. Orthodoxies may be more often cultural than religious, and may be more open to challenge than in the early Church, but they exert their influence nonetheless—for all autobiographers, but most effectively for impostors.

Certainly where contemporary impostors may create turbulence for the reading public, they also entertain the cynic or the ironist; faith and doubt have become detached from the big questions of life and death. By contrast, the textual battles of the early Church—and presumably the working lives of the men on whose erudition, scholarship, and faith the Church depended—were significantly more complex. Not least, the critical readings and translations of biblical and Church codices, and exposures of inauthentic texts, just like their companion forgeries or emendations, took place in the context of serious faith. So Erasmus, who developed sophisticated systems of internal checks on manuscripts, was not, as D'Amico tells, above "pious forgery" himself, issuing a treatise called *De duplici martyrio* as if by Cyprian, the third-century bishop of Carthage, to respond to what he saw as the religious extremism of the Reformation (36–37). In other words, because Erasmus was concerned to protect and perpetuate the true faith, he found himself an "author" (Cyprian) with a name that could be trusted, to authenticate the documents that he himself had written. His lineage, like his creed, was impeccable; but it was not, of course, authentic. In distinct contrast to contemporary experiences of imposture, both the author and the orthodoxy he upheld were public rather than private entities. Even where documents themselves were not as truthful or authentic as they could be made to seem, those that survived contributed to orthodoxy, which we can translate as that which is known and believed, or that which the culture of the time allows to be written and read. Necessarily, then, both writer and text claim authenticity but rest on the swampy terrain of doubt, needing to prove that they are who and what they claim to be.

The Doubt Police

Enter the doubt police, descendants of "the Spanish Inquisition." I see them rather like Monty Python characters stalking the heretics of our time. Like the investigative journalism of *the smoking gun*, or Rex Stout's literary detective, Nero Wolfe, and like literary critics from biblical exegetes and classicists to analysts of contemporary literature, they are Doubting Thomases, requiring evidence and proof. The doubt police distrust and decode texts, subjecting text (and writer) to close scrutiny. They expose fraud and they sustain orthodoxy, or the canon—that which can be relied upon for quality, that on which our cultures can be founded. We may want to include these professional doubters among the heroes of this history, especially as they share so many of the same interests and exercise so many of the same strategies as perpetrators of fraud. In Grafton's words: "Forger and critic have been entangled through time like Laocoon and his serpents; the changing nature of their continuous struggle forms a central theme in the development of historical and philological scholarship" (*Forgers and Critics*, 6). From the anonymous scholars in the ancient libraries of Alexandria to such identifiable sleuths as Lorenzo Valla, Jean Mabillon, Petrarch, and Erasmus, they developed, articulated, and used replicable means for detecting inauthenticity. Their work in specifying anachronism,[8] historicizing handwriting, and dating and decoding texts was significant to the task of bringing text and "author" into alignment, specifying the latter and making him responsible for the former.

With the Renaissance, when "even more than in previous periods, forger and critic marched in lockstep" (*Forgers and Critics*, 31), the doubt police inserts himself into the text, establishing, as scholar and detective, his own textual identity. He tends to be known and named. He identifies himself with his forensic genius, claiming and naming his own text. Orthodoxy is prevalent here, too, of course. There's no value to correcting an error or establishing an unexpected truth unless that truth provides some service. As an academic, I am moved to declare Lorenzo Valla the pre-eminent hero of this discussion; when textual analysis can shake the foundations of the known world, then surely the academic knows her moment of glory. Valla's personal claim to his findings, his courage in facing down the opposition, and perhaps some element of pride in his own abilities and self-interest in the service of his master—all these are elements of his textual records, standing in for the more personal history. Notably, Valla's work shifts the focus of concern from faith to politics, from religion to secular power, and insists on aligning the writer with the words on his page in ways with which autobiographers of the twenty-first century can identify.

Valla's achievement and abiding influence rest on his exposure of the Donation of Constantine as a forgery. Remarkably, his weapon of choice was textual discreditation; he unravelled the authority generally attributed to texts, which marked a significant development in the detective work that follows doubt. Valla was drawing on the work of Aristotle, Quintilian, Petrarch, and others, and was a man of his time in his understanding that language is key to knowledge and meaning. Not least, Valla understood language itself as situated in history and as changing with use. He saw "scripture [as] subject to the same laws of decay as any other literary artifact and [as] similarly recoverable by the same techniques of linguistic and textual explanations" (D'Amico 16). For Valla, fact and language or "res and verbum [thing and word] went together and demanded particularized treatment … Thus for Valla textual criticism, and historical thought generally, could uncover reality" (17). I suspect that Valla would not have been surprised by contemporary theorizing about language as a sign system with no direct equivalency to fact; his arguments seem less concerned with language as some clear window onto the world than with language as valuable because it means what it says. Like Anselm and other distinguished predecessors, Valla seems to have cared for a meaning that could be trusted. Historians describe Valla as particularly remarkable for the clarity with which he laid out the terms of evidence and judgment, producing in the process the model for historical jurisprudence and modern historical scholarship. In fact, Donald R. Kelley sees the paradigm shift caused by Valla's oration as equivalent to that caused by Copernicus or Kuhn, describing its effect as "a significant step in the development of historical studies when the instability of human nature became not merely an occasion for lamentation but an object of investigation" (24). The nature of the text, its source and purpose, significantly affect textual identity. Therefore, when secular power rather than religious authority is the issue, responsibility for fraud becomes, as we recognize it today, a human matter, and correction a human possibility. Nonetheless, contemporary impostors investigated (sometimes in law) for their manipulation of materials they offer as documentary evidence, continue to work under the ancient shadow of truth perceived as sacred.

Following Valla, the seventeenth-century Benedictine scholar Jean Mabillon codified the key questions, which are still operative today (and which sound curiously like airport security), for determining the authenticity of a document or the reliability of a person: Who wrote it? What does it say? How is it written? Why, when, and where was it written? Who were involved in it besides the principal agent? Leonard Boyle makes the point that Mabillon's questions are the basic ones still put to every document that requires verification. They begin with the need for the text to be authentic, and then proceed to doubt that it is. They are also, in principle at least, very old. Boyle traces Mabillon's procedures "back in origin to Aristotle's Ethics (Book 3), where the subject is human, deliberate acts, and to the *De intentione rhetorica* (1:24–27) of Cicero, where lawyers are instructed how best to describe and present a client in court" (Boyle 93). Here, that word "origin" again determines the long and respectable ancestry that I can claim for my present enterprise: the pre-eminently ethical concern that texts and people represent each other fairly, as well as the methods for determining that people are who they say they are, that their texts represent them truthfully, and that we can detect imposture when it arises.

Mabillon's work in the seventeenth century, with its careful matching of document and known fact, is the clearest predecessor for such contemporary processes as legal discovery and investigative journalism. According to Boyle, Mabillon was concerned with texts of every kind, "any and every form of written act, legal, notarial, or commercial, from Babylonian tablets and Greco-Roman papyri to medieval charters and modern business papers" (88). Verifiably reliable documents, he argued, were essential for the discipline of history but also for the integrity of political and religious institutions (Hiatt 17). Concern is no longer a matter only of religious orthodoxy; it now reaches into every aspect of human experience. Mabillon's textual criticism, or diplomatics, as he called it, included "every possible form of written documentary evidence, from a charter of the most solemn kind to a scribbled commemoration in a flyleaf of a psalter, and from a record in elegant Rustic of the components of a Roman fire brigade to the patchy diary of an emigré during the French Revolution" (88), bringing the value of the text, and its authenticity, home to the individual.

Corpus Delicti

In matters of religion, politics, and law, with the text and with the textual detective, all roads lead to the author, the maker of the text, the man (and increasingly the woman) whose relationship with the text—or whose textual identity—is both produced and organic. This alignment of author and text, this production of textual identity, ensures a substantial or physical object to avow or disprove, but is also embedded in common parlance. According to Grafton, the library catalogues and literary histories of the fourth-century Athenian book market classified genuine works as *gnosioi* or legitimate, the same term applied to legitimate children, and spurious ones as *nothoi* or bastards (*Forgers and Critics,* 12). I note that the word "corpus" refers both to the human body and to a body of work, and suggest that numerous instances render these two interchangeable. Do we, for instance, mean "Shakespeare" the man, or Shakespeare the plays? Which do we read or watch or hope to understand?

I have been considering attributions of authorship and the authorship of editorial critiques, so let me turn now to the more specifically autobiographical alignment of writer and text—in the first place, their very physical association. Early history is replete with examples of their shared physicality. For instance, Jay Rubenstein, who writes of the autobiography inherent in medieval biography, notes a significantly physical relationship between the medieval biographer and his subject: Adam of Eynsham was both Hugh's biographer and his embalmer. Eadmer embalmed Anselm; Reginald of Durham prepared Godric of Finchale's body for burial. "It is striking how common this pattern is," Rubenstein observes, and adds: "The biography was perhaps the final act of preservation, the life and legacy of a beloved master set in order to survive the world's decay until Judgement Day" (35). So much for the text and the immortal life, but Rubenstein also connects the very process of writing with the process of embalming: "The laborious process of writing and of publication in the Middle Ages—letters cut first onto wax and then transferred onto animal skins—was a much more physical one than is the case for modern writers. The analogy to embalming would have been far more obvious" (36). Corpse and corpus, man, biography, and body, are closely aligned from the beginning to the very end, to Judgment Day.

For judgment here on earth, textual transgression also comes home to the body. Courtney Booker refers me to the process of *transpunctio,* the traditional and formal procedure in early medieval Europe for ensuring that erroneous or fraudulent documents became inert when they were pierced through while gripped in the outstretched hands of their owner. So, for example, Janet L. Nelson cites the settlement of a dispute in Carolingian West Francia:

> Then, by judgement of all there present, the provost Saraman asked
> Otbert, the advocate of Norbert the priest, if he could prove false
> the documents which Amalgar still held in his hand. He replied
> immediately that he could prove them utterly false. Then by the right
> above established and with the witnesses above noted, he made the
> documents utterly false by piercing them there in Amalgar's hands and
> thus tearing them through, as it had been adjudged and decided in his
> favour by all. (57)

To make the punishment fit the crime, both the text and the man responsible for it had to suffer the same fate. Foucault notes that texts were assigned "real authors" "only when the author became subject to punishment" (124). This particular point may be open to dispute; even so, it serves sharply to clarify the alignment of author and text.

However, this "author" need not have been the writer; he might well have been the publisher, the printer, or the owner of the text judged to be fraudulent, heretical, or treasonous. Nor was this association limited to early history. Just as the Church had burned bodies at the stake, so in the secular state, censorship traditionally brought home the punishment for transgression to the body of the perpetrator. When in 1663 the printer John Twyn published a book that he himself had not authored, imagining the death of Charles II, "he was hanged, cut down alive, his 'privy members' were cut off, his entrails taken out, and with him 'still living, burnt before his eyes'" (Stewart 11). This gruesome punishment effectively collapsed printer and disseminator of the text into the author or originator, distributing responsibility in ways to which contemporary publishing houses remain sensitive, though they are subject only to possible lawsuits or the loss of sales when books must be withdrawn. Daniel Defoe was more fortunate than poor Twyn; when he was pilloried for his satirical pamphlet *The Shortest Way with Dissenters*, the London mob turned him into a hero. However, John Matthews was hanged for high treason in 1719 for publishing a pamphlet in support of James III (13). Conformity—or suffering and death. Foolish or courageous men were identified quite personally with the texts in which they expressed personal opinions that did not conform to the positions sanctioned by government. Today the author still appears in person; the author interview makes for good publicity, especially on television, where the face and body of the writer are visible. However, today the polarized ideologies of the *fatwah* and freedom of speech determine the physical safety of being thus identified "in person."

Will the Real Author Please Stand Up? *Le texte c'est moi*

Where history and biography are clearly about people and events separate from the writer, autobiography originates with the autobiographer. *Le texte c'est lui,* defining and standing in for the autobiographer. Just as Louis XIV of France saw no distinction between the state and his own person and prerogatives, so both the writer and the reader of autobiography, ignoring contemporary theory, assume this conflation of person and text as a matter of course. I propose, therefore, in the context of early European history, to rephrase Foucault's question about the author and ask not quite "what is an autobiographer?" but, more pertinently for my present topic, what issues attach to the use of an author's person or name when *le texte c'est lui?*

Exploring the earliest traces of individual identity in Western literatures, from the tomb inscriptions of the ancient Egyptians, through the literature and philosophy of the classical world and the Hebrew psalmists and prophets, Georg Misch identifies times and conditions for self-recognition. One of the most moving, and surely the most often cited, is the occasion when Odysseus, "the unknown stranger among the Phaeacians hears his own deeds outside Troy praised at the feast by the blind rhapsodist, and then, overcome by his feelings, himself relates his adventures" (Misch I:67). Historians have tended to qualify or discount the value of autobiographical testimony, but autobiographers seem always to have situated themselves as participants in, and authorities on, their own corners of history with their own particular stories to contribute. This story is mine, Odysseus says (in tears), and I am the one who must tell it. His telling reveals him as the man the story is about. His claim to this story strips him of the many (wily) disguises he has assumed on his long journey. Like his drawing of the bow at the end, Odysseus' telling of this story identifies, in his own body, the authenticity of his claim to be who he says he is. However, in transition from person to text, from the oral to the written narrative—which like an embalmed body can be preserved for all time—Odysseus' story creates a gap between the man and his narrative, a separation that opens room for doubt about perfect alignment. If the heretic can be identified with his text and tortured and killed, so, in reverse, can the textual narrative actually give its "author" room and time to duck and hide unless he chooses, like Odysseus, to come forward. Curiously, for the impostor the temptation to come forward seems almost irresistible. The story is so good, moving its readers to admiration and tears, that the impostor asserts a personal claim and defends it against all comers.

Historically, this individual identity could be hard to assert or discover. Distinctions between scribe and writer were harder to make or maintain in the

pre-modern world, with several factors blurring the role of the author and the possibilities of fraud: ancient habits of writing for the use of others; or use of others'
names in order to be read; or education, which fostered imitation of others for
the development of style (Stewart 78). However, Chartier notes that the assign-
ing of texts to particular writers actually predated the introduction of print and
became most apparent in visual representations of the writer in the act of writing.
The function of the author's portrait, which first emerged in miniature decorations
in fifteenth-century manuscripts (Chartier cites the works of Christine de Pisan,
Jean Froissart, René d'Anjou, Petrarch, and Boccaccio), "[was] to reinforce the
notion that the writing is the expression of an individuality that gives authenticity
to the work" (52). The "I," as Chartier puts it, became visible. This aspect of self-
representation and public recognition is, of course, paramount in our time, when
impostors must modify their personal appearance, or assume a disguise, or avoid
photographers because their faces, in particular, have become the flashpoints for
media attention. In fifteenth-century manuscripts, it was a novelty, which Chartier
associates with new understanding of what writing meant. In particular, the French
words *escrire* and *escripvain* took on their modern meanings to indicate not only
the copying but also the composition of texts. Similarly, use of the vernacular
suggests individual invention, original creation, from the fourteenth century on
(52). Both invention and creation, like the image of the author, introduce into early
literature (some of it very personal) the notion of an inner life and an individuality
that Misch identifies in the (problematic) writings of St. Paul.

In literary matters, the value of the particular hand, like the signature, also
precedes print. Chartier describes the concern of early-fourteenth-century writers with the production and transmission of their texts as well as their tendency
to produce their "author's book" made from an autograph copy, not a scribe's
copy. Protected from the errors that others might introduce, these authors' copies "manifest the author's intentions as the work had been composed with less
risk of betraying those intentions or vitiating them" (55). Petrarch, for example,
copied several of his own works in his own hand, establishing direct and authentic relations between poet and reader. When that pre-eminent liar, Rousseau,
signed documents that he intended should have legal force to express his anxiety
about works appearing under his name, he faced the further issue that his signature needed the countersignature of a witness to prove its authenticity. Laurence
Sterne signed four thousand bound copies of Volume 5 of *Tristram Shandy* as a
protection against forgery, Volume 5 being the one that contains the most plagiarisms from Burton's *Anatomy of Melancholy* (Mallon 16–20). Well may the thief
take out insurance on all his stolen goods. The handwriting or signature of the
individual author has never protected the reading public from abuse (as, one must
suspect, in the case of Jesus' letter to the Sanhedrin), but it does personalize the

claim to ownership of the text. It meets some burden of proof that the writer claims the text as well as the textual identity it provides.

What, in the end, can we take away from this survey of textual production in early modern Europe? That textual fraud has always been endemic to textual production? Curiously, such fraud is often benign in intent, meeting a perceived need because it can establish authority or maintain security in its community. That the complexities of both fraud and detection have refined the skills each one develops in order to outwit the other? Perhaps "the truth" can be caught only on the spear points of such encounters. Both fraud and its detection have engaged some of the finest minds in European history, ensuring that questions of fraud and authenticity underwrite, so to speak, the cultures we inherit. Surely, too, this historical evidence determines to a significant degree our own concerns with truth and untruth even in times and places where ideological positions are more tenuous than they used to be. So we recognize that truth is somehow sacred, that it belongs with the power that can enforce it, and that resistance to this power may also be true and honourable. Contemporary autobiographers know the value—not just to their own sense of integrity but also to their community and their culture—of asserting the truth as they see it. If, as many suggest, autobiography has become a salient force for the liberation of oppressed or minority voices, some sense of the past may enable both autobiographers today and their readers to recognize that we sign off only on matters we believe in, on matters that *matter*.

More Immediate Prequels for Current Imposture

These matters that matter have become increasingly secular over time. Curiously, with technological development and increasing literacy, personal narratives of all stripes have become simultaneously more permanent (as in print) and more ephemeral (in their connections to the life outside the text). Jack Lynch, who has written extensively about the textual impostures that flourished in eighteenth-century England, helps bring this survey of authorship and textual identity into the present by suggesting some parallels between then and now. If, as many scholars contend, modern autobiography first emerged in the eighteenth century, I am interested to understand what cultural conditions pertained for writers, readers, and autobiographers that textual (and personal) imposture should have flourished at the same time.

Finding concerns about authenticity and truthfulness in eighteenth-century literature quite paranoid, Lynch refers to rampant skepticism, or "Pyrrhonism";[9] but the numerous identity pirates he describes might also have enjoyed Stephen Colbert's 2005 coinage of the term "truthiness." An outcrop of both the current fashion in imposture and the political machinations of the U.S. government, "truthiness" describes claims to knowledge that lack evidence (so should be doubted) but that also make an emotional appeal (and are therefore believed). Truthiness refuses to be either truth or falsehood and establishes the flavour of possibility that attends imposture. Between them, Lynch and Colbert provide vocabulary for conditions of doubt or uncertainty (that embed memory of truth or a desire for secure knowledge) in which impostors flourish. Lynch invites this comparison between then and now when he argues in *Deception and Detection* that "the remarkable surge of interest in deception [in the eighteenth century] is the result of a series of cultural shifts that took place, and ... the reason many of these questions seem obvious to us today is that we live in a world shaped by the eighteenth century's struggles with deception: our laws, our philosophy, our history, and our criticism all emerge from the[se] debates" (10). My time travel does not, of course, discount imposture in many other times and places, but focuses here for the precise connection that Lynch provides.

As if he had stepped out of *Gulliver's Travels* or *The History of Rasselas,* George Psalmanazar arrived in London in 1703 with the extraordinary tale that he had come from Formosa, which was safely far away and which he described in lurid and exotic detail. Though this particular impostor ended up as a contrite, opium-addicted Grub Street hack, he began by supporting his astonishing histories and geographies of Formosa with texts and drawings that matched for audacity those of James Macpherson, inventor of the ancient bard "Ossian"; Thomas Chatterton, creator of the fifteenth-century poet Thomas Rowley; Daniel Defoe with Robinson Crusoe; or William Henry Ireland with his trove of Shakespeare plays. Simply to list these names in this time span is to suggest an impressive range of textual invention, deception, fraud, or satire—which operates by displacing or destabilizing established knowledge. It is also to suggest a wide range of motives, achievements, and effects. Lynch provides tables to demonstrate an astonishing increase through the eighteenth century in titles incorporating such words as "authentic," "genuine," and "real" (1–2); in doing so he is both responding to this phenomenon of invented texts and identities and, without doubt, continuing the widespread trespass on credulity.[10] By a wonderful chance, Psalmanazar succeeded for as long as he did because imposture was high fashion in that time and place. How so?

When Lynch refers to cultural shifts, he notes that textual identity took on new forms in the eighteenth century in part because of major developments in the dissemination of knowledge that suggest some historical parallels with current experience. So I begin with an issue that dogs every instance of imposture: its provenance, origins, or originality. For text, "origins" means who wrote it (but also carries theological connotations, as in Original Sin, about the insecurity of virtue or truth). New laws of copyright in England in 1710 gave writers particular ownership of their work. Where earlier writers could assume language and ideas as common, attributable to any appropriate name, copyright created an "author" or "origin" for the printed word and introduced, accordingly, the notion of plagiarism and theft of text as serious offences in civil law. That is, textual practices that had been quite common in the earlier period we have considered became quickly identifiable and subject to punishment when texts explicitly belonged to named authors.

More happily, copyright also enabled writers to move away from royal or aristocratic patronage (and conformity), to risk success in the market, and to distinguish themselves as professional writers. Following this copyright law, authors, not publishers, became the legal owners of their works. In a fascinating review of the history of literary ownership, Roger Chartier discusses the difference between the ownership of real property, "which was inalienable and freely transmissible" (34) and the justification authors needed to make for ownership of their work based on the notion that writing is labour, that the text is the production of the man. Notions of literary creation were central to the debate across Europe. This organic process "acquires an identity immediately referable to the subjectivity of its author" (37). Text became valuable, in other words, not simply as a material object but, more significantly, as an expression of personal originality. Profoundly personal claims to authority and "author-ship" (which had certainly been adumbrated by earlier writers) moved in the eighteenth century into the marketplace of letters.

Copyright laws have continued to be refined over time; I note in particular developments at the end of the eighteenth century and the beginning of the nineteenth, when Chartier describes strict rules on "author's rights, author–publisher relations, rights of reproduction, and related matters" (Chartier 30) because this was a flourishing period for (presumably authentic) autobiography. In the twenty-first century, the Internet has given rise to new copyright concerns, which raise, now as then, questions of original ownership and the accrual or deprivation of profit. Among the literary impostors I discuss in Chapter 5, only the copyright page traces Andreas Karavis to David Solway or Araki Yasusada to Kent Johnson, thus identifying ownership and responsibility for texts that are otherwise mysterious by establishing the address to which any royalty check should be sent.

As soon as the text becomes quite explicitly the personal expression of an identifiable author, autobiography, both authentic and fictional, becomes an inevitable form of literature. I have found Marcus particularly interesting for her discussion of this phenomenon. Citing Michael McKeon on travel narratives, William Warner on realism, and Philip Stewart on the contamination of historical records by fictional memoirs, Marcus explains how writers increasingly turned to first-person narrative to authenticate authorship and narrative truth. She also cites Philippe Lejeune's wonderful observation that autobiography mimicked the novel because the "autobiographer could only become himself by imitating people who imagined what it was to be an autobiographer. This curious game of mirrors," he adds, "shows that sincerity is something learned, that originality is a matter of imitation" (47, quoted in Marcus 258). Marcus concludes this section of her discussion with Sir Isaac Bickerstaff's famous attack on apocryphal French memoirs, and his insistence that the word "memoir" is the French for "novel." We may further the parallels between eighteenth-century and contemporary aesthetics by noting how the very concept of imposture depends on readers' concerns with authenticity, sincerity, and intent. (Even ironic postmodernists are unlikely to escape their grounding in such eighteenth-century or modernist concerns.) In short, frequent use of first-person narrative in this period introduced what was to become a new set of genres as well as significant genre confusion. Both contributed to constructions of the self and to opportunities for imposture.

For contemporary imposture, and for the investigation and exposure of contemporary imposture, the Internet has replicated London's coffee shop culture on a global scale. In both cases, information is immediate and widespread as well as hard to trace to its source. In an article wittily titled "What's in a Name?" Miguel Mota has written about contemporary textual and Internet uses of the name for identification of the author as a particular person. He contrasts Jeanette Winterson's highly politicized postmodern critique of traditional categories of identity and the Enlightenment subject in particular with her indignation when one Mark Hogarth registered her name (along with the names of several other writers) on the Web. She, who has written extensively about the multiple and unstable qualities of identity, was outraged to have her name "cyber-kidnapped." "It had never crossed my mind," she wrote on her website, "to confirm my identity. I know who I am. My books tell other people who I am. That used to be enough." Claiming that she is not attached to material possessions, she nonetheless suggests that "to be detached from [her] own name seemed to demand either schizophrenia or a Buddhist calm." In short, apparent authentication of origins matches person with author with autobiography—or with imposture.

Not surprisingly, copyright developed in the eighteenth century in tandem with a thriving print culture. Parallels with our contemporary Internet culture are, again, inescapable. Alvin Kernan, while suggesting that figures vary, nonetheless spells out a dramatic growth in the publishing industry. In 1695, a mere 20 printing houses were operating in the whole of England, housing no more than two presses apiece; by 1724, there were at least 7 printers in London alone, with a further 28 in the provinces. By 1785, London had 124 printers, some with as many as nine presses to a shop (59). This hectic and profitable business, much like today's Internet, was surely driven by commercial interests and fed by the laws of supply and demand. Certainly, much contemporary imposture has been similarly driven by a reading public eager for sensation and by publishers eager to make money regardless of autobiographical authenticity. (The scandals of James

Frey's *A Million Little Pieces* and Norma Khouri's *Honor Lost* are cases in point.) Furthermore, because writers, as Samuel Johnson put it so succinctly, wrote to make money, they in turn created what Johnson called "the common reader." Together, the working writer and the common reader ensured that personal narratives, among others, and narratives that claimed to be personal (as in Sir Isaac Bickerstaff's examples), could be both popular and profitable.

Today's common readers of books, which are still most commonly produced for profit, also bring to their reading some elements of the eighteenth-century experience that may be less obvious. I am thinking, for instance, of the association of the printed word with factual evidence. Kernan suggests that simple usefulness "acquired an aura of authenticity" in the eighteenth century: "Permanent records began to be printed, accurate information conveyed in newspapers, and the society's privileged texts—legal, sacred, instructional—stabilized and stored in print. Gradually this kind of authority grew into authenticity that is probably the absolute mark of print culture, a generally accepted view that what is printed is true, or at least truer than any other type of record" (49).

In general parlance, this early association of print with fact means that the authority of print does not really suffer even in our paranoid times. The authority of the printed word does not simply represent the scrutiny one may fairly expect that word to have received before it ever went into print; it also suggests an objective facticity of its very own, as if print were its own stamp of approval. In short, and generally speaking, because language (especially printed language) pertains to fact, it is therefore factual. The impostor then, like the impostor now, establishes a textual identity that is curiously protected by the authority of print.

Despite or because of texts having owners and print containing fact, plagiarism flourished in eighteenth-century England, giving rise to that anxiety about truthfulness implied in Lynch's "Pyrrhonism." We have seen these anxieties at work in ancient history. However, the eighteenth-century writer and audience, like writers and readers today, referred to the theft of another writer's work in the public arena that print had created. Certainly, plagiarism became an obsession with the Romantics (whose originality was matched only by their thievery). The cycle was either vicious or hilarious. Pope populated his *Dunciad* with plagiarists, all the while rewriting Dryden's "Mac Flecknoe," which was itself plagiarized from Andrew Marvell's "Flecknoe" (Groom 27–28). Focused as he is on deception in eighteenth-century literature, Lynch raises a question that recurs at different sites when he asks why it actually matters whether a work is authentic or not, given that it still exists as the same book that we found interesting when we thought it was authentic. He notes that "the great sin of ... famous forgers," to which I would add plagiarists and impostors, "is that they lived in an age when, perhaps for the first time it did matter who wrote it and when" ("Splendide Mendax"). This "first time" has not, for the common reader, become a last time. Many of the impostors discussed in the chapters that follow were challenged in courts of law, or sued, or threatened with suits for theft of language or identity.

As we respond to contemporary instances of imposture, or wax indignant about the shameless opportunism of publishing houses capitalizing on readers' interest in autobiography, or discover horrifying situations and personal stories, often created and widely disseminated online, we do well to recognize what we inherit from the past—in practical terms, certainly, but more importantly in terms of what counts as knowledge and dissemination of knowledge, the very reasons we have for trusting or doubting, and the conditions that exist for an impostor to "pull a fast one."

When impostors sign off, we sit up and pay attention and make a big fuss in the media precisely because they outrage our sense of propriety—the *propria persona,* the property of the individual aligned with his or her text, the long-established grounds on which writer and reader can agree on some sort of truth. Furthermore, and crucially, history demonstrates that impostors are most likely to appear when something important is at stake. At precisely that point where the community is most vulnerable, where the ground shifts between who we are and how we define ourselves, the impostor can strike. Counting on dis- and mis-alignments between author and text, or anxiety about current orthodoxies, the impostor may with satisfaction hear Foucault's rendering of Beckett: "What matter who's speaking?" (138).

3
Sensational Identities:
Made in the Media

Media tycoon William Randolph Hearst is credited with suggesting that one should never let the facts get in the way of a good story. Clearly, he understood the significant role the media play in feeding the public appetite for scandal (Boese 89). Scandal, after all, sells papers. Determined to print the Hitler materials even after he understood that Trevor-Roper was entertaining doubts late in the day (Harris 315), Rupert Murdoch saw both a mandate to entertain and certain profit. P.T. Barnum, self-styled Prince of Humbug, understood that the public did not mind being lied to so long as the lies were more sensational than the truth (Boese 64). In the case of impostors, this scenario plays itself out repeatedly: the popular media create and then address a commodity culture (the same that Adorno saw as destructive of individual subjectivity). Impostors understand this concept well, crafting identities and histories that manipulate volatile situations and therefore draw media attention (as in the case of the Hitler diaries, where the media themselves were the principal victims.) The impostor, then, uses or invents enough facts to convince the media, which are eager for the particular information, that he is serious and credible. Turning from scandals of the past to some contemporary impostures, I am impressed by how typically these are "made in the media." How many, I wonder, would receive any attention at all in a world without media? As things stand, the media provide the platform for astonishing success, the investigation that leads to exposure, and the stocks at the very least, if not the gallows and disembowelment of times past.

As with the fraudulent or doctored texts of the ancient world, so with contemporary media and impostors, fraud and sleuth depend on many of the same skills because they know how to "read" or interpret each other. Only since the age of the internet has the general public had access to more information than traditional media supply, and the internet, too, propagates both scandal and investigative journalism. This paradox cannot pass without comment: papers and radio and television programs sell on the strength of scandalous information, but they also assess and critique that information. Perhaps the media have inherited the mantle of the ancient poets, serving both to entertain and to instruct. This paradox affects impostors as well: the very publicity that creates them also destroys them. They seem to require publicity, but if they were not in the public eye, their escapades would be less likely to draw fire. (Even while Jerzy Kosinski with his scandalous Holocaust story was making news playing polo with the media darlings of his time, journalists were assembling the stories that would undermine his credibility.)

Furthermore, impostors and journalists share the key requirement that they be able to protect their sources. Journalists must do so in order to report freely without fear of political interference or reprisal. Impostors, for their part, cannot survive if their sources or origins are exposed; interference and reprisal would be swift and sure. And the scandal in each case ("scandalum" means "cause of offence," from the Greek *skandalon,* "snare, stumbling block") surely connects even in contemporary cases with the orthodoxies so carefully developed and protected in the early Christian world. Now, as then, communities protect themselves from the unauthorized version; text or man, it may be engaging but it cannot be normalized.

How, then, are these sensational identities made (and unmade) in the media? Recognizing that this inquiry carries over into every instance of contemporary imposture, this chapter focuses on just two particular issues: that of the Muslim woman, or the woman under the rule of Islam, as she is represented in the West; and that of the self-made American man who plays with the fire of drug addiction. Gillian Whitlock's *Soft Weapons* analyzes representations of "the Muslim woman" that have figured largely in the Western media since 9/11. This woman is the pre-eminent mystery, the veiled and therefore hidden but also vulnerable and virtuous "face" of Islam. She is exempt from the fear and rage that Muslim men inspire (burdened as they tend to be with the need to prove they are not extremists). She, too, is a victim, subject to the Muslim man and therefore to be rescued by the liberal West. The Muslim woman, accordingly, provides a flashpoint for imposture. Despite the work of remarkable women like Shirin Ebadi and Zahra Kazemi, who risk their lives in pursuit of justice, and Azar Nafisi (*Reading Lolita in Tehran*) and Hirsi Ali (*Infidel*), who complicate personal and literary representation, the opportunist cannot waste this fraught situation.

This chapter looks briefly at the cases of Jumana Hanna (in fact a Christian but from Iraq) and Norma Khouri because they are in so many ways typical of contemporary imposture that is made in the media and of older forms that enjoyed a slower groundswell. They provide, therefore, an opportunity to identify the relations between media and imposture, both in particular and in general—to ask what these relations look like and why they matter.[1] As for the self-made American man, my questions about James Frey and *A Million Little Pieces* pertain not only to the media but also to the publishing industry, to the trap presented by myths of origin and identity in autobiography, and to the Janus-faced relations between text and life. Furthermore, Hanna and Frey have more in common than may at first appear: both depend on the American dream of independence and freedom; and both know the readership for their roles and can assume positions that the media recognize, support, and develop. The ultimate question therefore becomes "Who are we that we believe these kinds of stories and care when they are shown to be fraudulent?"

Reading the Middle East in the Middle West

On 21 July 2003, Peter Finn, correspondent for the *Washington Post,* published the terrible story of Jumana Hanna. Under the headline "A Lone Woman Testifies to Iraq's Order of Terror," he reported that Hanna, an Assyrian Christian, had been subjected to extended torture and rape under Saddam Hussein's regime. Her husband had been tortured and killed, his body passed to her through the bars of a gate like so much butcher's meat. Human rights officials spoke of hundreds, possibly thousands of women who had been brutalized, and Hanna became the face for all this suffering, the only one to emerge alive from the Loose Dogs Prison in Baghdad. Following the *Post* story, Hanna was taken into protective custody, became a valuable intelligence asset to the Coalition Provisional Authority in Iraq, and was finally brought to safety in the United States. At a point when the Bush administration was failing to find weapons of mass destruction, and when public support for the invasion of Iraq was beginning to wane, Jumana Hanna became what the *Village Voice* called "a poster girl for the ex post facto justification of the Iraq war." Deputy Defense Secretary Paul D. Wolfowitz told a Senate committee that Hanna's courage in providing "very likely credible information" (*Post,* 23 January 2005) would help the coalition "root out" Baathist killers (Solovitch 3). On her word alone occupation forces did indeed arrest nine Iraqi officers, including one brigadier general (Sara Solovitch, "The American Dream," *Esquire* [2005], http://www.esquire.com/features/articles/2004/041222_mfe_dream_1.html TNA online).

Then in January 2005, Sara Solovitch published a feature article in *Esquire* in which she outlined the impact that the *Post* article had had, and the stages of her own increasing doubts about Hanna's veracity. This led to a follow-up article in the *Post* on 20 January 2005, "Threads Unravel in Iraqi's Tale." Not surprisingly, given that 20 January was Inauguration Day in the United States, the day when the president renews his oath of office, the debunking of this important story did not occupy headlines to the extent the original had done but was relegated to page A18 of the *Post*. Hanna's exposure as a fraud was less useful than her support of the U.S.-led invasion and less thrilling than her detailed accounts of the torture inflicted on her.

The *Esquire* piece, on the other hand, was substantial. Titled "The American Dream," it detailed the naïveté of the American investigators in Iraq, the persuasiveness of Hanna's behaviour, and the value of the knowledge she claimed to have. Solovitch herself had responded warmly to the possibility of writing Hanna's story for her, of ghosting an autobiography of her that would command a wide reading. But as a responsible journalist, she also pointed out that all of Hanna's information would need to be verified. She explained to Hanna that Norma Khouri's "runaway bestseller," *Honor Lost: Love and Death in Modern-Day Jordan,* had recently been exposed as a fraud and withdrawn from bookstores in Australia, where it had been published as *Forbidden Love.*

Norma Khouri—or Norma Bagain, or Norma Toliopoulos, who grew up in Chicago, not Jordan, and who was wanted by the Chicago Police and the FBI for extravagant financial fraud at the time of her rapid escape to Australia—had sold an estimated 50,000 copies of her title on "lost honour" in the United States and 200,000 copies in Australia (*Chicago Sun-Times,* 28 July 2004). Apparently bearing witness to the honour killing of her close friend in Jordan, Khouri's manipulative fiction, posing as memoir, was exposed by what the *Sydney Morning Herald* referred to as "old-fashioned but reliable gumshoe techniques of investigation" (28 July 2004) and withdrawn from bookstores. The resulting media flurry spread across the English-speaking world through the summer of 2004, though it was especially intense in Australia, where it reopened discussion of a long history of imposture. By 2007, Anna Broinowski had released her documentary film of the Khouri scandal, *Forbidden Lie$.* Throughout that film, Khouri insists on the truth of her story. Repeatedly, Broinowski's research proves otherwise. In fact, Broinowski reveals a long succession of scams in addition to this one of the fraudulent memoir, and a number of people hurt. Not least, women's groups in Jordan expressed outrage at the damage that Khouri had done to their own work. Imposture of this kind is scandalous not only because it is opportunistic but also because it causes extensive and often quite specific harm. Clearly, Solovitch, though moved by Hanna Jumana, also belonged to the gumshoe school of journalism. Her enthusiastic offer to ghost Hanna's story produced in the end a Broinowski-style exposure.

Hanna was touchingly grateful that Solovitch would be so careful. "You are my voice," she told Solovitch, "you are my candle … You are not my writer; you are myself now. Because I don't have the language, you are my mouth" (Solovitch 3). Clearly, she was brazen, but this ventriloquism rapidly went awry. Some fairly elementary research began to unravel the skein of lies that Hanna had told in order to manipulate both her fame and the wealth of her "American dream," which somehow included a steady supply of Belgian chocolates. Her husband was not dead. American investigators had found no bodies at the mass grave she had pointed out to them. She had not attended Oxford, where they do not offer the degree in accounting that she claimed to have taken, and so on. Hanna proved, in fact, to be a talented con artist who had imposed herself on the American military and government, the American media, and the American public.

The reasons for her success, of course, are not far to seek; we also encounter them in the success of Norma Khouri's *Honor Lost* or *Forbidden Love*. As with Hanna's story, one reporter for the *Sydney Morning Herald* of 28 July 2004 noted that *Forbidden Love* had "mustered a wave of Western revulsion against the supposedly widespread Muslim practice [of honour killing] at the very time the West was clamouring for justification of anti-Muslim sentiment." Khouri's case, like Hanna's, belongs to the genre that William Norman Grigg in the *New American* called "Atrocity Porn." Both women had targeted a Western audience with extravagant tales of Muslim men from whose brutality they personally had suffered. Both bore righteous witness to atrocities to which the West—where women apparently enjoy respect and power—needed to respond.[2]

The speed with which these stories spread and the international coverage they received are very much contemporary phenomena, indicative of the power of the media in numerous roles: as conveyors of information that contributes to rapid and significant action on the part of both government and business; as sensitive contributors to contemporary culture, recognizing exactly what material will create a feeding frenzy and what the cultural value of that material is; as communicators of contemporary orthodoxies (Solovitch was onside until her homework punched holes in Hanna's bucket); as our gumshoe detectives following in the steps of Valla, Mabillon, and the doubt police of old. However, like the impostures they help produce and destroy, the media seem very serious (appearing in print) but also shockingly evanescent. How many of the websites on which I have relied, I wonder, will be easily accessible to future readers of this work? For all the excitement and interest these stories generated across quite diverse reading communities, I wonder whether the media productions, like Hanna and Khouri themselves, are not, in the end, a flash in the pan.

These two women and their stories do not seem complex, but they clearly indicate the precision with which this kind of headline-grabbing autobiographical imposture constructs and interprets its chosen readership. P.T. Barnum knew what he was talking about. I am concerned about how these versions of the

"Muslim" East make sense in the "Christian" West, how they mediate our under-standing of ourselves. In Hanna's case, of course, where she has no book to peddle but emerges from a scene of atrocity, the media are the earliest witnesses to her appalling experience and therefore the first mediators between her and her public. They are therefore the dupes if not the actual co-practitioners of her autobiographical fraud. Between them, these two impostors make clear both how ready their audience was to be duped and how the media played robbers and then cops in the imposture and its subsequent exposure. They had to bring to heel the excitement they themselves had unleashed.

The Young Pretender, James Frey

Almost every instance of imposture involves both life and text, raising questions of origin and intent. Who is the impostor really? Where, or in what, does the text origi-nate? At what point do life and text come unstuck from each other? In *The Making of Medieval Forgeries,* Alfred Hiatt includes a section on "Forgery as Historiogra-phy," in which he examines situations where technical forgery may support actual fact. So, for instance, medieval written records may in many instances validate (or cause problems for) information previously stored only in oral tradition. Some such elements of information or custom underpin the histories of Kosinski, who appears in Chapter 6, and of Jumana Hanna and, indeed, James Frey. Their false stories are not simply and entirely fiction; they rest on some kind of foundation, some kind of fact, but not enough fact to justify the edifice they build. Impostors are people, of course, but they are not who they seem to be because their origins are in doubt or disproven; and in autobiography, mere seeming is not enough. Even if given to failures of memory or imaginative reconstruction, autobiographers must be who they say they are and who others believe them to be if they do not wish to be challenged as impostors.

Hiatt refers to Harry Bresslau who, in the nineteenth century, distinguished between "diplomatic forgery," or "'any piece of writing, which due to the intention of its producer, gives itself for something other than it really is,'" and "historical forgery, [which] asserts something that never in reality took place, but whose issuer does not assume a false identity" (5–6). These fine distinctions, which could be significant in a court of law, help me think about different impostors as engaged in subtly different kinds of deception. Most usefully for my concerns, Hiatt then cites Giles Constable, who suggested replacing "the terms 'forgery' and 'fraud' with 'imposture' or 'fiction'" (7). Both Hanna and Frey became rich on the basis of their fraudulent stories, but I suspect that Frey in particular was more interested in imposture and fiction than in forgery or fraud. Both imposed on the gullible public by fabricating "historical forgery," their own living presences being the thread through events that never took place. In Frey's case—as in Kosinski's, and in Wilkomirski's—he also produced a piece of writing that, due to his intention, presented itself as something other than it really was.

I did not read *A Million Little Pieces* when it came out or even when it became a bestseller. I was immersed at the time in the reading required for classes and research, so I depended on reviews and discussion for many books that were attracting the attention of friends and neighbours. However, by February 2006, I noticed that we were into week five of the scandal that had followed James Frey's autobiography after it was shown to be a tissue of lies. My desk soon became littered with printouts from the links from the links on the Internet. Family and friends were e-mailing these sites to me on a daily basis, an international Web of our own for gossip and for sharing news from the *New York Times, LA Weekly,* and *Slate,* the *Washington Post,* the *Minneapolis Star Tribune,* the *Vancouver Sun,* the *Globe and Mail,* the *New York Post,* the *New Republic,* the *New York Observer,* ABC News, CTV, Canoe.ca, *Westcoast Life,* the *News Tribune,* the *Denver Post,* the *Saskatoon Star Phoenix,* and so on and on. James Frey pronounces his name as if it were "Fry," which led to headlines such as "Deep Freyed" (*Globe and Mail,* 14 January 2006). The headlines were playful even when discussion was irate: "A Million Little Corrections" (*New York Times,* 11 January 2006); "Picking Up the Pieces" (*Slate,* 12 January 2006), with its echoes of Blake Eskin's book, *A Life in Pieces,* on that other impostor, Binjamin Wilkomirski; "A Million Little Fibs?" (*Globe and Mail,* 11 January 2006, R1); "Link by Link: Before the Fame, a Million Little Skeptics" (*New York Times,* 23 January 2006); "Reality Bites" (*Slate,* 7 February 2006); and "Frey Faces a Million Little Grudges" (*Denver Post,* 14 February 2006). Journalists also indulged in literary allusion, invoking association for their readers, contextualizing this text, ensuring that the issue of personal scandal remained grounded in the world of literature. Though Frey's work is completely innocent of irony, early critics invoked comparison with David Eggers, as Joe Hagan did with his title "Meet the New Staggering Genius" (*New York Observer,* 3 February 2003), and Chris Lehmann, with "A Heart-Stopping Work of Sentimentality" (*Slate,* 21 April 2003). Early in the media frenzy, Edward Wyatt, who seems to have been assigned the Frey desk for the *New York Times,* opened his column of 11 January 2006 with a play on Ayn Rand's title, *Atlas Shrugged:* "And on the second day," he wrote, "Doubleday shrugged"—which I understand to mean that money and power drove the story of this story, with repercussions for the publishing industry extending far beyond a single text.

For many of these media sites, I acquired many entries, yet I am sure my file is incomplete even so. The Frey scandal mushroomed out of control, spawning connections with contemporaneous impostors like JT LeRoy and Nasdijj and, in editorial discussion, with the many impostors who preceded them. Even Elie Wiesel was drawn in, partly because *Night,* his memoir of Auschwitz, followed Frey's *A*

Million Little Pieces on Oprah Winfrey's Book Club, and partly because *Night* has actually been described as a novel ("mainly because of its literary style"), though Wiesel insists "it is not a novel at all. I know the difference." In a memoir, he insists, "experiences in the book—A to Z—must be true" (*New York Times,* 17 January 2006). While introducing numerous other issues, the Frey scandal became at bottom *about* this expectation of the A–Z truth to life of memoir and the outrage that follows the exposure of lies.

Quite apart from the lively discussions among bloggers that supplemented editorials in the news media, the fallout from Frey's imposture has affected contemporary autobiographers whose seriousness had not so far been called into question. Linda Joy Myers, Mary Karr, and Vivian Gornick have all been required to defend the fictive elements in their work—to argue for the authenticity of elements that develop the meaning or value of their life experiences. Unfortunately, heated debate on truth and lies does not depend on or devise particularly subtle understanding of the meaning of either one. Leah McLaren, for example, defended Frey in the *Globe and Mail* (14 January 2006): "If you want the truth, go read the Income Tax Act. If you want a good story, read Frey's book." McLaren's equation of truth with factual information that has been deliberately concocted and is subject to change is unhelpful but apparently widely shared.

James Frey's *A Million Little Pieces* purports to be about his recovery from drug addiction, a painful and deeply relevant topic in a prosperous and aimless society. As a young, middle-class white man, Frey writes from the privileged position of the traditional norm, the position from which all others need to distinguish themselves (as in Jew or African American or Aboriginal or Muslim). Not surprisingly, then, he seeks attention in the only way that is open to him, by developing the trauma of his private life, his addiction to drugs, and leading his readers to the new frontier of self-help: he kicked his brutal habit without professional help, on his own. To write a story that the public would notice, he created out of his boringly "normal" identity an encumbered identity—one that, like Jumana Hanna's, made a very clear kind of sense and that sought a very clear kind of response. Because drug addiction represents helplessness and failure, Frey was able to describe the weakness (and violence) of the victim, the horror (and violence) of his experience, his devalued status, and the remarkable courage that returned him, forever changed, to the world of "the normal," from which he could bear witness to his experience.[3]

Responding to a draft of this chapter, Geoff Hamilton, who works on the psychopath in American literature, accepted but also improved on my reading of Frey as reversing the American Dream in his journey from privilege and success to near-lethal disaster. Frey, he suggests, is actually pursuing another very clear trajectory such that this reversal "isn't finally a reversal at all, as the Dream being articulated is the old American one of the antisocial individualist who fights for a radical autonomy along some rugged frontier: Frey gives us something like Slotkin's 'regeneration through violence' For Dummies."[4] Hamilton sees the receptivity of American readers as key to understanding *A Million Little Pieces,* suggesting that it also draws heavily on what Mark Seltzer has called America's "wound culture" in order to make "James Frey" a hero of popular culture.

Apparently endorsing Seltzer's point, Oprah Winfrey selected *A Million Little Pieces* for her Book Club in October 2005, referring to it as "a gut-wrenching memoir that is raw and it's so real" (*Globe and Mail,* 11 January 2006, R3). This memoir, at that point the first non-fiction title in Oprah's ten-year-old club and her fastest-selling selection (*New York Times,* 27 January 2006), became what *the smoking gun* called "a phenomenal hit," Amazon's top pick for 2003 (*New York Times,* 23 January 2006), racking up more than 3.5 million sales, sharing the *New York Times* bestseller place for more than fifteen weeks for the end of 2005 and the beginning of 2006 with the latest Harry Potter. Then, targeted by *the smoking gun,* this memoir was exposed as fraudulent in many of its key elements. While retaining the limelight, it ricocheted from fame to notoriety. Despite or because of its notoriety, Frey's work continued on the *Globe and Mail*'s national bestseller list through 2006, sharing space with *Night* as well as with *The Da Vinci Code, The Jesus Papers, Holy Blood, Holy Grail,* and *The Gospel of Judas.* In the final listing for 2006, on 6 January 2007, *A Million Little Pieces,* having stayed on the list for fifty-five weeks, ranked as #1.

The extent of the scandal was quite astonishing. Colleagues who knew I was interested in imposture began accosting me on the stairs, in the washroom, and at the water cooler wanting to know if I was having fun. (Yes, I would be having fun if I could keep up.) The Frey scandal opened up for all to see the kinds of issues that had been concerning me for a while. "Do you think," Michelle, my massage therapist, asked, "that we should be reading memoir the same way we read fiction? For me," she said, "the two are quite different because I believe what I read in memoir. I'm not reading a fictional story, I'm reading about a real person." Exactly the kind of question I had been working with. Clearly, I had to do some solid research here—at least as solid as Michelle's—and read the book itself. "What on earth do you want this one for?" asked my friend at special orders in the bookstore, clearly implying that my habits tend to be more salubrious. "Are you buying this one in spite of yourself?" asked the woman at the till, whom I don't know at all. After all the hype, I fell asleep within thirty pages. However, serious research is always a hard slog, and my interest in imposture is more than a little connected to my own fears about being an impostor myself. As I approached retirement I took comfort in a friend's kind reassurances that if I got away with it for just a little while longer, I'd have had "them" fooled.

James Frey, who made more money in about three years than I have made in a lifetime, is not so lucky. He has been exposed. He now faces loss of revenue on several fronts (no film, likely damage to further book contracts, ongoing lawsuits for misleading readers and purchasers of his book (see www.CTV.ca, 9 February 2006; *Globe and Mail*, 4 February 2006). When the sheer volume of media attention began to subside, he began losing currency for his celebrity status as well. The *Saskatoon Star Phoenix* noted (13 February 2006) that Frey "has understandably been dumped by Barnes & Noble as a judge in its annual Discover Great New Writers Awards." Sadly, his name has lost its moral value (a quality special to the memoirist and less likely to be invoked in the case of the writer of great fiction). Unlike Clifford Irving with *The Hoax,* or Timothy Barrus, who is planning a book about his construction of "Nasdijj" (*Globe and Mail*, 4 February 2006), or Geoffrey Koop, former partner of Laura Albert, creator of "JT LeRoy," "who plans to write about his experience of this duplicity" (*New York Times,* 7 February 2006), Frey is not, apparently, planning to write about his roller-coaster ride as "James Frey." He has told CTV that "writing a book about this experience would be trying to capitalize on it in some way and that's not something [he] want[s] to do at all" (CTV, 28 January 2006).[5] Frey, in other words, clings to the only moral high ground left to him. (Notably, when Oprah lambasted Frey on her show on 26 January, she also allowed him his moment of moral redemption at the end; he has learned his lesson, he told her, and will never make this mistake again.) Nonetheless, like so many impostors before him, he has made significant money out of his brief, meretricious, and unrepeatable success. Sales continued strong following the high drama of Oprah's excoriation of Frey for lying to her and to his millions of readers, reminding me of Barnum's observation that "the public loved the spectacle of frauds unmasked and deceivers brought to justice" (Boese 5). Imposture, which is invariably, maybe necessarily, sensational, links inextricably with the making of money and with the reading public's desire not for bread but for blood and circuses.

Sensational Identity in Autobiography

Rather like Jerzy Kosinski, who figures in Chapter 6, James Frey became notorious for the fiction that he connected very specifically to himself and his own life, the kind of fiction that steps through the looking glass into imposture. The scandal of Frey's exposure pertains quite specifically to autobiography, which convention has established as the truthful (perhaps read "honest" and therefore trustworthy) story of one's own life; as well as to autobiographical identity, the narrated self or central character of this story, which the author maps onto his or her living self. Despite all the problems attendant on such a possibility, autobiography is understood to be "true" when readers can trust that the story and experience, author and character, match each other, that they may believe the person behind the text. Unlike the elusive "author" of other forms of literature, the autobiographer, as I suggest in Chapter 1, must be perceived as the source or origin of the autobiographical text. Any breakdown in this perception, any doubt about the symbiosis between teller and tale, opens up questions of imposture. Significantly, given the limited story forms available for use and, therefore, the predictable story forms that narrators fill with different content, the onus for integrity in autobiography falls on the teller, not the tale. Can readers hold the autobiographer accountable for the tale? (This question has been raised repeatedly throughout the Frey scandal.) Can he or she truthfully claim to be the original for the narrator and protagonist of the story? Is the autobiographer the source of the experience narrated? The impostor is the person (not the text) who claims another person's story or claims to be the living source for a story that is not true.

Given the vagaries of narrative, perspective, and memory, "true" autobiographies may, of course, involve disagreements about what happened or about how what happened is perceived. Autobiographies that purport to be true may even give rise to debate initiated by others involved in the lived experience and who have their own versions to relate. I think, for example, of Paul Steinberg's *Speak You Also*, which was an explicit response to Primo Levi's *If This Is a Man*; of shared texts, such as Blaise and Mukherjee's *Days and Nights in Calcutta*; or of Butler and Rosenblum's *Cancer in Two Voices*. Less happily, Mary McCarthy famously claimed on *The Dick Cavett Show* (18 October 1979), that everything Lillian Hellman had written was a lie, including "and" and "but," a situation fanned both by the celebrity status of the participants and by the lawsuit that followed. However, "true" autobiographies come unravelled (as Frey's story has) not for ands and buts but rather because fact checkers have found no matches at all or have found outright contradictions for key elements of the story, thereby (as in Frey's case) unravelling the origins and authorization for the claims being made.

Frey's story is extreme, but it resonates in a culture where drug and alcohol addiction are distressingly commonplace. In keeping with so foundational an autobiographer as Jean-Jacques Rousseau, who considered his own self-exposure so scandalous that no one else would ever attempt such a thing, Frey declares his own faults so unsparingly that readers assume they are true. As if he had been attending to William Zinsser's insistence on the necessity of truth in memoir, Frey insists on the importance of truth the whole way through his text. Truth is his mantra, and he is prepared to defend it to the last cliché. For example, he is outraged by a Rock Star speaker whose self-promoting talk is "not in any way, shape or form related to [the truth of the experience of addiction] and that is all that matters, the truth … The truth is all that matters" (178). However, Frey has refused to take the transparency test. He says he has taken steps "to legally expunge court records related to the seemingly most egregious criminal activity of his lifetime," and he would not grant *the smoking gun* access to all the records, "medical, psychological, financial, criminal, and otherwise" that he said he had given to Doubleday and spoken about with Oprah (see www.thesmokinggun.com, hereafter TSG). Rousseau may have wished for the fans that Frey has gained but may also have been fortunate to write before the Doubting Thomases of the press could go to work on his story.

Initially seeking only the mug shot of this former prison inmate for their rogue's gallery, and failing to find it, *the smoking gun* began a six-week investigation that included three interviews with Frey. The second one, on 14 December 2005, left Frey so "rattled" that he called on Martin Singer, the Los Angeles attorney to the stars, who subsequently threatened *the smoking gun* with a multimillion-dollar lawsuit if it "described the author as a liar and/or that he fabricated or falsified background as reflected in *A Million Little Pieces*" (TSG 2). As in so many other cases of autobiographical imposture, the law plays a part as it is invoked to establish credible identity or to punish fraud. (Both Clifford Irving and his collaborator Richard Susskind went to jail for their forgery of Howard Hughes's name, as did Konrad Kujau for his fraudulent Hitler diaries.) Repeatedly the law demonstrates that it serves selective interests and is an important maker and breaker of confident identities in Western culture. However, *the smoking gun* published its story (including the lawyer's letter, which had been submitted to it with a publication ban) on 8 January 2006, with no legal consequences. Subjected to Oprah's outrage on 26 January, Frey admitted, with interesting indirectness, that he thought that "most of what [*the smoking gun*] wrote was pretty accurate, absolutely" (*New York Times*, 27 January 2006). While this is a shame-faced rather than a ringing endorsement of *the smoking gun* report, the impostor exposed cannot depend on the law to secure his failing credibility.

Frey (man and text) comes unravelled on three separate but related grounds: the actual facts that he claimed were true, the effects within the text of such non-facts, and his own aspirations for literary distinction. In the first instance, *the smoking gun* report was the sleuth, the modern Mabillon, using "old-fashioned but reliable gumshoe techniques of investigation," like the journalists who uncovered Khouri. Describing Frey in its headline as "The Man Who Conned Oprah," it suggests rather more nefarious failures of accountability than mere failures of memory. It summarizes its findings about the facts in a key episode in *A Million Little Pieces* as follows:

> There was no patrolman struck with a car.
> There was no urgent call for backup.
> There was no rebuffed request to exit the car.

> There was no "You want me out, then get me out."
> There was no "Fucking Pigs" taunt.
> There were no swings at cops.
> There was no billy club beatdown.
> There was no kicking and screaming.
> There was no mayhem.
> There was no attempted riot inciting.
> There were no 30 witnesses.
> There was no .29 blood alcohol test. There was no crack.
> There was no Assault with a Deadly Weapon, Assaulting an Officer of the
> Law, Felony DUI, Disturbing the Peace, Resisting Arrest, Driving without
> Insurance, Attempted incitement of a Riot, Possession of a Narcotic with
> Intent to Distribute, or Felony Mayhem. (4)

The problem identified here is the simple impossibility of matching Frey's story with that of witnesses or with documented evidence. *The smoking gun* exposed Frey's story as, quite simply, factually untrue.

Another problem is the effect of one lie on the narrative that follows. (I understand "lie" to mean that which can be shown to be not true and which the writer himself knew to be not true when he wrote it. A lie, in other words, is not the same thing as a failure of memory or the associative enrichment of a lived experience.) Where *the smoking gun* investigators tried to verify facts as information, refuting a sequence of autobiographical claims by interviewing the people involved and running exhaustive checks on police and court records, Tom Scocca worked with the effects of such misinformation on the truthfulness of the text itself (and its alignment with its author). Beginning from Frey's correction of fact—his admission that he had not spent time in jail—Scocca takes just the opening sentence of *My Friend Leonard,* the bestselling sequel to *A Million Little Pieces,* and unravels the lies that follow from one false statement.[6] The opening sentence of *My Friend Leonard* reads: "On my first day in jail, a three hundred pound man named Porterhouse hit me in the back of the head with a metal tray." "In other words," Scocca writes:

> "On my first day in jail*, a three hundred pound man** named
> Porterhouse*** hit me in the back of the head**** with a metal tray*****."
> *The author never went to jail.
> **Weight is an estimate; also the author, not being in jail, never met such
> a person.
> ***Not his real name: also the author never met such a person.
> ****Because the author's head was not present in jail, such a blow did
> not actually land.

*****The composition of the tray is a guess, because the author did not actually get hit by it, because the author was never in jail.
(*New York Observer*, 23 January 2006)

Where *the smoking gun* went after verifiable truth for a series of events, Scocca wanted just one true thing—Frey's spending time in jail. In both cases, Frey's preference for sensation over fact led to this gruelling (even if profitable) exposure. Frey himself, Oprah when she was supporting him, and his publisher, Nan A. Talese, defending flexible expectations of truth in autobiography, all gave higher priority to emotional than to factual truth. However, in terms of autobiography, if not only the "ands" and "buts" but also the A to Z of experience are false, one must ask to whom this emotional truth belongs, or on what it is founded, who is telling this story, and why.

Sadly, for a man who briefly won iconic status on the grounds of his personal experience, Frey actually had pretensions as a writer. As with Holocaust autobiography and all writing based on trauma, life experience wins over the aesthetic quality of the story. Both publishers and public are drawn to the moral rather than the aesthetic value of the story they believe to be true. When moral ground and aesthetic quality combine in one text, the autobiography is rich indeed. However, in Frey's case, that moral ground was all he seemed to have: it was the reason for his being published and for his being noticed. His claims, therefore, to literary excellence create confusion for himself (what is he up to?), for his publisher (what is she up to?), and for literary critics who rely rather more than they should on the publisher's imprimatur and who fail to see that the emperor is wearing no clothes. Each one conflates life with text, somehow believing that the moral value of the life necessarily amounts to the aesthetic value of the text. Keeping my eye on that mobile quantity known as autobiography, I realize that good writing can enrich the resonance and meaning of life story; but I also doubt that crude attention to sensational experience translates at all readily into good writing. Writing pretensions, in effect, introduce new kinds of doubts, about the writer's self-awareness, motives, or responsibility to truth.

Frey, who has described himself as working in the tradition of Hemingway, Burroughs, and Kerouac, would certainly like his work to rate as literature. He told the *New York Observer* as early as 2003 that he (like Kosinski) aimed to be "the greatest writer of [his] generation" (*Slate,* 21 April 2003). For a while, his aspirations were aided and abetted by the media response. According to the acclaim he has received that is printed at the opening of *A Million Little Pieces,* the *New York Press* wonders, "Can Frey be the greatest writer of his generation?" and concludes "Maybe." Similarly mixing caution with extreme praise, *Elle* suggests that "Frey will probably be hailed … as the voice of a generation." When Frey repeated on *The*

Larry King Show (11 January 2006) that he followed in the tradition of Hemingway, Fitzgerald, Bukowsky, and Kerouac, King pointed out that these great literary figures all wrote fiction. "At the time of their books being published," Frey responded, "the genre of memoir didn't exist" (Mary Karr in the *New York Times,* 15 January 2006). Unfortunately for Frey's moral standing, the genre of memoir has since been invented, with two possible results for truth telling: either one writes true and honest fiction or one writes true and honest autobiography. Sadly rare is the talent that combines these skills, bringing the insight of imagination to the recounting of fact. For Frey (as for Kosinski), misplaced pride in his literary skill means that both man and book fail the test of truth. Here, too, autobiography straddles a middle ground; we may object to the impostor who is not, as a man, who he seems to be or says he is, and the poverty of his work may well be part of what exposes his imposture.

Literary talent invites and provides a different kind of knowledge from that provided in non-literary autobiography. Wayne C. Booth makes the point for fiction very clearly when he explains that we do not have to believe the information that Regan and Goneril have behaved thus and so but we must understand that ingratitude is sharper than a serpent's tooth (17). Frey's prose fails to take that second step (which does not belong to Shakespeare alone but also in varying degrees to Hemingway et al.) in which information that may not be verifiable does at least convey a clear meaning. Frey asks us to believe, for instance, that his high school sweetheart was killed when the car in which she was riding collided with a train. Sadly, Frey's treatment of this train crash depends on a prose that is mannered and therefore lacking in the kind of insight or impact associated with literature: "She got hit by a Train and killed," Frey writes. "She got hit by a fucking Train and killed … She was my only friend. She got hit by a Train and killed" (81–82). Unfortunately, both for his literary aspirations and for his claims to be telling the truth, Frey lacks both the creativity and the self-criticism that are important to good writing as well as the self-knowledge that comes with fine autobiography. Pretentious writing, coupled with constantly righteous and pitying self-regard, undermines the authenticity he wants to convey.

In short, the grounds for refusing Frey's claims both to truth and to artistry come full circle and implicate each other: he has not used true information; since his work depends on untrue information, it is fiction; as fiction, it is derivative and lacking in merit; as poor fiction, it cannot sell unless it sells as fact; however, the facts are not true. When the press then turns on the impostor hiding like that Wizard of Oz behind the text that is shown to be false at every level, what normative values do they invoke or validate? How do they restore the equilibrium that they have helped disturb? Where does the publisher fit into the situation? Are we looking at an anomaly or at a systemic collapse of checks and balances on the orthodoxies of life and life narrative?

Frey's explanation to Oprah, now written into the disclaimer inserted in new editions of his work, suggests that he had "tried to present [him]self as a far braver, stronger, and more heroic person that [he] really was—or [is]." As Frey's luck would have it, Meghan O'Rourke notes that even this moment of apparent introspection and honesty lacks personal authenticity in that it closely echoes the disclaimer extorted from one Jimmy A. Lerner in 2002, when he, too, made false autobiographical claims in *You Got Nothing Coming* (*Slate,* 7 February 2006). No sad disclaimer can rescue either man from the charge of inventing the person he would like to be. However, not wanting, by any means, to sound as outraged as Mary McCarthy on the subject of Lillian Hellman, I must wonder why Frey should plagiarize even this apology, whether the chicken and egg of life and narrative are so confused for Frey that he no longer knows, in fact, who he really is, in which case, of course, he cannot write a life story—but he, like so many other impostors, has chosen autobiography as a genre that sells.

Autobiography or narratives of identity have become central to the publishing industry, alongside such other non-fiction categories as books on political science, science, diet, and health (Deborah Rybak, *Minneapolis Star Tribune,* 27 July 2003). Like Elie Wiesel in his response to *The Painted Bird* as fiction, or like Dorothy de Santillana at Houghton Mifflin, who accepted that manuscript, Nan A. Talese, Senior Vice-President of Doubleday and Publisher and Editorial Director of Nan A. Talese/Doubleday, is clear that she would not have published *A Million Little Pieces* as a novel. I must assume that she and I are in accord about its poor quality as text. Nonetheless, counting on the life story that autobiography can privilege above quality of text, Talese took on *A Million Little Pieces* and marketed it as memoir. She defended it as memoir on Oprah and in other media, dodging charges of lies (if not of quality) by saying that memoir cannot be held to the same standards of factual truth as history and biography. I have seen a number of versions of The War of the Taleses but refer to the *New York Times* of 12 January 2006, which quotes Gay Talese taking issue with Nan Talese's position, insisting that "nonfiction takes no liberty with the fact, and it should not. I think all writers should be held accountable." Nan Talese responds that she "adores Gay" and that they have been having this debate for forty years. I return later to their debate, which is central to my project, but I note in passing that this couple stars in the New York world of literature and publishing, can command media attention, and can make and break the likes of James Frey.

Autobiography may sell because readers want accessible personal history, but bestselling titles suggest that readers care in particular about experiences and stories that are in some way extreme. Certainly, critics and journalists have complained about the plethora of self-indulgent memories of suffering. Michael

Posner wrote about what he called "Chronic book syndrome" in the *Globe and Mail* (20 November 1999, D20–21), referring to "the Medical Misery Library (a subset of the much larger Victimology genre)" as an increasing trend in publishing. "Pick a disease," he wrote, "any disease." More recently, Karen von Hahn wrote a piece on "addiction addicts" (*Globe and Mail,* 18 February 2006, L3), suggesting that "we are all living in a large group-therapy session" and that nothing "in this our new public 'empatheatre' … no matter how low-down, is shameful, so long as it is shared, and not spared." However, she notes that "when it comes to tales of addiction, perfidy is an outrage. Addicted as we are to our addiction stories, they don't really work for us unless every sordid detail is the sad and miserable truth." She is not the first or only one to observe the arc of redemption that follows appalling abasement, thus identifying narratives of popular culture with religious and psychological "confession" and with the narrative forms of autobiographical confession that trace back, even in popular culture, to St. Augustine and St. Paul.

If autobiography sells, and if—as media moguls know—sensation sells, then the agents and publishers of sensational autobiography share the impostor's success. They also share with the media both his making and his unmaking. However, they seem not to share the media's other responsibility to investigate. Writing in *The Australian* during the Khouri scandal, Frank Moorhouse wondered about the

> need for a tightening of publishing practices [and] the increasing demand
> for integrity of information (and integrity in the communicating of human
> experience). Integrity of information is the business of reputable book
> publishers and it is what distinguishes them from the internet (as it is at
> present) and from self-publishing, and still, to a degree in the public mind,
> from film, television and journalism. Hence the discussion in copyright
> theory of the value and need for publishers' trademark integrity, the
> reputation of their imprint, their colophon. Publishing is not just show
> business—some may be, some is definitely not.[7]

In the case of Doubleday and *A Million Little Pieces,* show business seems to have won over the integrity of their procedures, rendering them, too, complicit in this particular imposture. However, because culpability for imposture once again aligns the man with his text, only the author is held responsible.

For all this fracas, Frey alone has taken the heat, with merely some questions raised for his editor, Sean MacDonald, or his publisher, Nan A. Talese, or his agent, Kassie Evashevski of Brillstein-Grey. However, it seems that both they and even Oprah had been given early warnings about the extent of these fabrications and, in Oprah's case, warnings about the risks of promoting a work that offered dangerous false hopes to addicts. Ian Brown of the *Globe and Mail* is not the first journalist to discuss the unmasking of scandalous problems in the publishing industry, in particular publishers' failure to hire fact checkers. As early as July 2003, Deborah Caulfield Rybak of the *Star Tribune* was checking with experts about whether various things in *A Million Little Pieces* "could have happened as described." Nan Talese told her then, some two and a half years before the scandal broke, that the publisher had slipped up in not inserting a disclaimer page. However, Talese also suggested that publishers' lawyers are concerned only about possible libel suits, not about factual verification. Furthermore, Edward Wyatt in the *New York Times* (24 January 2006) wrote that "more than three months before questions were raised about Mr. Frey's memoir by the Smoking Gun Web site … before, in fact, Ms. Winfrey first had Mr. Frey as a guest on 'The Oprah Winfrey Show'—producers at the program were told by a former counselor at the foundation that runs the Minnesota treatment center reportedly used by Mr. Frey that his portrayal of his experience there grossly distorted reality." A senior producer for the *Oprah Winfrey Show* conducted an extensive interview with this addiction counsellor, Debra Jay, who had herself been a frequent guest on the program. None of this concern was apparent in Oprah's promotion of Frey's work or in her impression that it was "all completely true." In short, as Wyatt concludes in the *Times* (28 January 2006), "the questions about how publishers should deal with the truth or falsity of the books they publish are likely to continue to resound through the book business." If these institutional elements of the publishing world can indeed be implicated in the promotion of a book that they understood to be problematic, we cannot separate autobiographical imposture from the financial expediency or institutional greed at work beyond the impostor himself. "James Frey" has created a fictional self, but this fiction, further created by the media, seems to have been shamelessly endorsed by those who failed, on the basis either of fact-checking or of literary analysis, to tell counterfeit from true currency.

Frey alone takes the heat. Others failed to police his narratives—the same others who stand to profit from his publications—but he alone is the autobiographical impostor. Like so many others, he has gambled—that he might be recognized as a great writer, that his personal story could, with some significant adjustments, press the magic button for his time and place, that he could ride out the notoriety of exposure and continue to prosper as writer, or autobiographer, or both. However, whereas con artists can testify to the possibility of continuing success in various fields of fraud, the autobiographical impostor is limited by life itself. Frey did remarkably well to produce two books before final exposure. Most produce no more than one. Doubleday, Brillstein-Grey, and Oprah will all continue as before, but the man, James Frey, like other impostors, must now walk the earth naked because burdened with a text he cannot wear.

A Brief Taxonomy for Imposture

Finally, to demonstrate how inextricably connected imposture and the media tend to be, I suggest a brief taxonomy. While this taxonomy draws quite specifically on media and imposture, it also addresses the relations between any given reading public and the texts it is invited to believe. Suggesting some critical elements of faith and doubt, it offers some generalities to bear in mind for the less specifically media-related impostures that follow in the rest of my discussion.

First, in Jumana Hanna's case, where she had no book to peddle but emerged from a scene of atrocity, I have suggested that the media were the earliest witnesses to her appalling experience, therefore the first mediators between her and her public, and therefore the dupes if not the actual co-practitioners of her autobiographical fraud. Solovitch, for example, was initially so committed to Hanna's cause that for many weeks she resisted the little doubts that kept causing her concern. Serving as "the mouth" of the suffering woman with a story to tell, Solovitch ran the further risk of collapsing the distance between the two women. As Michael Getler wrote in the *Washington Post* on 23 January 2005: "Reporting stories of people caught up in war is important and valuable but also tricky ... It helps to tell readers when some of what is being said can't be verified and is being told through interpreters, if that is the case." Readers, in short, need reminding that the media mediate the stories that readers receive as true.[8] If readers are naive, they reduce language and narrative, in the world or about the world, to transparent information devoid of subtlety, critique, or self-reflection. In this context, I note that Western readers are often media junkies and that news therefore creates its own communities of story and response, be it online, on television, on the radio, or in print. The successful impostor, manipulating a volatile situation that everyone knows about, addresses a community that lacks the means or the will to critique and that is wired to respond. The media's adoption of stories like Hanna's ensures a groundswell of emotional response as well as a cultural solidarity that crosses internal divides in the receiving public. Comfortingly, we all feel the same way about what we have been told.

Second, because, as we have seen, particular times and places are sensitive to particular identity performances, these impostures are topical and timing is key to their success. With Western anxieties about Islam, Hanna and Khouri were spot on. We do not tend to hear about impostors whose timing is off. Furthermore, the particular identity performed must be foreign to its targeted audience. Ironically, these well-timed irruptions of the unfamiliar into the familiar world prove to be not merely fascinating but actually credible—precisely because they are foreign. They seem to offer an insider's narrative about people or places or times or experiences with which their chosen reader is unfamiliar, or about which that reader may have particular concerns:

Third—and again, pertinent across the board—the successful impostor assumes what I think of as an "encumbered" identity, an identity associated with clear baggage, clear issues, above all, clear definitions, as in the case of racial, religious, or ethnic discrimination, which I explore in Chapter 4. The impostor depends on essentialist mythologies of identity and authorship. To this end, the impostor adopts a single position in his narrative, as distinct from a continuous ground of identity. Where human experience and even the most naive life stories tend to include uncertainties and blurred edges, this identity has one uncomplicated meaning, inviting an uncomplicated response. Such identity depends on stereotype, which is easy to replicate. Only when someone in the community takes offence and exposes the fraud do the more complex possibilities of this assumed identity become part of the discussion. (Jerzy Kosinski's case brought Polish nationals and Jews into dialogue, and Helen Demidenko's case in Australia did much to bring Jewish and Ukrainian communities into dialogue with each other.)

Fourth, all the impostors that investigative journalists have exposed began by drawing attention to their particular strategic identity, inviting readers and reviewers to recognize and thereby validate it. "The counterfeit," Hugh Kenner suggests, "does not claim a reality it does not possess, but only an origin—that is, an authorization" (165). Because the impostor must protect her true "origin," she depends on such confirmation as media attention provides, as surely seemed possible between the first Hanna story in the *Post* and Solovitch's defection, or the early reviews of any successful impostor's work and the processes of detection that transform a star into a scandal. Imposture cannot operate unless it is believed, and readers who believe do so because of the limitations of their own starting place outside the strategic identity in question.

Fifth, autobiographical impostors perform a helpless or devalued identity for the benefit of those with power, inviting sympathy and identification. I am interested that this symbiotic relationship between the impostor and her reader disguises the power reversal that the impostor is enacting (she seems weak while in fact taking control); she appears to be perpetuating the very power relations that created the (faked) traumatic experience in the first place (in which she was a victim and needed help), thus ensuring the credibility of the fake. In other words, the impostor succeeds because the power she achieves through weakness appeals to and does not threaten her apparently dominant reader. The innocent (ignorant) reader is eager for this knowledge, greedy for this story, and is invited to shelter or protect the provider of such autobiographical intimacy, narrowing the distance between impostor and recipient, making the believer complicit in the fraud.

So, for example, Chapter 4 examines how the fraudulently Native perspective of Grey Owl in Canada circulates within a white readership, as has also been the case with the presumed Aborigines "Mudrooroo" and "Wanda Koolmatrie" in Australia, and Chief Buffalo Child Long Lance, Little Tree, and (more recently) Nasdijj in the United States. Closer to the white and Western experience, the child survivor of Nazi concentration camps has significant post-Holocaust value (as, in their different ways, did Kosinski and Binjamin Wilkomirski). If Western readers establish the market norm, then "exotic" ethnicity and, in particular, suffering become the tea and spices of contemporary trade.

Sixth, I note the very central role that autobiographers have come to play in popular culture in the West, introducing to my friends and neighbours the newly acceptable reality of lives previously beyond our ken and moments in history that we had previously ignored. However, because this information is apparently personal and therefore vivid, seeking a personal identification and response, it deflects analysis and criticism. One result can then be our soundbite understanding of complicated situations, in which we receive political and historical events essentially in terms of individual experience. The media know this very well. Most of my news of recent events in Egypt, Israel, Lebanon, and the Gaza Strip, Darfur or Zimbabwe, Iraq or Afghanistan has come to me in terms of the anxieties or tragedies affecting particular families. I return later to Susan Sontag's suggestion that psychology and private crises have replaced history and public crises. In short, I suspect that North American cultures today understand themselves and their world in terms of the personal or private story.

Finally, these impostors, burdened (or encumbered) with the race or ethnicity that is currently most problematic, emerging from volatile situations of specific and intense conflict about which moral responses are clear, are sensational identities in every sense of the newspaper headlines that hail their appearance.[9] However, the media do not simply instruct the communities they serve but also reflect them, and therefore do something far more in these instances of sensational identities than thank their lucky stars and grab the headlines. I suggest that the media attention given to autobiographical impostures *constructs,* to a significant degree, the moral value of the imposture, what, in each instance, it means, and the moral values of the reader who responds to it. In the Demidenko case, for example, media coverage explained publication and prizes for this poor piece of writing in terms of the anxiety prevalent in the mid-1990s in Australian culture. Could this young country come of age, they asked themselves, with a newly broad-minded acceptance of multiple perspectives, if its people bucked the trend of Holocaust narratives and recognized this story of fascist collaborators in Ukraine during the Second World War?

In short, in a curious replay of native informants, impostors play back to their readers the assumptions with which readings begin, tapping into cultural anxieties, mapping a psychological shift between white or Western dominance and its Other suffering through a time of crisis or need. Western cultures do not emerge from this exchange looking particularly pretty: anxious, ignorant, and naive in terms of politics and politicized narratives, guilty of dominance, comfort, and fecklessness. Were the contexts for these impostures not so serious, I would say that each individual instance shows us up as fit subjects for farce. More seriously, I wonder how autobiographical impostures, by crying wolf, may short-circuit authentic narratives from communities that need, in fact, to be heard.

4
"The Song My Paddle Sings":
Grey Owl and Ethnic Imposture

Archibald Belaney was born in Hastings, England, in 1888, and raised by his grandmother and two maiden aunts. He was educated in part at home, where he developed considerable ability on the piano, then attended Hastings Grammar School until the age of sixteen. Leaving England for Canada in 1906, young Belaney ended up among the Ojibwa, or Anishnabe, as they call themselves, at Bear Island on Lake Temagami, where he learned to hunt and trap and where he guided visiting hunters as well as those who were increasingly interested in commercial uses for the wilderness. Belaney married Angele Eguana in 1910, worked on his Ojibwa—which apparently became fairly fluent—adopted the Ojibwa lifestyle, began colouring his skin, grew his hair, and considered himself adopted by the Ojibwa (Smith, *From the Land of Shadows,* 40–43). He also took the name Qa-She-Quon-Asin, or Grey Owl, the name I use here because that was his choice and because it is the name by which he became well known.

Several wives and a world war later, Grey Owl underwent another dramatic conversion from trapper to conservationist, making the survival of the beaver in particular and of the wilderness in general his fervent mission (see *Tales of an Empty Cabin,* xiii). With no more furs in his pack, Grey Owl began writing and speaking in order to make a living, quickly achieving international acclaim as a remarkable "Canadian Indian" and as a wilderness writer. (I use the term "Indian" throughout this chapter because the characters I deal with called themselves Indian and because the literature of their times referred to Indians.) Lovat Dickson, the Canadian who published Grey Owl's work and who organized and promoted his speaking tours in England, considering himself in the process a close friend, was devastated by the exposure of Grey Owl as an impostor after his death in 1938. "The secret of his success," Dickson concluded, "was his genuineness and his simplicity"—strange terms, surely, to describe an impostor; but, Dickson insisted, "these terms are the right ones" (Dickson, *Wilderness Man,* 234). Dickson's response indicates how effectively Belaney drew on widely held myths of "the Indian" and then articulated in his life and writings the nostalgic romanticism of his time. For me, Grey Owl is the morally benign impostor who "gets away with it"; not only did his charade cause no one harm, it actually created an imaginative or narrative future both for Canadian Indians and for Canada as a nation. Unlike the other impostors I am considering, Belaney's Grey Owl drew on the past to critique the present and to suggest a future that resonates in our environmentally conscious times as both prescient and entirely acceptable.

For these reasons, Dickson's reaction to the man he knew "in person" resonates far beyond Dickson's own immediate experience. Certainly in the context of the extensive literature of ethnic imposture in the United States—and, most particularly, in Australia—Grey Owl is a disinterested phenomenon: both a neurotic Englishman who escaped from suburban decency and a romantic visionary who tapped into some of the deepest needs of his time and place. A tall tale, perhaps. In my attempt to explain it, I situate Archibald Belaney among some of the many others who have adopted strategic stories or identities—that is, stories or identities that were for them specifically useful. I also consider the historical context in which his choice of a Native identity and his development of the concept of "native wilderness" were so particularly engaging. In this process I depend on my discussion so far, which places our ducks in a row (rather too simply) as: specific culture + recognizable and acceptable story + "author" + identifiable human being = autobiographer, whether true or false.

Ethnic Imposture

I do not wish to collapse race and ethnicity into one simple category, but recognize that while race, racial issues, and racism are frequently part of my topic, my real questions in this chapter involve ethnicity. Grey Owl did not assume another "race" but he did acculturate himself into another ethnicity. Nonetheless, genetic purity was a racial issue that constantly troubled Grey Owl's imposture. Writing at a time when Nazi Germany was defining Jews in terms of proportions of ancestry, and when the southern States were identifying blacks according to the "one drop" rule, Grey Owl's wife Anahareo responded to his being treated as a full-blooded Indian by saying: "One never reads of a full-blooded Englishman, Swede, or German" (Anahareo 179). Ironically, at a time when identity was perceived in such essentialist terms (with "white" so evidently normative, requiring no comment), those who adopted new identities, or who freed themselves from what they felt were tainted identities, or who needed to prove the authenticity of their claims, did so in essentialist terms, reinventing their own past and giving themselves new ancestors.

To pre-empt challenges and assert his authenticity, Grey Owl began by claiming that his father had been a Scotsman and had served as an Indian scout in the wars against the Indians in the southwestern United States. His mother had been Apache. Or, again, his father had been a friend of Wild Bill Cody and had joined the Buffalo Bill show in England for Queen Victoria's Jubilee in 1887. This show had enthralled young Archie Belaney when it came to Hastings in 1903 (Smith, *From the Land of Shadows,* 15). During the war, he told Lieutenant Ewart Banks that he was half-Indian and Mexican and that he had shot the man who had killed his brother and had therefore to flee Mexico for the north woods of Quebec away from civilization (57). In his correspondence with *Country Life* in 1932, Grey Owl gave his father's name as MacNeill and his birthplace as Hermosillo in Mexico (Dickson, *Wilderness Man,* 225). Grey Owl's varied and sometimes contradictory explanations about his background provided specific context for his hybrid identity; they encompassed his ethnic claims and measured out his "race" in order to ensure that he could be recognized, so to speak, by his public and accepted as "Indian."

Not that reinventing the past was a new experience. When the former slave Olaudah Equiano included information on the Middle Passage in his autobiography, *The Interesting Narrative of the Life of Olaudah Equiano, or Gustavus Vassa, the African, Written by Himself* (1789), he invented for himself an authenticating origin in Africa that gave authority to his abolitionist work as a free man. Equiano's story is complex and contested and involves his own possible involvement in slave trading before he saw the error of his ways. However, the likelihood of fictive origins for this icon of the Black Atlantic and of African American history has been unsettling both in Africa and in the United States. It has also underscored the value of strategic identity as a tool in autobiographical persuasion. Whereas a former slave might be persuasive on the evils of slavery, an African from Africa, claiming as his own the worst experiences of capture and transport, would surely be that much more so. As historians seem not to doubt the American or European elements of Equiano's autobiography, we may read his earliest experiences as opportunistic fiction supporting the larger structure. Equiano was what he said he was, but he dramatized for consumption the ways in which he was or became so.

Strategic adjustment of information may serve lofty purposes, as presumably for Equiano, but appears more commonly as downright lies and invention dished up to an eager public in the simple hope of financial gain. Race and ethnicity become in these instances quite valuable commodities. So, for instance, Toby Forward, the English vicar, who published *Down the Road, Worlds Away* in 1987 as if he were a young East Indian woman called Rahila Khan, identified his achievement quite precisely: "We ... found a gap in the market and we set about filling it"

(quoted in Callaghan 197). Or, as Ien Ang puts it, "the displayed self is a strategi-
cally fabricated performance, one which stages a useful identity, which can be put
to work" (quoted in Rocio Davis 43). Like Equiano—indeed, like any more complete
impostor who has crossed my path—Forward recognized the value of the role he
was playing. He was producing a public identity that the public wanted or needed
to believe in. Accordingly, while acknowledging variations and degrees of imposture, I need to ask: What audience does the "self-made" man address? Of what
does he need to convince them? Why this story in this time and place?

Ethnic and racial identities pose quite particular problems of perception that
are historical, political, and social in origin. Painting with a fairly broad brush, I have
been suggesting that ethnic identity in the West tends (as Anahereo noted) to
be everything other than white, which means that ethnic imposture usually plays
to a white audience. Repeatedly, in my experience, the ethnic community itself
is not fooled. As the Ojibwa writer Drew Hayden Taylor writes of Pierce Brosnan
playing Grey Owl in Richard Attenborough's 1999 film (the Irishman playing the
Englishman playing the Indian), Brosnan, despite coaching, "kept dancing with an
accent" (120), an accent which, the stories of Grey Owl himself (and, in the United
States, Chief Buffalo Child Long Lance) suggest, Native audiences were aware
of but that white audiences did not hear or see. White is normative. White is an
ethnicity-free zone to which all alternatives are "visible" because they are "other."
Furthermore, this white perspective is blinkered by its assumptions about racial
purity as well as by its simplistic markers of racial or ethnic identity. In his effort to
live the black experience in the Deep South, the white man John Howard Griffin
dyed his skin and shaved his head in order to pass as a black man among whites,
who saw only his skin color. (Griffin's story marks a curious development in the
mediation of black experience by white activists, as in white authentication of
black slave narratives.) However, he was astonished that he apparently passed as
a black man in the black community, too, where he himself had failed beforehand
to notice the racial variety that blackness encompassed (Bonazzi 38–39). If even
the self-conscious white man, in the comfort of his own racial orthodoxy, fails to
see elements of white, and much else besides, in all "others," then the impostor
has an open playing field. Ironically, Griffin discovered, when his experiment was
long over, that the black people to whom he had confessed his "real" identity
when he was among them had been polite and interested but had not believed
him (Bonazzi 64). Why, after all, would any but the most self-loathing black claim
to be white when he was so evidently not?[1]

Certainly, one can say of racial or ethnic imposture that it creates new opportunities for people in untenable situations. So, for example, Sylvester Long felt
trapped in the "coloured" category by the racial practices of North Carolina at
the end of the nineteenth century.[2] Transformed, however, into Chief Buffalo Child

Long Lance, he became, just slightly earlier than Grey Owl, the most famous Indian in North America, welcome even among people who were violent on the subject of racial purity and who, even while despising blacks, were charmed by the Indian mystique (Smith, *Long Lance,* 149–54, 196). Unlike the white supremacist Klan member Asa Carter, who invented a deeply nostalgic Cherokee boyhood for himself, Sylvester Long lived his Indian life flamboyantly, for sure, but to some extent truly; he was not interested in lynching people of colour, and he actually did have Cherokee ancestry. For Archibald Belaney, who transformed himself into Grey Owl, the trap from which he needed to escape seems to have been his privileged English upbringing. Biographers and critics have speculated on psychological wounds, particularly those caused by the mysterious absence of his father, but I prefer, in his case, to draw on the "call of the wild" and the romance of "the Indian" in the early twentieth century. Apart from the simple fact that Grey Owl and Chief Buffalo Child Long Lance were both men, "the Indian" seems also to have been an exclusively masculine myth; Indian women, after all, demeaned as "squaws," lacked both mythical status and romance. Curiously, despite the new opportunities offered by Indian identity, imposture in both of these cases involved some sense of loss and nostalgia; like their white audience, in other words, these wannabe Indians did not imagine a future for the authentic "Indian," and here's the rub.

"The Indian"

Indians represent the past. Most notably, they represent the past for white readers raised on James Fenimore Cooper and Longfellow's Hiawatha. They represent, in other words, the white man's version of the Indian past in which the Indian was the denizen of nature, at home in a wilderness pastoral that Europeans had lost centuries earlier. This wilderness ideal gained remarkable purchase in the early decades of the twentieth century as North Americans, too, moved from rural to urban and industrial cultures and as war in Europe gave indecent burial to cultures of hope. Daniel Francis (*Imaginary Indian*) details representations of the innocent and vanishing time of the Canadian Indian through the end of the nineteenth century and the early decades of the twentieth, referring to the paintings of Paul Kane, Frederick Arthur Vermeer, Edmund Morris, and Emily Carr. Stern or romantic portraits, buffalo hunts, and abandoned totem poles blended romance with a poignant nostalgia. Carr's paintings of Native villages along the coast of Vancouver Island, Haida settlements on what were then known as the Queen Charlotte Islands (now Haida Gwai), and Tsimshian villages in the Skeena River Valley brought her to prominence in an exhibit at the National Gallery in Ottawa in 1927 just a couple of years before Grey Owl began publishing with *Country Life* in England. *Klee Wyck,* Carr's memoir of her travels among Indian villages, won the Governor General's Award for non-fiction in 1942, just four years after Grey Owl's death in Alberta. To a remarkable degree, both were heretics with a cause, turning their backs on the white mainstream of their own origins and becoming, unwittingly, part of a phenomenon of their time, celebrating the Indian as part of a vanishing world.

The Indian is also Aboriginal to the white psyche, not simply because he lived in North America for millennia before white people arrived (and then began "disappearing"), but also because white immigrants discovered in his ways of life an apparently natural authenticity that was most appealing. Grey Owl won over numerous audiences, including the Royal Family in Buckingham Palace, with his understanding of this appeal. "'You're tired with years of civilization,' he told them. 'I come to offer you—what? A single green leaf'" (Dickson, *The Green Leaf,* 13). With theft, imposture, or appropriation, the newcomer needed to adopt Equiano's strategy and find authenticating origins in a past that, in this case, his own culture was erasing.[3] Part, then, of the Long Lance and Grey Owl context takes the form of wilderness writing that popularized for an increasingly urban readership the life skills necessary to wilderness survival. Ernest Thompson Seton, for example, both wrote and lectured on his wild animal friends and "the Indian as I know him." Seton had grown up in Manitoba close to the Cree, who had guided him on deer hunts and taught him woodcraft, much as the Ojibwa of northern Ontario guided and taught Grey Owl. Finding the prairies much changed by farming and settlement on his return as an adult, Seton began working with boys in Connecticut, taking them camping, tracking animals, living Indian style. His 1902 article on this experience for *Ladies Home Journal* marked the beginning of the Woodcraft Movement, which was adopted with a rather more militaristic slant by General Robert Baden-Powell as the Boy Scout Movement in England. Seton's second wife also studied North American Indians; together, they founded the Seton Institute and took their daughter Beulah with them on lecture tours on which she performed Indian dances in costume (Polk 39–60). (As she was not pretending to be Indian, we have no record as to whether she danced with an accent.) Writing about what she calls "The Grey Owl Syndrome," Margaret Atwood suggests that Seton "[did] not attempt the rather modest feat of turning himself into an Indian, but pursued the greater ambition of turning everybody else into Indians, instead" (42). Quite apart from the romance of returning from the urban to the natural world, this kind of adoption of indigenous customs serves to authenticate the European in North America.

In stereotype, the North American Indian gallops bareback in war paint, a ferocious savage. Or, facing extinction, the man on horseback figures in a wild landscape, a silhouette against the sky. Daniel Francis suggests that Buffalo Bill's Wild West Show (in which Long Lance learned his horsemanship [Smith, *Long Lance,* 9], and which young Belaney admired in Hastings) "reduced the complexity of Native cultures in North America to a single image in the popular mind, the mounted, war-bonneted Plains chieftain" (94). So says Hollywood (see Berton

156–57), and so say the frontier stories of Western expansion across North America. Sitting Bull, the Sioux chieftain who defeated Custer at Little Bighorn in 1876, took part in the Wild West Show, as did Black Elk and the Canadian Métis leader Gabriel Dumont. After the massacre at Wounded Knee, the U.S. government pressured Native men to perform in the show in place of serving time in jail (Francis 92). In other words, authentic Indians performed Indian for North American and European audiences, incidentally in the process training Chief Buffalo Child Long Lance and inspiring Grey Owl, so that they too were capable of performing Indian.

Popular romances or dime novels in North America became native to Europe as well, with Balduin Mollhausen in Germany in the 1860s and 1870s, Gustave Aimard in France, and Karl May in Germany, whose tales of the Apache Chief Winnetou were translated into twenty languages and read by about 300 million people, including such notables as Hermann Hesse, Heinrich Mann, Albert Einstein, Adolf Hitler, and Günter Grass (Francis 73). So established did the stereotype of the Plains Indian become that when the Kwakiutl of Bella Coola from the west coast of Canada toured Germany in 1886, they were assumed to be Chinese or Japanese impostors because they carried no tomahawks, wore no headdresses, and lived in no skin tipis (Francis 94; Raibmon 8).

In short, at home and abroad, the romance of the frontier from the nineteenth century through the twentieth ensured for "the Indian" a strong position as authentically North American even as indigenous peoples themselves were decimated by disease, segregation, assimilation, or genocide. So children of all ethnicities have grown up playing "cowboys and Indians," the white child choosing to whoop it up in face paint, and the Native, I am told, preferring to be a cowboy. Even today, friends and colleagues have wished me happy riding when I say I am working on Native imposture. Deeply influenced by stereotypes, Chief Buffalo Child Long Lance might have wished me happy riding too, except for his foray into Grey Owl country and his immersion in the paddling tradition celebrated by Pauline Johnson (who deserves her own story) as "the song my paddle sings." Avoiding the warrior stereotype so readily available to impostors, this of the woodsman travelling in pristine wilderness by canoe and portage is the one that Grey Owl chose. So he aligned himself also with stories of trappers, or *coureurs des bois,* and miners, who depended on Indian guides, who opened up the Canadian North and West for Europeans, some of whom made a fortune and many of whom have left their mark on the Hudson's Bay Company and the maps of European expansion in Canada. Atwood cites M.T. Kelly on the literature of Canadian exploration, which demonstrates a particular pattern: "The adventurers may be known as heroes, yet they were always led, guided, literally carried and often saved from death by native people" (40). The unsung Native saving the foolish but adventurous white man suggests a curious hybridity for Grey Owl, whose life and writing belong in this wide array of historical situations, from which they draw a vivid and curiously credible narrative. So, what about his writings? I have been discussing the context in which Belaney made his choices and found some camouflage and turn now to the "Grey Owl" that he wrote into being.

Grey Owl (Qa-She-Quon-Asin), Pilgrim of the Wild

Biographers and critics seem to agree that the evolution of "Grey Owl" was circumstantial, gradual, and in some curious way authentic to the Englishman who had transferred his allegiance from England to Canada, from urban to wilderness culture, and (somehow) therefore from white man to Indian. However, this imposture involved not simply an eventual decision to live one life rather than another but also the need to produce and defend the ethnicity of choice. He did so, of course, as a white man. A voracious reader, Grey Owl manifests his late Victorian background in his writing style. He echoes *Pilgrim's Progress* ("How We Crossed the Slough of Despond," *Pilgrims of the Wild,* 81) and the Bible ("the simple kindly people, companions and mentors of my younger days, whose ways had become my ways, and their gods my gods" (210). Apart from its fine observations of wildlife in general and beaver in particular, *Pilgrims of the Wild* (1935) is emphatically dated by a lush sentimentality that evokes such work as H.E. Marshall's *Our Island Story* (1905) and history entries in Arthur Mee's *Children's Encyclopedia* (1908–64). Both nostalgia and high moral fervour suggest an Englishman's loss of imperial confidence more persuasively than an Indian's sense of displacement. Surely "the Unforgotten Days of Long Ago" (*Pilgrims* 7) reflect not what indigenous peoples had lost but, rather, the romance of the Indian that inspired young Belaney's desire to adopt an Indian identity.

By the time he began writing in the 1930s, he had also lost a lot of his own dream; he was, by then, living as an employee of Parks Canada rather than as a trapper in the wilderness, and drawing on his keen sense that his original wilderness was being overrun and destroyed. Of his early submissions to *Country Life,* he writes that his "soul slipped back to wander once more, at will, in a land of wild romantic beauty and adventure that would soon, by all the signs, be gone beyond recall" (139). Furthermore, his wilderness is animate; just as it inspires him, so also it represents him. His grove of pines is "brooding" (154), or again, the pines "tower[ed], mighty in their silence; and standing there immovable in their impenetrable reticence, they seemed to meditate, and brood upon the past" (201). His "apparently endless black forests of spruce" are also, like Carr's, for all the wonder of their discovery, curiously Eurocentric, "cathedral-like with their tall spires above and their gloomy aisles below" ("The Passing of the Last Frontier" quoted in Smith, *From the Land of Shadows,* 84). Though Grey Owl describes his struggle with the English language and his immersion in works of reference, books of synonyms, and a dictionary, as well as *Hiawatha*, the poetry of Robert Service, Emerson, Shakespeare, and the Bible, as if he were indeed educating himself into writing (Pilgrims 207, 216), he is surely drawing on life with his aunts and Hastings Grammar School when he tells how Jelly Roll, his tame beaver, refused to live in a tent, "preferring domiciles of her own manufacture" (170). Smith refers to Grey Owl's "compound-complex sentences of Dickensian proportions" and notes the rash of Latinate vocabulary and foreign phrases with which *Men of the Last Frontier* begins (102–3). Neither high nor low literature gives Grey Owl Latinate phrasing; along with the sentimentality, he surely gets that from the time and place of his boyhood, his personal history leaching through his acquired identity—language in text, one might say, betraying the man.

Warning against reading authors rather than texts (a tricky task in autobiography studies), Albert Braz suggests that Grey Owl's imposture does not stem explicitly from his writing, which involves "less outright duplicity than strategic evasion" ("The Modern Hiawatha," 54). Certainly, in his approach to *Country Life* on 6 May 1929, Grey Owl wrote of Indians as "them," not "we," signing himself "A.S. Belaney" (Dickson, *Wilderness Man*, 158–59). Nor did this first work use the first-person pronoun, though his correspondence with *Country Life* was studiously naive and he remained insistent that grammatical and spelling errors not be corrected (Dickson, *Wilderness Man*, 201–2). Furthermore, when *Country Life* changed the title of this book from *The Vanishing Frontier* to *Men of the Last Frontier,* he was angry, writing to them on 14 January 1932: "As it stands I have written a book about myself, a thing I studiously avoided" (218). His books do not include the stories he created in conversation about his parentage and personal history. However, the situation evolves, as do the autobiographical details. By 1935, with *Pilgrims of the Wild,* he was referring to being Indian and to having (with a nod to his white readers) what may seem "perhaps some queer ideas" (163). He also reckoned (sounding again quite remarkably like that other late Victorian naïf, Emily Carr) that for his present work "it seemed that a few good healthy unequivocating 'I's' standing up honestly on their own hind legs, would do no harm whatever" (185). On one happy occasion, he commented on his forgetting that he was "a gloomy half-breed" (212). Such phrasing is fairly explicit. Whereas I agree with Braz that Grey Owl is generally more concerned to write about his world than about himself, the writing process seems to bring out the Indian in him.

In part, no doubt, this Indian identity was strategic for marketing purposes. Anahareo, the wife who persuaded him to abandon trapping, writes that "everything Archie did, the more Indian he became in the eyes of the public, and he went along with it and became more Indian than Tecumseh himself" (180). This public element is surely central to imposture. Repeatedly we have seen how impostor and public fit each other, how they create and clarify each other. Whereas Grey Owl had lived privately for twenty years as an Indian-educated trapper, the writing and speaking that made him a public figure involved his self-authentication as Indian, and his writing became significant to this performance. His continuing correspondence with *Country Life* included the injunction that they refer to him as an Indian (Dickson, *Wilderness Man,* 225). He signed himself Grey Owl for the first time in 1930, changing even his handwriting (48), and he told *Country Life* in 1931 that he had "Indian Blood," and, later the same year, that he was an "Indian writer [who] writes as an Indian" (Smith, *From the Land of Shadows,* 85). By the time he was also publishing in *Forest* and *Outdoors,* he had made the transition, writing to *Country Life* not about "them" but about "us" (Dickson, *Wilderness Man,* 212–13). However, as with all aspects of imposture, written performance requires attention and high maintenance.

Grey Owl was outraged by a review of *Men of the Last Frontier* that suggested a ghostwriter must have been involved, wondering "how in the world ... a half-breed trapper [could] pick up such an elegant style" (quoted in Smith, *From the Land of Shadows,* 106). He wrote to Hugh Eayrs, his Canadian publisher, the sort of authenticating letter so common among impostors about his still having "the original pencilled copy of the first M.S., scrawled over with notes and alterations, written on exercise book paper, with no marks of an editor's pen, but the cuts of the teeth of a beaver who once stole the entire M.S., & took it to make his bed'" (107). His writing becomes the first line of defence for his own authenticity, the beaver trademark validating both the text and, by implication, the life.

Speech, too, became part of Grey Owl's construction of himself. Bill Guppy, who had first taken Grey Owl to Lake Temagami in 1906, saw him again in 1908 and was impressed by how Indian he had already become, noting that just "the blue-grey eyes, the voice with its English drawl and its educated accent, showed his exotic origin" (Dickson, *Wilderness Man,* 58). Guppy's use of the term "exotic" to describe an Englishman marks distinctions of perspective that Grey Owl himself had to negotiate with care. The Englishman who was exotic, or from elsewhere, outside, was studiously making himself exotic to the folks back home. Reporting on Grey Owl when his authenticity was being questioned near the end of his life, the Indian agent in Chapleau described Belaney's arrival as a young Englishman who told of his father being an Indian fighter in Mexico and his mother an Apache, but who "spoke like an educated young man, not a fugitive from the Wild West when the Indians were being subdued" (245). However, when he arrived in England on his first speaking tour, a "picturesque figure in Indian dress, with the thoughtful face of the philosopher," according to the *Times of London,* the *Manchester Guardian* referred to his having the "true nasal twang of the Canadian Indian" (Smith, *From the Land of Shadows,* 1). Certainly, accents slide with time away from home base, and I do wonder how many "Canadian Indians" the *Guardian* reporter had ever spoken with, but I also cannot doubt that Grey Owl worked at his own transformation. Nurse Parson, who looked after "Private Belaney" when he was wounded in the war and who corresponded with him after his return to Canada, observed that he "spoke English very badly. He wrote me dozens of letters. His spelling was simply awful. No educated Englishman could spell so badly. His father, he said, was a Scotsman, and his mother an Apache Indian" (quoted, 60). Such observations made by individuals on particular occasions did not coalesce into a critique of Grey Owl's persona until after his death and exposure. His self-creation seems to have survived well enough in general terms and from one situation to the next.

In his private life as in the development of his authorial persona, Grey Owl was translating his language from educated English to Canadian backwoods and then claiming the tools of self-education (Shakespeare, the Bible, and so on) in the backwoods in order to address his educated English audience. Language, spoken and written, was crucial for the talks and the books that developed Grey Owl's persona, promoted each other, and promoted Grey Owl's conservationist agenda. Furthermore, that agenda depended on the authenticity of the man, in person and in text, whom language was so instrumental in creating. Language, spoken and written, also created the audience that, through the Depression and under threat of war, wanted to hear what he wanted to say. In short, language became the vehicle for recreating the wilderness and the ideal "Indian" that industry and European migration were displacing.

Yet for all the credibility that Grey Owl earned in white communities, he seems never to have fooled any Native people. Language, here, is only a part of the issue. Smith notes that the very use of the name Grey Owl is problematic because the Ojibwa name identifies a small grey screech owl that is not thought of as a grey owl at all and that does not really translate as He Who Walks by Night, poetic and alluring as that sounds in English. However, as Smith suggests, only the Ojibwa would have noticed, and they made no fuss (Smith, *From the Land of Shadows,* 91–92). Given that Grey Owl spoke Ojibwa, he must never have imagined them as his audience. (According to Agnes Lalonde, his daughter by Angele, her mother's uncle actually called him *ko-hom-see,* or "little owl," the one who sits taking everything in [41]). When Grey Owl raised his arm in greeting to King George VI, telling him he came in peace, he spoke first in Ojibwa but then used the Sioux greeting "How Kola," for which he could claim neither an Apache background nor an Ojibwa adoption but only the predictable audience recognition of the Plains Indian (125).

Furthermore, like Pierce Brosnan (and perhaps justifying Pierce Brosnan), Grey Owl seems to have had trouble with both his singing and his dancing. Native communities were constantly bewildered by his style. John Tootoosis of the Poundmaker Reserve in Saskatchewan was puzzled by Grey Owl's having no words for his singing. Stan Cuthand recalls Grey Owl dancing at the ceremony in August 1936 when Lord Tweedsmuir was adopted by the Plains Cree (as the "Teller of Tales"): "It was at this dance that people recognized Grey Owl as not having the genre and ethos of an Indian. He looked awkward and out of place as he danced with the rest" (160). Robert McWatch, a Cree visitor to the community at Biscotasing, thought that Grey Owl's knife wielding and axe shaking were "half-crazy," and the Ojibwa from Fort Mattahami to the north thought his dance was evil (73). According to the fur buyer Jack Leve, the local Ojibwa and Cree "didn't know his brand of Indian lore" (73). Regardless, Grey Owl's creation of the Indian life persists both as ideal and as commodity for the white visitor; Biscotasing in northern Ontario, known locally as Bisco, now offers Grey Owl camps for tourists in search of wilderness (Mitcham 25).

So why was Grey Owl not exposed before his death? Why, at that point, was it a white journalist and not Native communities that exposed him? For answers, we should return, perhaps, to the context in which he produced this remarkable translation or appropriation of identity. I have suggested that the myth of the disappearance of the Indian formed part of the context in which impostors like Grey Owl and Long Lance could offer themselves as "the last of the Mohicans," so to speak, spinning their own romance out of their generation's nostalgia for idealized, better, purer, more natural times. Relegating this ideal to the past left present-day Native peoples at a severe disadvantage: impoverished socially, culturally, and economically, displaced and despised. According even to Marius Barbeau, who, as an anthropologist and ethnographer, had dedicated his life to the study of Native peoples, the Indian was a dying race. In 1931, while Grey Owl was launching the writing career that would ennoble both the wilderness and the Indian who lived in it, Barbeau was writing in *Queen's Quarterly* about Indians as squalid and ignorant (Smith, *From the Land of Shadows,* 161). However, Grey Owl went on to explain to King George and anyone else who would listen that Indians should be placed in charge of the wilderness spaces of Canada. He worked with John Tootoosis on appeals from the Poundmaker Reserve for negotiations with the Department of Indian Affairs (which was simultaneously investigating Grey Owl's authenticity).[4] Tootoosis told Smith some forty years later: "I knew that he was doing good for the country with the wild game, so I never let him know that I didn't believe in him" (151). Similarly, the Espaniels in Bisco, who took Grey Owl in when he was seriously ill, certainly knew and cared for him as a white man, but remained silent (71–72). Armand Garnet Ruffo, of Espaniel and Ojibwa descent, wrote a verse biography based on archives and family lore, which includes Grey Owl being rescued by the Espaniel family after the war: "Everybody can see plain as day he's suffering," Ruffo has Alex Espaniel saying:

> Maybe a better way is to say there's something chewing
> At his insides, the beast of war hunched and hissing,
> All that he's seen and done over there in the trenches
> Coiled inward [...]
> Then one day we see him sprawled outside his shack
> Shivering, too weak even to get up and feed himself [...]
> And my son puts him over his shoulder
> And we take him to our camp
> On Indian Lake. (Ruffo 33)

The community was kind; and, as when the Sarcee celebrated the poet Charles G.D. Roberts in 1928, or Lord Tweedsmuir in 1936, Native peoples honoured those who knew and appreciated the wilderness and their lives in it.

If Native people offered Grey Owl friendship and guidance, shrugged at his exaggerated claims of belonging, and refused to expose him, they may also have shared the surprise felt by whites (and by the blacks to whom Howard Griffin confessed his imposture) that he would actually choose so undesirable an ethnicity. Nostalgia for a dying way of life is one thing, but the lived experience of racism is another. Smith notes that Robert J.C. Stead's *The Empire Builders and Other Poems,* which came out in a fourth edition in 1910, includes "The Mixer," a poem about how Canada turns its immigrants into Canadians. It is good rousing stuff, full of the old imperial bombast, but it also includes a distinctly racist element that schoolchildren would surely have recited with the same thoughtless fervour with which they celebrated Canada's geographical scope: "From Atlantic to Pacific, from the Great Lakes to the Pole." Only today, perhaps, when the jingo sounds dated, may we be startled by these lines:

> Not a sacrifice so great but they will gladly lay it down
> When I turn them out Canadians—all but the yellow and brown.
> (in Smith, *From the Land of Shadows,* 45)

Ken Conibear, a Rhodes Scholar from Alberta, had been raised in the Northwest Territories and was therefore familiar with Native Canadian issues. Given the task of chaperoning Grey Owl on his second, 1937 tour in England, he noticed that Grey Owl travelled with a sun lamp (290n57); also, he was puzzled that so fair-skinned a man would actually seek recognition for Indian blood where most, given his colouring, would have hidden it (186). Grey Owl's repeated references to himself as "just a half-breed" (in conflict with media headlines about his being full blood) were clearly a ploy to divert the curiosity of someone like Conibear. However, "the half-breed" belonged in neither camp and was insulted by both. At a time when "Negro" and Jewish blood was being measured by the drop, Grey Owl's choice was practical (he had blue eyes) but hardly an obvious source of pride. When reasonable evaluation in the media followed the initial scandal of Grey Owl's exposure, the *Toronto Star* of 20 April 1938 noted: "The case of Grey Owl reminds us a little of the new race phantasies which poison life in Germany. There it matters everything what a man's grandmother was, and less than nothing what his own achievements in life have been" (Dickson, *The Green Leaf,* 39). As we have seen, Archibald Belaney chose, so to speak, to reinvent his grandmother in order to achieve objectives that mattered to him. He sought to embed himself in the ancestry, traditions, and communities that made sense of his own life and that would count as authentic for a voice from "the wilderness."

Grey Owl's Wilderness

As a boy, Belaney had been drawn to the countryside and the wildlife around Hastings, developing remarkable skills as he, like so many other white children, played at being an Indian. When he left for Canada in his late teens, he moved rapidly from work in the city to opportunities in the backwoods. Bear Island on Lake Temagami, just north of Georgian Bay, seems to have become central to his sense of himself as an Indian. Here, on one of the largest lakes in Ontario, with more than 1,200 islands, Bear Island, which also had a Hudson's Bay Company trading post, was summer home to the Ojibwa. The future Grey Owl went to the source for the woodcraft that Seton was teaching young boys in Connecticut. The Ojibwa were welcoming. He learned to hunt and trap and became expert with a canoe. He lived among them, learned their language, adopted moccasins and deerskin, and began to wear his hair long; as Angele Eguana's uncle put it, he became ko-hom-see, or the little owl who watches and takes everything in. He worked as a fire warden and, for the summers of 1910 and 1911, after his marriage to Angele, he worked as a guide at Camp Keewaydin (Longfellow used the name Keewaydin for the northwest wind in *Hiawatha*) on the northwest of Bear Island. Grey Owl wrote to *Country Life* in 1929 that he had been adopted by the Ojibwa in 1909 or 1910, but Smith makes clear that he was exaggerating this adoption (*From the Land of Shadows,* 103, 261n14, 262n16). The ceremony he specifies had simply been a thanksgiving festival at which whites were welcome.

However, if the Indians were not actually vanishing, their wilderness was. Prospectors were arriving, lumberjacks, mills, and machinery. Allison Mitcham notes that no logging had been permitted in the Temagami region before 1924 except for salvage from two minor burns (95). Then surveyors laid out a townsite at the northeastern end of the lake for a summer resort. In Dickson's words, the Indians were beginning to serve new masters (*Wilderness Man,* 70–71). Grey Owl records at the opening of *Pilgrims of the Wild* the damage to the country around

Biscotasing, just a little west of Bear Island, with sawmills and pollution increasing after the First World War. Writing from his Parks Board cabin on Lake Ajawaan in Alberta two decades later, Grey Owl ends *Pilgrims* with delight in the "uninterrupted wilderness, flowing onward in a dark billowing flood Northward to the Arctic Sea," but contrasts this space with his earlier experience: "No railroad passes through [this Albertan wilderness] to burn and destroy, no settler lays waste with fire and axe. Here from any eminence a man may gaze on unnumbered leagues of forest that will never feed the hungry maw of commerce" (280–81). Grey Owl's sense of sanctuary is surely ironic for the contemporary reader who depends on the oil boom that has transformed Alberta in the past few decades. As he looked back on Ontarian wilderness with nostalgia, so readers of the twenty-first century may look back on Alberta.

The Northern Ontario Railway that had taken Grey Owl into the interior and brought the tourists who wanted hunting and guides, had helped destroy what young Belaney had gone north to find. Anahareo writes of the incursion of the railway, tourists, and white settlement into the northern wilderness: "Archie hated with a burning hatred to see the forests go under the axe and the land under the plough" (98). For him, the outboard motor was a health problem: Did tourists and the new breed of hunter not recognize that men overheat with portage and then need to paddle in order to stay warm? (71). She describes their search for a suitable beaver sanctuary at Birch Lake, and how they "paddled and poled for mile upon mile through devastated country. Even when [they] reached the Horton branch, there was still no end in sight to the ravaged, timberless land" (95–96). Visiting Biscotasing in 1978, forty years after Grey Owl's death, and then again in 1991, Mitcham describes extensive logging and pollution. Signs at Lake Biscotasing and at Lake Temagami alternate between warnings of pollution and invitations to fish. "This beautiful wilderness," she writes, "is hemmed in by powerful mining garrisons—from Sudbury and Elliot Lake in the South to Cobalt and Timmins in the North, Noranda and Abitibi to the East" (25). No logging is allowed within a few hundred feet of roads and waterways, so that cultivated woodland along the shores of the lakes hides the bald spots beyond. People now use motorboats instead of canoes, snowmobiles in place of dog teams, and INCO controls the headwaters of the great rivers (39). Bitter land-use disputes involving the provincial government, loggers, developers, and Native people developed in the 1970s and remain unresolved as I write.

From Wilderness to Nation: Grey Owl as Canadian Icon

Mention of land claims, which have occupied the courts across Canada for several decades now, and of increasing concerns since Grey Owl's time about the loss of habitat for numerous plant and animal species, may give some sense of how timely Grey Owl's intervention was. He did not simply find a way of life that suited him—he found an endangered way of life, an endangered world, and he set out to rescue it. His publications and his speaking engagements resonated abroad as well as at home, creating both a paradise being lost and a remarkable opportunity for Canadian self-identification. When James Harkin, Commissioner of National Parks, seized on Grey Owl's iconic status to offer him a very public custodial position as Chief Conservation Officer, he was smart about what Grey Owl could achieve; Grey Owl's prominence and influence would lend weight to the very concept of protected park lands. The young lawyer John Diefenbaker was one of many visitors at Ajawaan Lake, Grey Owl's beaver settlement in Prince Albert National Park, where he lived and wrote from 1931 until his death in 1938 (Smith, *From the Land of Shadows,* 111). Grey Owl himself approached various government sources for funding for his very popular films about beaver, including the Department of the Interior, which supported him (Dickson, *Wilderness Man,* 217); Canada's Governor General, John Buchan, Lord Tweedsmuir (Lady Tweedsmuir was impressed) (Smith, *From the Land of Shadows,* 160); and Prime Minister William Lyon Mackenzie King, who represented the Prince Albert constituency and had been helpful in the creation of Prince Albert National Park in 1927. (Mackenzie King listened politely but had his doubts.) In terms of both his regular salary and his state-funded conservationist projects, Grey Owl was an employee of the Canadian government and necessarily, therefore, part of Canada's face at home and abroad. As an Indian messenger from the wilderness determined to protect the beaver, he was ideally situated to represent an emerging sense of Canadian nationalism.

Subsequent history does not suggest that the Canadian government of the 1930s was so circumspect as to value wilderness as an ecological or even a commercial good. Rather, I suspect that Canada, as a maturing colony, still about fifty years from patriating its own constitution, was discovering the qualities that emphatically distinguished it from England (or what many of my neighbours as late as the 1970s still called "the home country").[5] Curiously, Grey Owl's focus on the beaver blended with this sense of colonial history and came to represent an emerging national identity. This identity—or Grey Owl's part in its creation—blended the wilderness, the indigenous past, and Native traditions of respect for the lives taken in the hunt (Dickson, *Wilderness Man,* 72). Befriending the beaver and striving to save the beaver from extinction run parallel to Grey Owl's advocacy for Canadian Indians, who, according to Dickson, called the beaver "little Indians" (198). However, because beaver pelts had been, since the late seventeenth century, central to the wealth that Europeans could glean from Canada, the association of the beaver with Canada had already by then a long and varied history. In 1678 the Hudson's Bay Company put a beaver on the shield of its coat of arms. In the same year, the Governor of New France suggested the beaver as an emblem for that colony; thus the "Kebeca Liberata Medal," struck in 1690 to celebrate the French defence of Quebec, shows the beaver at the feet of a seated woman representing France. Among the numerous situations in which the beaver identified industry and publications as Canadian, perhaps the best known is the first Canadian postage stamp (1851), known as "the Three Penny Beaver"; since then, various Canadian stamps and coins have carried the beaver. Finally, in 1975, the beaver received Royal Assent for its role as the official emblem of Canada. What more could *Castor canadensis* require—except, perhaps, survival, and this is where Grey Owl's story plays its part.

As a hunter and trapper, Grey Owl had depended on beaver pelts. However, when in 1928 Anahareo persuaded him to abandon the hunt as a violent and brutal way of life, Grey Owl underwent a form of conversion from predator, surviving as hunters and trappers did in those days, to protector of this species and, by extension, of the Canadian wilderness where such species thrive. He was in fact won over by the two beaver kits that Anahareo insisted on bringing back to their cabin. When writing and public speaking became his new source of income, he wrote and spoke about "McGinnis" and "McGinty," as they called the two kits. When both beaver failed to return to the cabin one day, perhaps trapped by another hunter, Grey Owl's sense of loss and his extensive search for them were both personal and symptoms of more pervasive grief—for the wilderness and the Indian way of life. Beginning *Pilgrims of the Wild* at Beaver Lodge in Prince Albert National Park, Grey Owl told the story of these two beaver kits as itself beginning "in the Unforgotten Days of Long Ago" (7). From backwoods trapper leading a private life of choice, Grey Owl became a public missionary with a national and international mission. "Grey Owl, the Canadian Indian who … established world fame for himself as a conservator of game and as a modern Hiawatha," became "one of the most sought-after lecturers alive" (Anahareo 174). Grey Owl had travelled another trajectory as well, from remittance man (like his father before him) surviving in the colonies far from "home" to Indian interpreter of the Canadian wilderness—for Canadians, certainly, but also very particularly for the English. Furthermore, going back to England "as the Indian they expect [him] to be" (Anahareo 173), Grey Owl put his Indian imposture to work for his cause, to some significant degree creating Canada in his own image.

The Afterlife of Grey Owl

Imposture has, on the whole, a brief shelf life. Because it is so particularly pertinent to its time and place, its shock value is specific. In most cases, very little survives by way of impact or history. If I consider my cast of impostors, Jerzy Kosinski's Holocaust writing is no longer so frequently taught; as of the spring of 2011,

James Frey has dropped out of common chatter ("Wasn't he the man who …?"); and Nega Mezlekia and David Solway have gone on to other things; but curiously, not so with Grey Owl. Exposure of his imposture had surely been gathering like storm clouds toward the end of his life, and that storm broke as soon as he died in 1938; yet he remains vivid in Canadian consciousness and is well remembered abroad. My reading is that Grey Owl's imposture was distinct from others in a number of significant ways: he assumed an ethnic identity but seems not to have offended those whose identity he borrowed; his imposture may have satisfied his own needs, but it also served a selfless cause; his environmental concerns have become more rather than less topical. Furthermore, the man who drank to excess, quarrelled, and fought, and who repeatedly abandoned his "wives" and their children, may be found entirely authentic as a man, as well as weak and irresponsible, but "the Indian" who lived in the wilderness and understood its wildlife seems to be forgiven his imposture because of its resonance for himself and for his audiences. In that sense, he may be described as having written himself both into and out of existence.

Exposure did, of course, lead to scandal. Angele Eguana and her daughter Agnes Belaney had been prepared to identify Grey Owl after they heard him speak at Massey Hall (Smith, *From the Land of Shadows,* 213), and now came forward to claim some inheritance from his estate.[6] Anahareo travelled to England to meet his mother because she could not believe he had no Indian blood (214–15). In England and across North America, the press was astonished: so public a figure, so convincing an imposture. Dickson, who had believed in this prodigy who had made the fortune of his publishing house, caught a sense of widespread loss when he declared: "We had been duped. There was no Arcadia" (*Wilderness Man,* 255). Notably, however, there was little condemnation. On 22 April 1938, the *Times of London* considered the scandal "supremely unimportant" because romancing about birth and boyhood would leave the "central truth" untainted (Dickson, *The Green Leaf,* 38). Within a week of Grey Owl's death, the *Winnipeg Tribune* suggested that "[a] great chuckle has gone across Canada at the suggestion that the national leg has been well and truly pulled" (Smith, *From the Land of Shadows,* 214). J.A. Wood, Superintendent of Prince Albert National Park, wrote to Dickson, whose first flurry of research surely stemmed from his own shock at imposture, that he did not care whether Grey Owl was "an Englishman, Irishman, Scotsman or Negro" (an interesting choice). What mattered and would be remembered were his efforts to protect the forest, to end cruel hunting practices, and to rehabilitate the Indian (Dickson, *The Green Leaf,* 30). After a brief flurry of attention, the Grey Owl story, like the Grey Owl cabin, suffered only from neglect.

However, after the war, on 1 August 1951, *Maclean's* published an article by Trent Frayne called "Grey Owl, the Magnificent Fraud." Frayne explores Grey

Owl's imposture as tied to his disgust at white civilization after the trauma of the First World War, which was when the Ojibwa in general and the Espaniels in particular had saved him. Given *Maclean's* focus on Canadian issues, I assume the editors did not pull Grey Owl out of a hat but associated his story with political developments in that same year concerning Indian status. In 1951, the Federal Indian Register was created in Canada in order to identify and verify Indian status (not necessarily the same thing as blood inheritance, but a government tool for determining "Indian" benefits). Also focusing on matters of Canadian interest, the *Canadian Geographical Journal* of May 1972 ran its own article, in which Vera Fidler borrowed extensively from Frayne. But by then *The Gazette* (Montreal) had run a piece on how the "Ecology Fad Returns Grey Owl to Fashion" (8 April). Cantwell's article "Grey Owl: Mysterious Genius of Nature Lore," in *Sports Illustrated* (8 April 1963), demonstrated a casual but continuing interest in this specifically Canadian "Indian" who had made the outdoors both so Canadian and so romantic. Maybe Grey Owl survives because, in Christopher Irmscher's phrasing, he made respectable the "elegiac lament for lost harmony cast in the form of an autobiographical tale of self-discovery" (109). Surely this is the Grey Owl that Jane Billinghurst captures (1999). His imposture tapped a very general malaise and was true to his own deepest needs.

For myself, I am attracted to the notion that Grey Owl survives as an "Indian" most particularly because "the Indians" themselves came back from their vanishing point. Penny van Toorn notes the remarkable proliferation of personal Aboriginal stories from the early 1970s onward (as official government intervention in their lives began to slacken). These minority voices belong in part with the autobiographical narratives of other minorities that transformed the field of autobiography studies at the same time: women's voices, black voices, immigrant voices, and personal perspectives on previously unspoken experiences such as illness, disability, homosexuality, and AIDS. However, van Toorn also associates the proliferation of Canadian Aboriginal narratives with quite specific Canadian politics. After Pierre Elliott Trudeau was elected prime minister in 1968 with the mandate to bring about "a Just Society," Jean Chrétien, his Minister for Indian Affairs, produced a White Paper in 1969 that sought to abolish Indian status, thereby equalizing or assimilating "the Indian" (30–32). Whether or not Ottawa in fact provoked the personal and political literature that followed, indigenous Canadians, now asserting their history and variety by calling themselves "First Nations," certainly began producing an extensive literature in all genres in which they explored their own experiences and perspectives for mainstream consumption. Interest in Grey Owl resurfaced quite noticeably with this emergence of First Nations literature, and has ridden this wave, which has become part of the mainstream of Canadian literature, ever since.

In the early 1970s, for example, Macmillan of Canada brought out new editions of Grey Owl's books. In 1972, CBC-TV produced a Grey Owl documentary.
Anahareo's *Devil in Deerskins* and James Polk's *Wilderness Writers* both appeared
in 1972. Lovat Dickson's *Wilderness Man* was published in 1973, as was Robert
Kroetsch's novel *Gone Indian,* in which one Jeremy Sadness disappears into the
interior, wanting to be Grey Owl. Toward the end of the twentieth century, with
post-colonial studies hitting their stride, Donald Smith published scholarly biogra-
phies of both Long Lance (1982) and Grey Owl (1990), and Albert Braz and Carrie
Dawson came to the subject with fresh, unsentimental, but certainly appreciative
appraisal. This mostly non-Native interest in Grey Owl marks Canadian interest in
the man and his connections to Native cultures in Canada, but it could not be so
appreciative if Native responses too had not been favourable. White academics
would have needed to defer, for instance, to any sense from Native communities
that Grey Owl had truly trespassed. I have already referred to the Attenborough
film released in 1999, in which Pierce Brosnan plays Grey Owl. One of the most
memorable scenes in this otherwise rather sentimental film has a serious gathering of Native peoples, surely about to expose the impostor, welcoming him
instead with warm and prolonged laughter. Smith's research in particular suggests a dramatic truthfulness to this scene. Cuthand, Tootoosis, and McWatch
may have found him absurd, but they also liked him and let him be. Furthermore,
just as Indians were, as Braz puts it, "instrumental in [Grey Owl's] metamorphosis"
during his lifetime ("The White Indian," 172), so also the First Nations, speaking
quite clearly now on their own behalf, seem to have welcomed Grey Owl after
his exposure. I have already referred to Ruffo's biography in verse, which, even
as it explores the psychological complexity of the man, celebrates Grey Owl's
closeness to Ruffo's own Espaniel family, claiming him as kin. As an epigram at
the opening of his work, Ruffo quotes the distinguished American Indian writer
N. Scott Momaday, who gave a conference paper titled "The Man Made of Words,"
in which he said that "an Indian is an idea which a given man has of himself. And
it is a moral idea, for it accounts for the way in which he reacts to other men, and
to the world in general. And that idea, in order to be realized completely, has to
be expressed" (49). Momaday was speaking of the concept of "the Indian" and
not specifically of Grey Owl, but when he adds that "the greatest tragedy that can
befall us is to go unimagined" (55), he seems to give impostors like Grey Owl (or
Long Lance) permission to share a moral position with the Indian and, therefore,
to express that position.

Less generous, more critical understanding associates Grey Owl's imposture, like that of all make-believe Indians, with erasure of the authentic Indian. The
nostalgia that colours all of Grey Owl's writing and public speaking assumes that
the Indian way of life is over. In *The Men of the Last Frontier,* Grey Owl describes

his own adoption by the Ojibwa in dramatic terms that equate his birth as an Indian with their death. He steps out when called upon into the "full drama of sound and ritual," and "not one feral visage relaxed in recognition, as, absorbed in the mystery of their ritual, they intoned the almost forgotten cadences ... The weird cries trailed off into the empty halls of the forest ... They are a fading people" (226). This section ends with Grey Owl feeling the need to return to the lake, where an ancient man comes ashore in a canoe, saying that he has called and called and that Grey Owl has been the only one to hear and return. They had formed the blood brotherhood of the beaver, and now Grey Owl will be the last. As the old man paints a picture of a vanishing race, he "seemed no longer a man, but a prophet, the patriarchal ruler of a vanished people" (245). With the coming of the railway and destruction of the ancient forests, these "scattered bands of broken, bewildered people [have been] driven like leaves before the wind" (246). Grey Owl buries the old man in his canoe, appropriately facing west. I cannot imagine what Momaday or Ruffo or the Ojibwa of northern Ontario, pursuing their land claims through the courts all these decades later, make of Grey Owl's burial of the old man. However, they seem not to object to his naming himself the heir of old traditions or the spokesman for his time on Native issues. The people who might most reasonably object to this imposture seem to share Grey Owl's own evaluation of himself as described in a letter to Lovat Dickson: no, he is not a full Indian, so he should not wear feathers "unless perhaps one, on occasion" (Dickson, *Wilderness Man,* 80).

In the end, I suggest that Grey Owl is the impostor who gets away. He fooled only his white audience, and not all of them, and not all the time, and they wanted very much to be fooled. He created for them a concept of authenticity that took them back to childhood or, even better, gave them a sense of possibility. Ironically, this future-oriented thrust for the apparently vanishing past must be one of his finest achievements. For the Native communities of Canada, whom he did not fool, he inspired a new orthodoxy: that one might wish to be Indian not only in rejection of white civilization but also because Indian could be authentic and significant in its own right and because it carried as identifying baggage that respect for the natural world that is now a matter of both fashion and pride.

5

"Frautobiography," or, Discourses of Deception

Foucault's question "What is an author?" and his own response from Beckett, "What matter who's speaking?" resonate throughout discussion of imposture in autobiography. I set out to demonstrate in Chapter 2 how volatile the relations were between an apparently identifiable author and his text in early and medieval Europe and with the copyrighting of personal narrative in print through the eighteenth century. So, for instance, I could name St. Paul as a model for Christian conversion but also recognize the unlikelihood that he wrote all that is attributed to him. Similarly, I cited instances of prevarication and forgery in authoritative documents in which named authors wished to support religious orthodoxy or to avoid censure for their own opinions. I had to ask both what was in a name and how the author could be identified with his text: by style, attribution, authenticated claim, signature, and even portrait. Equally, I asked, how could the author *avoid* being aligned with a particular text? In a sense, one just plays the reel backwards to eliminate physical image, signature, claim, attribution, and possibly style. However, I am working not just with author and text but also with the author as created in the text, and have found that construction and verification of textual identity remain problematic long after copyright laws have supposedly clarified one part of the situation. Copyright, after all, establishes who claims to have written the text; but copyright does not ensure that the author has also been telling any kind of truth. We have seen that Norma Khouri and James Frey were identified as creators of false histories and castigated along lines that, short of physical torture and execution, have obtained for two thousand years. They were not who they said they were and their stories were not connected in good faith to the world outside the text. This chapter brings some of those same questions about varieties of imposture to bear on distinctly contemporary, postmodern texts in which textual identity, the person *behind* or the character *in* the text, is particularly fraught.

A footnote on the term "frautobiography" will not suffice. If I myself, as the anxious "author" of this discussion on textual identities and the creation, purloining, and misplacing of textual identities, am to escape censure, I must begin by fully acknowledging my source. So far as I know, the term "frautobiography" first appeared in a paper that Travis Mason and Duffy Roberts gave at the Modern Language Association conference in Philadelphia in December 2004. Witty, sophisticated, and self-reflexive, this paper was called "Invitation, Construction, and Collaboration in *Doubled Flowering* as 'Frautobiography.'" To complete the transparency of my disclosure, I must add that the Mason and Roberts of this MLA convention began their work on *Doubled Flowering* as Travis and Duffy in my English seminar titled "Plagiarism, Hoax, and Fraud in Autobiography" in 2003, where they produced a fine early draft of this MLA performance, for which they earned an equally fine grade. I am borrowing their coinage, "frautobiography," because it can cover a multitude of textual sins (or what Susan Stewart has called "the.crimes of writing") that extend beyond this problematic text and provide the focus of this chapter.

Doubled Flowering is a strange confection, which presents itself as the translation of fragments of the poetic remains of Araki Yasusada, a Hiroshima survivor—who has since, conveniently, died. It interests Mason and Roberts for three main reasons. First, it depends on collaborative authorship, not just as that involves more than one author but also in that no use of language and certainly no text springs like Athene fully armed from the head of Zeus; rather, it negotiates its existence in relation to conversations, written and oral, that precede it. Second, *Doubled Flowering* depends—as all imposture must—on the collaboration of the reader. It functions, in other words, as a reading process in which the text matters rather more than the person behind the text, who has been such a large part of my concern to this point. Third, *Doubled Flowering* invites the reader to participate in "a collaborative aesthetic" that does not rely on interpretation (as in literary criticism) or on a referential aesthetic (as in autobiography), but opens a new "creative and critical space from which to challenge conventional binaries and reading strategies" (2). In other words, Mason and Roberts see "frautobiography" as a literary heresy that takes on the orthodoxies of its time in order to adjust the nature of "truth." Furthermore, they distinguish "frautobiography" from simply fraudulent autobiography, suggesting that its purpose is not so much the perpetuation of fraud as a continuous play in which readers collaborate both in the process and in the unmasking of whatever the scandal or secret may be.

This weighting of text over personal identity does not devalue my concerns in previous chapters; rather, it shifts their balance. Where I have been asking who is the author, how does the author align himself with his text, and what can the text say about this pre-textual human being, I now focus mainly on situations that begin and end with the text, situations in which the author is so well concealed or ambiguous as to avoid simple or confident detection, or situations in which personal identity depends absolutely (as for Wilkomirski) or very significantly (as for Kosinski or Frey) on textual construction. However, as my examples demonstrate, these discourses of deception that challenge or complicate questions of individual identity also absolutely require that individual personhood and authorship exist. This understanding, in fact, is the orthodoxy against which discourses of deception rebel—creating scandal, of course, and, very likely some shifting of the certainties (about personhood and authorship) that they resist. My examples also demonstrate that "frautobiography" is by no means a harmless or non-referential undertaking but gives rise to the anger, injury, and appeal to the law that follow from more evidently opportunistic imposture.

"Frautobiography" shares with *The Jesus Papers,* Kosinski, Wilkomirski, and Frey the common ground of some kind of identity theft, or some claim to ownership of a text or story that cannot bear the burden of proof. Adjusting Hamlet's wisdom for my purposes, I might say "there's nothing either true or false, but discourse makes it so." In order of appearance, my discourses of deception are plagiarism (focusing on the strange histories of Paul Celan and Neal Bowers), ghosting (and the disturbing cases of Jennie Erdal and Nega Mezlekia), and ironic pastiche and authority in hypertext (and the creations of Andreas Karavis and Araki Yasusada). Each deception flourishes within an enabling cultural and literary context and challenges—as Mason and Roberts suggest—both the aesthetic and the referential assumptions of the reading public. Furthermore, because I have shown that plagiarism and ghosting in particular are quite ancient forms of authorial estrangement, and that ironic pastiche was flourishing over two hundred years ago, and have suggested that hypertext has provided opportunities that eighteenth-century artists and con artists would have thoroughly enjoyed, I approach each of these forms of pretense or imposture as parts of a historical and theoretical whole. While plagiarism, ghosting, and textual play are sufficiently distinct activities to merit individual attention, they assemble under the banner of "le texte c'est lui," the replacement of the author with the text.

The Literary Politics of Plagiarism

As part of an erudite, intense, and sophisticated correspondence, Jorge Luis Borges has his imaginary author, Pierre Menard, write about his plagiarism of the thoroughly real (albeit fantastic) Don Quixote. Borges observes that Cervantes is an unlikely choice for Menard, this (fictional) Symbolist from Nîmes—and then introduces a magnificent series of "begats" that spoofs the creation both of authors and of their creations. However, Menard has explained to him (the creation being in close contact with his creator): "My affable precursor [Cervantes] did not refuse the collaboration of fate: he went along composing his immortal work a little *a la diable*, swept along by inertias of language and invention," whereas he, Menard, has "contracted the mysterious duty of reconstructing literally [Cervantes's] spontaneous work" (34). Figuring as part of Menard's elite, intellectually incestuous world, Borges finds that "the text of Cervantes and that of Menard are verbally identical, but the second is almost infinitely richer" (36). "Would not the attributing of *The Imitation of Christ* to Louis Ferdinand Céline or James Joyce," he concludes, "be a sufficient renovation of its tenuous spiritual counsels?" (38). How does mismatching author and text renew the text or affect reader response? Scholars in the early Church could answer that one. Situated in their own particular times and places, at home in their own orthodoxies, how do readers of any period since then respond to evidence of literary influence, or allusion, intertextuality, borrowing, or theft? To recognize influence or allusion, of course, is to become complicit with the text, to become part of the play of language and thought. Borrowing, like attribution, was once an acceptable form of propagation and authentication, whereas theft can only occur when ownership is clear. Borges plays with the whole complex of plagiarism in ways that make the academic response seem particularly pedantic but also make clear that the very concept of plagiarism depends on the concept of an originating author.

Academic plagiarism is quite simply and universally a punishable offence. Plagiarism (from the Latin *plagiarus,* "kidnapping") involves using someone else's intellectual labour, without acknowledgement, as one's own. Instructors can now submit students' essays to search engines that identify, in technicolour, both what and to what extent students have plagiarized. Honourable academics lard their own writing with footnotes (as I do here) to indicate how learned we are (like territorial dogs, we are marking our genre), or how complex each simple point may be, but also and particularly to make visible our debts to those who have gone before. Our claims to originality depend on our demonstrating where, exactly, we are not original. (The footnote is also an especially simple tool for the fraud to simulate, as Borges does.) In *The Footnote: A Curious History,* Anthony Grafton refers to a dissertation produced in 1743 by one Gottlieb Wilhelm Rabener, which consisted entirely of footnotes (120). Similarly, the bibliography of an academic publication pegs the text into its community of publications, providing both verification for particular discussions and many avenues for further research. (I have noted before and reiterate here how important community, like nation, can be to the impostor, who seeks the authentication of belonging.)

However, whereas words like "original" and "verification" call the doubt police back into action, not only for the presumed first use of the text but also to protect the originator of the text—that is, the man or woman who first wrote those words—"plagiarism," as Nick Groom points out, "is a perversion of theories of origin: it is a narrative of discovery that seeks to disguise its origins and present itself without precedent" (25). Plagiarism presents itself, in other words, as the original origin that overrides any earlier origin. This, too, if we work with Foucault's "author-function" or with Françoise Meltzer's discussion of authorial originality, is slippery terrain. Meltzer describes her (well-annotated) book, suggestively titled *Hot Property*, as demonstrating, case by case, "a moment when 'originality' itself is a construct, or even as a mythology, risks being destabilized, or uncovered as the greater fraud underlying the immediate one" (1). As for Borges, or Menard, language use is always both tied to the real world and, simultaneously, a deliberate fiction.

Most usefully for my discussion, Meltzer focuses on minority discourses, which tend to resist the orthodoxies of their time even while embedded in or dependent on dominant discourses. She identifies women and Jews, who have had difficulty with owning their own language or names or property (one could well include other groups of human beings), and the ways in which their constructions of themselves have been devalued. Meltzer concludes with a footnote on the problematic names of Otto Rank, Paul Celan, and Theodor Adorno, and by insisting that the terms "displacement" (for which she depends on de Certeau) and "origin" be

> understood as figures of speech that simultaneously possess a political,
> fatal power. They are both discursive formations … and words that literalize
> themselves. There is a lost place in being displaced; a stated point of
> origin in the metaphysics of origin; a ground to stand upon as a speaking
> (landed) subject; a spatial and material character to text; specific legal and
> financial consequences … to terms such as "naming" and "property." (164)

In each situation, the positive concept, as for property, offsets its negative, as in appropriation. Furthermore, discursive formations like plagiarism, in my present instance, have real and political implications in the world beyond the text. We have noted, historically, that men have died for what they wrote. In more recent history, origin and authorship continue to have life and death effects.

The Holocaust poet Paul Celan provides one of Meltzer's key examples of the politics of plagiarism. How, she asks, does the speaking subject risk speaking when life and the power to speak have been so completely denied? I return to this question in Chapter 6. Meltzer quotes Celan's claim that the German lyric depends on an "'I' who speaks from the particular angle of reflection which is his existence" (45). She understands him to be making a literal claim because, for the Holocaust survivor, the text remains the only possible position from which to speak: "poetic speech … is the only *place* left for existence" (48), the book is the apparently safe haven (53). When, therefore, Claire Goll, widow of the German Jewish poet Yvan Goll, wrote in 1960 to the editors of a journal accusing Celan of plagiarizing her husband's poetry, she was, in effect, removing the last ground on which Celan could stand (63–64). Evidence for and against this charge continued through the 1960s, and the literal truth may never be known. Celan told his friend Margul-Sperber that this accusation amounted to an attempt to destroy him—not just his poetry but his very self.

This charge of plagiarism was readily accepted in Germany, where Celan had been popular in the 1950s, but with no recognition that he was Jewish or that he wrote about the Holocaust. "In Germany," Meltzer writes, "the drive to accuse might be seen as a convenient way of expelling a poet whose growing international fame was making it difficult, at best, to continue repressing the Holocaust in his work" (76). However, in the United States, where Celan became known in the late 1960s as "the Jewish poet of the Holocaust" (75), the charge of plagiarism was barely credited. Arguing for plagiarism as a category dependent as much on cultural context as on content, on the reader as on the writer, Marilyn Randall notes that "'plagiarism' … is not an immanent feature of texts, but rather the result of judgments involving … the presence of some kind of textual repetition, but also, and perhaps more important, a conjunction of social, political, aesthetic, and cultural norms and presuppositions that motivate accusations or disculpations" (4). In short, as we have seen in virtually every example so far, readers and critics tend to accept and believe that which accords with their already established position in the real world, thus nurturing or rejecting the writers who suit their own (possibly quite unconscious) purposes, thereby repeating the complicity of the reading public in every act of imposture.

Just as the act of plagiarism has political effects, so, too, the charge of plagiarism may have political causes. Ironically, the poem in question was "Death Fugue," which has since become a commonplace in German textbooks and anthologies, and the presumably purloined phrase "black milk" has become a cliché (Meltzer 77). One of Celan's American supporters, John Felstiner, has noted that Goll's poem was published in New York in 1942, when Celan was in a Romanian labour camp. However, he does trace pre-Celan uses of the phrase to the work of Rose Ausländer, a fellow Romanian, and to the work of Immanuel Weissglass, a friend of Celan's. Perhaps the phrase can trace its origins for all of them to Lamentations 4:7–8, where white faces, purer than snow, turn blacker than soot and cannot be recognized in the street (74–75). One problem with language being the only space left for survival is that language is always already borrowed, part of another context, but available for new uses and new meanings that are not always welcome. As Thomas Mallon puts it in *Stolen Words,* "to some extent every writer's desk top is like a Ouija board, his pen pushed across it by whatever literary ghost he's just entertained" (3). Questions about source and originality that pervade this chapter are sometimes political, often difficult to secure, and are therefore unlikely to find clear or singular answers.

However, murky as these areas may sometimes be (to my mind, the student paper that shows up on my screen in technicolour bears the full burden of proof of plagiarism), I note Celan's observation to Margul-Sperber that this accusation amounted to an attempt to destroy him, not just his poetry but his very self. The American poet Neal Bowers makes very much the same claim in *Words for the Taking: The Hunt for a Plagiarist*. Bowers details the painful process of discovering that his work had been plagiarized, in each case just slightly altered, and republished (sometimes more than once) by one David Jones, using a variety of pseudonyms. "In more than 20 years of college teaching," Bowers writes, "I had never seen a more flagrant example of plagiarism" (26). What he identifies, in the process of his detective story, sleuthing out his plagiarist, is both the impossibility of claiming his own words as his own—as appurtenances of his own memories and thoughts and emotions—and the very personal violation that he, as victim of plagiarism, suffers. Because his poetry emerges, albeit with hard labour, from secret reserves in his own life, much more than words has been taken. Marilyn Randall notes this distinction when she writes of plagiarizers as essentially mediocre writers unable to produce the original (the "master" piece), and suggests that the distinction lies not in the textual product (*pace* Pierre Menard) but in the personal attribute (27–28). "True authorship," she writes, "is incompatible with plagiarism because authors are by nature—that is, ancient tradition—not only originary, but sincere, that is, authentic" (28). Randall jumps through a lot of hoops with that pronouncement, including her parenthetical nod to originality itself not being absolutely foundational, but Bowers would bear her out. His poems are a part of his self.

Specifically, Bowers's poems include very personal material, such as his exploration of his grief at his father's death and his dedications to his wife. The plagiarist makes free both with the language of the poetry and with the emotional life it expresses, desecrating private space, which deeply offends Bowers's wife, who feels assaulted by a stranger. Bowers says his private life has been invaded (29), that the wound he has suffered is far deeper than any to the ego. He refers to one poem as "a bittersweet bloom" that he had planted on his father's grave. "The thief dug it up, pruned it to his liking, and damaged the roots in the process. Worse, he replanted it in the soil mounded over my father and pretended the loss was his" (30). For Bowers, at least, if not for the readers and critics of his poetry, the differences between Cervantes and Menard are pronounced. For Bowers, words on the page connect umbilically with the experience that gave them birth. Furthermore, like Celan, Bowers claims that damage to his poetic persona, his written "I," damages him as a man. Responding to J.M. Spalding in an interview, he explains the personal harm the plagiarist has caused. "Almost every thought of my father," he tells Spalding, "evokes thoughts of Jones. That's the thing for which I can never forgive Jones" (Spalding, "Interview"). As for Jones's direct approach to Bowers's wife in correspondence, simultaneously unctuous and threatening (once battle is engaged, no holds are barred), she finds it frightening and manipulative. Contrary to Jones's assumption that women will be more sympathetic to his sad story than men, Bowers's private investigator, also a woman, finds Jones repellent, "a wrong guy" (65). Insofar as text relates to body, women may be more attuned than men to varieties of rape.

Two results of Bowers's search seem particularly relevant to my discussion: first, the context in which the plagiarist can do as he pleases, and second, the absurd (and for Bowers alarming) conflation of predator and victim. I have suggested that context is crucial for the perpetration of any imposture, that the literary stalker, in this instance, can only function (repeatedly) in a particular climate, which his actions then clarify or make visible. In this case, for instance, despite the common understanding in universities that plagiarism is entirely unacceptable, Bowers's colleagues are amused by the plagiarism of his poetry. They suggest he should feel flattered (42), or that the plagiarist may suffer from photographic memory (43). Some poetry editors to whom he writes warnings about Jones masquerading as "David Sumner" do not bother to reply. "Several responded that they had no intention of returning the Sumner poems they had on hand unless they were proved to be plagiarisms, which was comparable to accepting a chronic forger's check and assuming it to be good until it bounces" (48). They are skeptical about the accusation (53), or they feel that the true poet should be humble, less anxious than Bowers evidently is to claim his poetry as his own (101). Or they regard his "predicament" as merely "a 'poetry snit'" (102). However, such responses miss the point entirely, which has less to do with Bowers being angry and upset than with the generically crucial alignment between "the true poet" and his work. Cervantes might have been amused by Menard's copy, but Menard's copy can only pretend to exist because Cervantes's copy precedes it. Similarly, Sumner cannot claim the memories and emotions that inspire Bowers's poetry, or the wife to whom Bowers dedicates his poems, except as copies or fictions, so his "copies" absolutely depend on Bowers being the "true poet."

Because the poetry is personal, theft of the poetry afflicts the man quite personally. Various colleagues, for instance, who fail to identify Bowers the man with his productions as a poet, do not fail to identify him with his plagiarizer, adding to the ways in which Jones/Sumner is stealing Bowers's identity. Just as the original poet needs to bear the burden of proof in character as well as in text, so the community that fails to take his complaints seriously is "hard to dismiss because they attacked [him] personally—and for nothing more than having the temerity to speak out against the theft of [his] work. Like abusive nurses who slap the patient when he moans, they meant to teach [him] stoicism and silence." In short, these responses suggest that he is deserving of victimization "not because [his] poems were good but because [he himself] was weak" (132) or somehow personally at fault. Wondering whether this predator (literary and sexual) is seeking another identity (or several identities, as his female persona makes clear), Bowers is uncomfortable about being his vehicle. Damage to authorship of his poems extends to authority over his own life.

If Bowers's complaint is egregious, the community is not only upholding the plagiarist but is also, in ways that Bowers finds disturbing, conflating the two men, failing to distinguish that Jones is garbed in Bowers's wardrobe (78). As with failures of character (rather than text), the poet himself is the one suspected of misinterpretation, self-aggrandizement, or lies, the one who becomes "a pariah" (54). "More than a few friends," Bowers writes, "advised me not to alienate editors by pushing my case too hard. Others cautioned me not to link my name too closely with plagiarism, even as a champion of right, because in the long-term people might not remember which side of the theft I was on" (54). In the extended and absurd correspondence between poet and plagiarist, Bowers identifies yet another slippery or incestuous connection between them, realizing that Jones's lies tend to accrete around grains of truth. Worse, the constantly proliferating plagiarist inhabits his head, affecting the way he himself thinks about his own work and his own chances of being a plagiarist or failing in originality himself. "Most writers," he notes, "are haunted by the fear that they may inadvertently appropriate someone else's work" (103). "The problem is originality," and that is the bottom line (105). Or, as Randall puts it, "mistaken identity, in the realm of intellectual production, is a crime against the relation of authenticity subsisting between the author and the work" (31) so that plagiarism is an "index of the intimate and timeless relationship of identity … between personhood and intellectual activity" (95). So, disturbed and fascinated, Bowers and his wife and Anne Bunch, their private investigator, search for clues to the original or "true identity" of the man who is absorbing their life as a fake, as if to separate him from the original poet as another man in another body with a bewildering and distinctly alien psychological makeup. (The man himself never emerges from their searches except in disturbing traces of his history as a pedophile, which, for Bowers, adds a horrifying element of identity distortion to identity theft.)

The battle, in fact, is largely psychological. Recourse to law proves to be predictably expensive and quite useless. What, their lawyer wonders, is the worth of a poem? Why would anyone want to steal a poem if its value was purely intrinsic? How could Bowers be so upset if he had not in fact lost anything? (61). This Doubting Thomas of a lawyer takes the case and cites the Criminal Code to

Jones/Sumner—that is, Section 2319, "Criminal Infringement of a Copyright"—which could involve up to $25,000 in fines and/or a year in prison (72). However, Jones/Sumner rapidly sidesteps the lawyer to engage directly with Bowers and his wife, and the lawyer takes his fees and retreats from the fray. Bowers's problem, in law, apart from the fact that Jones has no money and is therefore effectively "'judgment proof'" (75), is that both the law and the lawyer have difficulty working with poetry valued at $2.00 a line. Bowers's stint as sleuth in his search for justice (recognition merely, as the poems can never be returned to him in their pristine, pre-Jones state) concludes with the discovery that Jones has now turned to plagiarizing someone else's prose and to various devious measures for eluding the charge of plagiarism when challenged.

The battle between poet and thief is also psychological in that the form of "frautobiography" set up by plagiarism depends, in each instance, not only on the relations between author and text (who first wrote these words?) but also on the relations of reader to text (how do readers of Menard or Celan or Bowers understand the text?). As good postmodernists, Mason and Roberts define their coinage as above all a reading strategy, pertaining to neither a literary nor a referential aesthetic but opening up a new space for the play of meaning. In this new space, one may indeed ask, "What matter who's speaking?" but our question will not satisfy the poet who feels that both his textual and his lived identity have been stolen. However, because the issues are so pre-eminently textual, Bowers gets nowhere when he thumps his physical chest; his text has already gone walkabout and he who spun that text out of his life experience has been left behind.

In effect, Jones wins—whatever it is that a plagiarist wins. Unlike Paul Celan, he is too elusive as a man to receive personal shame or to be identified as receiving it. He messes with another man's work and life and moves on apparently unscathed. Curiously, Bowers is supported not by law but by tribes of journalists who respond to an essay he writes for *The American Scholar* in the fall of 1994. "Because their world is a pragmatic one built on facts," Bowers realizes, "journalists see plagiarism for what it is—the theft of someone else's creative and intellectual property. Journalists who plagiarize are ruined" (128).[1] Journalists have no time for the plagiarist's being misguided or confused or subject to photographic memory; they call a thief a crook (128). Of course, they also have a nose for a good story, and Bowers finds, having received more attention for two stolen poems than for twenty-five years of publishing poetry, that he has become "better known for what was taken from [him] than for what [he] had given" (128). Frautobiography that turns on theft and loss, or identity and confusion, all within the text, may in the end leave only human scars. The money involved being, as Bowers's lawyer notes, so ludicrously small, and the sources for text (as his colleagues note) being so ambivalent, only the man remains. Or two men, both rather diminished by their separation from the text: the one who wrote from his heart, and the one who seized the words and ran. Depending on where and in what context the reader finds any of these poems, they refer to an author obscured or in hiding but no longer directly to life experience. Having travelled the long and winding road from conventional borrowing or appropriation, plagiarism of personal words that pertained to a personal life now dismantles the autobiographical project. If readers care no more than Bowers's colleagues, then he and all other autobiographers, all surely vulnerable, may as well take down their shingle.

Ghosting: "An ill-favoured thing, sir, but mine own"

Touchstone's brief exchange with Audrey in *As You Like It* on the nature of poetry reads or plays as witty metatheatre today but was surely some kind of insider joke for Shakespeare and his friends (*As You Like It,* III.3). Truly, Touchstone says to the simple country woman he plans to marry, "I would the gods had made thee poetical." "I do not know what 'poetical' is," Audrey replies (as part of a prose section of this very poetical play). "Is it honest in deed and word? is it a true thing?" Touchstone's response conflates poetry with lovers and both with "feigning," so that Touchstone and Audrey together conclude that if Audrey is not fair (or poetical), then at least she is honest. When Touchstone later presents Audrey at the court in the Forest of Arden, he calls her "an ill-favour'd thing, sir, but mine own" (V.4), claiming honest (original, authentic) connections with his rustic wife to compare and contrast the two of them with all the unlikely coupling around them. The world Touchstone makes, in language and in life, is his own creation, original to himself; his wit, as his name implies, provides the play's measure for reality.

However, like the plagiarist, both the ghostwriter and the named author of a ghosted text would need to say that the work, which might be a perfectly well-favoured thing, is certainly not his own. More honourably, for sure, than the plagiarist, the ghostwriter severs connection between the original or presumed author and the words on the page. When "David Sumner" seems to write about his father's death, he is stealing the father, the death, and the words of Neal Bowers. When the ghost writes, she (in both the instances I propose to examine here) is paid for specific work that she knows from the start will be published under her employer's name. Like plagiarism, this practice of ghosting that ensures non-writers can tell their stories surely has a distinguished history dating back to the days when scribes pushed their pens across the page in the service of a higher authority. Jack Stillinger mounts an extensive argument to demonstrate that more recent myths of the solitary author have been generally and altogether overvalued. Keats did not actually pay the friends and editors who amended his work. John Stuart Mill acknowledged but did not hire Harriet Taylor. Wordsworth (who regularly plagiarized from his sister Dorothy's journal) and Coleridge and Eliot and

Pound all developed working relationships that were crucial to the work that was then published under individual names and generally read as the work of one poet. Responding to New Criticism and to the subsequent death of the author, or the abstraction of the author into author-functions, Stillinger argues persuasively for the importance of the historical or biographical author who cannot, however, by the very nature of language and publication processes, function entirely alone. Either my family and friends, editors and publishers, are all involved in this book that you are reading, which displays only my name on the cover and title page, and we as author and reader may enjoy the simple illusion of my singular author-ship, or I may acknowledge the people who have contributed to my thinking and writing, humbly, like Touchstone, taking responsibility only for the faults. Or, again, I may conceal the ghost in my closet, the one that spooks only me in the small hours of the night and that you should never know about. What happens when that ghost emerges from the shadows to displace the "living" author, when the historical or biographical author that Stillinger values is not the one named on the title page? Who owns the words on the page, or the experiences the words describe (or create), or the public recognition that the words acquire? What kind of a ghosted author, claiming these words, has to take his bow, saying "a suc-cessful, well-reviewed, maybe a prize-winning thing, but not mine own"?

Ghostwriting: (a) The Gleam in the Eye of the Tiger

Unlike plagiarism, I have suggested, ghostwriting is an above-board, acceptable business. Numerous autobiographers with publishable stories to tell but no story-telling skills hire ghostwriters to write for them. The ghost receives a salary but does not receive or expect any acknowledgement for the finished work. The term "ghost" is well chosen. The ghost remains invisible, lacks substance, may be sensed, but does not manifest herself. However, the ghost belongs in discussion of frautobiography when she turns the tables, so to speak, exposes herself as the source of language, and takes a substantial, visible position from which to examine both the working relationship and the character whose solitary name has appeared on the ghosted book or books. For whatever reason, she can no longer accept her own invisibility and invites examination of various associated problems: Does experience trump language? Despite the apparent inseparability of experi-ence and language, do we not find ourselves asking whose story is it anyway? Or does the very experience of producing language constitute the material of the ghosted work? To whom, in short, does the story belong? Curiously, per-haps inevitably, my two examples involve educated, Western, anglophone women employed by flamboyant men, from Palestine and Africa respectively, for whom English is not a first language and for whom success in their adopted country is of paramount importance. In other words, both examples involve many more subtle and powerful issues than an economic transaction of skills for cash; here, as in every situation we have examined, the context creates the imposture. Where many a ghost may be an aspiring artist who ghosts as a day job, my two examples have come out of the closet to claim the stories that readers had not known were theirs—as well.

Amazon books lists *A Timeless Passion* (1995) and *Tara and Claire* (1997) as novels by Naim Attallah, both, as it turns out, ghostwritten by Jennie Erdal, and both published by Quartet Books (owned by Naim Attallah).[2] In May 2007, Quartet Books also published the 750-page hardcover autobiography of Naim Attallah, titled *Fulfilment and Betrayal.* Possibly, as of course befits an autobiography, he himself, betrayed by the ghost who had written the two novels, wrote the autobiography himself. However, in *Ghosting: A Double Life,* Jennie Erdal traces her twenty-year working relationship with Naim Attallah in which "they" produced important works of translation, massive collections of interviews with famous people, and even these two novels, which were well received. *Ghosting* is part exposé of an elaborate secret and—more interesting for my discussion—an exploration of the process by which the ghost must inhabit the mind of the named author and, in ironic reversal of conventional hauntings, be possessed by him. So *Ghosting* is in fact Erdal's autobiographical work. Hired initially to develop a Russian list for Quartet Books, Erdal was drawn into a curiously symbiotic relationship with this flamboyant man, who called all his female employees "Beloved," and whom she called "Tiger," after the tiger skin and head that blazed as a centrepiece on the wall behind his leather-topped desk. Her job, in other words, began with the elaborate trappings of fiction and of performance, and developed into a bizarre saga of his literary aspirations and her practical fulfillment of them.

For about twenty years, very much longer than most ghost experiences last, Tiger was like the fisherman's wife of the fairytale, wanting ever grander and larger and more magnificent achievements until he exhausted all the magic power available to him. Stories about Tiger make for both tender and hilarious reading. However, Erdal's sustaining question is how she, a self-effacing Scotswoman with a degree in Russian and philosophy and a family to raise, worked for this exotic and demanding employer, mostly from home near St. Andrew's in Fife, taking calls from Tiger on a dedicated line. Ghosting opens with a love letter, "a window on the soul," that Erdal wrote for Tiger on the occasion of his wife's birthday, one of many that he would then copy onto "embossed notepaper, using a Montblanc pen and blotting paper, signing it with a flourish at the bottom" (xi–xii). (A Montblanc pen is also Tiger's parting gift to Erdal when she leaves him.) Ghosting opens, in other words, with the disconnect between a man and the words to which he signs his name, a man and the words that his ghost understands to be expressive of his thoughts, his feelings, and his character, and that he accepts as expressive of these innermost aspects of his self. Audrey, I am sure, would have needed the same kind of help to translate her spoken affection for Touchstone into text, which brings me back to the question whether poetical is a true and honest thing. In each case, the personal feeling translates into the particular genres that are commonly understood to mean what the inarticulate "author" wishes to express. Translating from the inadequately rendered personal desire to the publicly readable formula that retains (or creates) individual tonalities is the task of the ghost.

Erdal begins as a translator from Russian to English because Leonid Pasternak's daughters persuaded her to translate his memoirs, in which she then interested this London publisher, who became her employer. From there, she developed Quartet's Russian list, landing *Red Square* for Quartet within hours of Brezhnev's death. Translation is in many ways an obvious place for the ghost to begin; it provides her training in invisibility. Erdal's personal history also prepares her well. Growing up in Scotland, trained from childhood to speak and use "English," she so adjusted her accent and her vocabulary as to acquire an early and intense understanding of language as a vehicle for the self. Immersing herself in other languages through school and university, she enriched these accents and vocabularies into significant appreciation for the subtleties and processes of cultural differences and of value or meaning. Not surprisingly, therefore, she is fascinated by translation. "Cervantes," she writes, "compared translation to looking at Flemish tapestries from the wrong side. I suppose he meant that, while it's possible to make out the general shape and colour of the pictures on the front, a lot is lost and obscured by all those dangling threads." However, while Cervantes may be right about the differences between the "right" and the "wrong" side of the tapestry (and while Borges's Pierre Menard clearly left no dangling threads), Erdal suggests that "even the wrong side of the tapestry can be worth seeing" (81). Recognizing that love of words and response to linguistic nuance are prerequisites, the translator "should be able to engage the reader in much the same way as the original, to replicate the author's vision and the particular spirit of the work" (82). Discussing the qualities of excellent translation, Erdal looks for the grammar of cultural difference, the expression of people and their thinking, that "soul" onto which Tiger's love letter had provided "a window." The translator, after all, is forging "a deep connection with the author," turning his words "into something new, unique but not original, creative but not inventive, a palimpsest of the first creation" (86). Unlike the plagiarist, the translator works not from the outside in but from the inside out.

In Tiger's case, where no first creation existed, Erdal also became a ventriloquist, inventing and producing language for Tiger to speak (in the interviews for which he became renowned) or to write. She anticipates his likely responses or responds to them as if he had made them. Ventriloquism and make-believe conversation become an insider language for supplying both the answers and the questions. In effect, she speaks both parts of their conversation. The crucial difference with Tiger is his apparently insatiable desire for her to efface herself and speak exclusively for him, to interpret his inarticulate fantasies into expression that the world would recognize. When his ambitions rise to fiction, however, Erdal feels as if she has begun to sign away her soul (196).

Fiction, of course, involves not information but invention. For the ghost, it involves creating the invention of another mind. "The fact that I was writing as someone else," Erdal explains, "with a mask on, as it were, inevitably added yet another layer of complexity. I did and did not feel responsible for the words on the page, I did and did not feel that they belonged to me; I did and did not feel that I could defend them in my heart" (140). Fiction raises the "central difficulty ... the question of sincerity" (141). "I tried to think myself into what I imagined Tiger's style might be, but the more I searched for his voice, the more I caught my own breaking through; the more I tried to realize his literary aspirations, the more my own seemed to intrude ... The more I struggled to be free, the more I felt constrained by Tiger's expectations" (142–43). Erdal is daunted by the task of a second novel. "'If we do just one, nobody will bloody believe us,'" Tiger tells her, using that first-person plural in which they always spoke of their collaboration. "'They will think the first one was a fluke!'" (163–64). Looking for the heart in place of the formula, trying to please her customer, who is not the general reader but, in this case, "the soi-disant author" (175), Erdal faces the question again: Whose heart? Fiction has to come from inside one's own skin. Otherwise, one is trying to "fake sincerity" (175). For Tiger, on the other hand, the fiction "they" wrote was in some profound sense the autobiography of his fantasy life. He was the hero. The hero's mother could not be dead because that would be so offensive to Tiger's mother. Nor could he betray his wife (who seems not to have known about his ghost). His vision was absolute but left his ghost no room in which to manoeuvre; she was to realize his private version of his own inner meaning.

The separation between author and ghost becomes inevitable once Erdal understands that this writing is unlocking secrets inside herself, that she is in some way examining her own past and "trying to make sense of it" (215). "Through writing," she discovers, "we are not so much creating a new pattern as uncovering one that is already in us ... Writing is always personal. You reveal yourself to yourself" (215). In other words, whereas plagiarism silently moves text from one originating author to another, and Erdal's experience of translation bridges between source language-and-text and targeted language-and-text, ghosting produces the one and only source text with only one apparent author. However, that author takes the risk that the invisible ghost will become visible first, as in this case, to herself, then to her author, and then to her author's readers as well. When Erdal decides to "give up the ghost" (215), to acknowledge her own voice, she does so by examining precisely those threads of the tapestry that Cervantes found problematic. If we read these threads as the significant pattern rather than the wrong side of another pattern, we are switching the point of view from the eye of the tiger to the eye of the word weaver creating what is, in the end, her own world. Collaboration cannot be more "fraught" than this. Nor can the written "life" be more obscured to its own writer than when that writer does not, in effect, exist.

Ghostwriting: (b) Collaboration and Consuming Lives

By comparison with Erdal's exposure of Attallah, the outing of Anne Stone as Nega Mezlekia's ghost is crude and hostile. Where Erdal explores language, translation, and identity to arrive at her own story, Stone and Mezlekia went to court over her role in the production of his memoir, in the process opening up major questions about the role of the ghost, the construction of the author, and the politics of a white woman writing (in this case) for a black man. Erdal treats Attallah's idiosyncratic use of English as a feature of his culture and his personality, part of what she needed to "translate" and, in translating, somehow to retain. So it falls to reviewers and commentators, with varying degrees of irony and racism, to make the point in Attallah's case about the exotic outsider seeking his place at the centre. John Morrish, writing most appreciatively about Attallah's support for various endangered literary ventures, also describes how Attallah was known as "The Ayattallah" and "Naim-Attallah-Disgusting."[3] In a similar vein, Celia Brayfield, who describes herself as "a novelist and retired ghost-writer," refers to Attallah as "the literary equivalent of Mohamed Al-Fayed, a Middle Eastern plutocrat who owned what he mistakenly imagined to be a cornerstone of elite British society, but who did not understand how that society works and what its ethos is." Describing his success, she assumes that "the fact that he was foreign actually helped. The English like their sacred monsters to be exotic and larger than life, and only turn on them—think of Robert Maxwell or Mohamed Al-Fayed—when they are perceived as having gone too far."[4] These same possibilities arise for Nega Mezlekia in Canada and do not speak well for Canadian pride in multiculturalism. On one hand, the refugee receives the warmest welcome, and on the other he remains so distinctly foreign as to be a pariah. For all their differences, both situations shed light on the foreigner within the gates, the limitations of welcome to English or Canadian identity—in person or in text.

Issues of person or text permeate discussion of Mezlekia's work in terms not only of national identity but also of the many ways in which he constructs himself and the ways in which the Canadian media have constructed him by means of his writing. Mezlekia's "memories of [his] Ethiopian boyhood" are called *Notes from the Hyena's Belly.* Wild hyenas roamed Mezlekia's hometown at night, ensuring, in the words of the boy's teacher, that there was no homelessness: "Sleeping outdoors in Jijiga was the ultimate suicide. It was a vanishing act. The hyenas would cut you up into pieces quicker than the gods could put you together. They would devour you, your shoes, bracelets, linen and anything else you had touched. Beggars knew this; they might go hungry, but they always had shelter" (52). Mezlekia grows from boyhood to youth as a guerrilla fighter, only sometimes able to help his family in their desperate poverty, and finally leaves for Europe and then Canada to study engineering. Because his story deals with extreme experience, and because he has lived to tell his story, sheltering in a foreign language and a foreign country, Mezlekia develops the close connections that I continue to see between the body of the man and his words on the page, but by no means simply so.

Mezlekia himself, Anne Stone, and the media attention to their quarrel all emphasize the construction and conflation of author and man. Neil ten Kortenaar, in a thoughtful article that situates *Notes from the Hyena's Belly* in the context of African writing, begins by noting what Mezlekia supporters have tended to refer to as "the voice of the text," seeming to suggest not just that the words on the page belong to Mezlekia but that they somehow *are* Mezlekia (42). He notes that both Mezlekia and Stone, in their different relations to the text, seem to protest too much about their ownership, indicating the precarious nature of authorship and the personal value of claiming it. Such urgent claims may be made for any text, but ten Kortenaar also points to the "fearful shadow of the ethnographer's relation to the native informant" (43) that dogs this text as well and that may allow Stone, as a white Canadian, the authority of language and deprive Mezlekia, the black immigrant, of the future he wants as a writer. However, citing Couser on the "cloven tongue" so characteristic of collaborative autobiography that "conflates two consciousnesses," he suggests that nothing here beyond the standard problem of the adult man looking back on his own past need provide this fissure (45; see also Couser, *Altered Egos,* 208). In short, had Stone not emerged from the shadows, Mezlekia might simply have launched his career as a writer with remarkable success. (Attallah, too, enjoyed his day in the sun.) Once Stone became part of the story, questions arose about personal history, narrative, and authorial responsibility.[5]

The brutal civil wars of the 1970s and 1980s in Ethiopia consumed both of Mezlekia's parents, many of his friends, certainly his own youth. So far, Mezlekia's story is entirely his own, though the reader may ask to what extent it could exist prior to the language that creates it, suggesting accordingly the significance of Stone's role. However, the history of this book as developed in the media suggests that Mezlekia's story, the role of Mezlekia's story in Canadian literature, and perhaps even Mezlekia the man, all are open to reconstruction. In fact, Mezlekia's frautobiography shows up Frey's experience for the very simple situation that, in the end, it was. With Mezlekia, autobiography is about a life that cannot always stay hidden behind the text and that changes outside and beyond the text in ways that affect the reading of the text. When Stone claimed to have ghosted this autobiography, she created a split between text and man far wider than that between the adult and the child on whom he looks back. She claimed the text but not the life. However, in making this claim, she unleashed a public event that reimplicated the teller in the tale and resituated the narrative in experience that now overflows from the "original" story. In effect, her intervention clarifies how this tale connects with other tales, those that are told and those that are lived; how (once again) media involvement can alter the trajectory of a text and therefore a life; and even how the tale connects with place, as in the case of Grey Owl, and with the political relations between and among places.

Mezlekia's book was published by Penguin Canada in March 2000. It is an extraordinary and very beautiful book in which an often whimsical and occasionally passionate narrator blends the traumas of civil war in Ethiopia with ancient history, contemporary politics, Amharic myth, community, and family. Then, on publication, a Montreal lawyer, Lauren Carrière of the firm Leger Robic Richard, sent a five-page letter to Penguin claiming infringement of copyright on behalf of Anne Stone, who claimed that she and not Mezlekia had written all but the last twenty pages of *Hyena's Belly* (Michael Posner, *Globe and Mail*, 6 December 2000). Penguin's lawyer, acting for Penguin and for Mezlekia, disputed Stone's claim, and the story seems then to have gone underground. I can find nothing more in the media until *Notes from the Hyena's Belly* won a Governor General's Award for non-fiction in November of the same year.[6]

Enter national pride, literary prestige, and high financial stakes. Canada's highest national literary award draws major attention in Canada every year. On 14 November 2000, Adrienne Clarkson, then Governor General of Canada, honoured Nega Mezlekia along with Michael Ondaatje, originally from Sri Lanka, in a gala ceremony at Rideau Hall in Ottawa. CBC reports explain that both men's writings deal with violence and terror in their places of birth and that both hope readers come to understand the turmoil and horror of which they write. Ondaatje said that his novel, *Anil's Ghost,* had been the most painful and difficult book he had ever written and that it had taken him seven years to complete; Mezlekia, that *Notes from the Hyena's Belly* had been a very painful process and had taken him ten years to write. Adrienne Clarkson spoke of the "compass" that literature provides, "speaking to the moral imperative of humanity." These parallels that effectively compare Nega Mezlekia with Michael Ondaatje end with the re-emergence of Anne Stone. But the story-so-far can be angled in a number of ways: two writers win the big Canadian prize with works of fiction and non-fiction about Sri Lanka and Ethiopia respectively; two immigrant men of color produce powerful works in English about traumatizing violence in their countries of origin; Mezlekia, the African newcomer, wins big alongside Michael Ondaatje, who has become a Canadian icon. No small part of this developing story about Mezlekia has to do with his success (or not) as a Canadian and his chances of becoming a Canadian icon as well.

Stone's claim that she had not received appropriate recognition for her part in *Notes from the Hyena's Belly* damaged these chances. Stone retained a new lawyer (*Globe and Mail,* 6 December 2000). David Widgington of Cumulus Press asked the Canada Council to strip Mezlekia of his award. On the other side, hands-on editors and ghostwriters protested Stone's unseemly self-promotion. Editors, Margaret Wente wrote in the *Globe and Mail* (7 December 2000), are always the "unsung heroes" of a work, "handmaids" or "midwives" of books that could not have been written without them. As Rick Archbold wrote in *Quill & Quire* in January 2001, even though editors often do write, rewrite, or rescue other people's books, they are supposed to be invisible. Their invisible contributions are recognized in the Tom Fairley Award, the only award designated for editors (and the only Canadian literary award to which no money is attached). In other words, where Stone might have hoped for her name on the cover of *Hyena's Belly,* or where she might more reasonably have hoped for some acknowledgement, she would never see a book on which she had worked "emblazoned," to quote Archbold, "with a spiffy gold seal proclaiming [her] distinction." Stone may well be chafing at the personal success that has befallen Mezlekia. Other editors describe how very odd it is to hear putative authors claiming in celebrity interviews not only the text but also the experience of writing it and the occasions it has provided for exploration of the dark regions of their souls and so on. How the ghosted autobiographer can seriously make such claims is hard to imagine, but the more mundane issue is money. The bottom line is "this life for sale."

As with every other situation I am considering, part of the Mezlekia story has to do with the processes and politics of publishing and with money and recognition. Stone had been paid $6,000 for her work, but clearly this is small potatoes compared with the book's new potential for major sales—quite apart from the award money. Furthermore, the ghostwriter, whose name does not appear on the cover, fails to receive any royalties from the Public Lending Right Commission, which pays out to the name or names on the cover of a book according to the appearance of the book in public libraries. Failure to acknowledge does, then, cut the ghost out of all sorts of profits. Furthermore, Stone, an aspiring writer herself, might have increased the sales of her own work had she been able to piggyback on Mezlekia's success. Martin O'Malley noted on CBC-TV that he had never "heard of Mezlekia's *Notes for the Hyenas's Belly* or Stone's own modest novel *Hush.* Now [he'll] look for them in [his] neighbourhood bookstore, which is the wonderful thing about literary feuds"; and "as feuds go," he adds, "this one's a peach" (25 February 2001). Neal Bowers would appreciate the irony of this feud being so visible, and his lawyer might have been interested, given that visibility in this case depends on dollars.

So Stone had several possible reasons to renew her claims after Mezlekia won the Governor General's Award. She began a media rampage at the end of November 2000, which became a daily event between 7 and 13 December and continued into February 2001. Curiously, as with media attention for Hanna Jumana, Norma Khouri, and James Frey, the effect of Stone's advancing her claims in the media was to shift attention from the text, and even from the author and his editor or ghost, to Nega Mezlekia the man. The case was receiving media coverage anyway as both Stone and Mezlekia worked through their lawyers to ascertain the justice of their conflicting claims to authorship. Mezlekia claimed to deplore Stone's use of the media—as well he might despite the publicity his book received, and beyond his concern that he was being "held up to public ridicule and contempt" (CBC, 24 January 2001)—because Stone's work for him clearly extended far beyond *Hyena's Belly* and included other elements of his autobiographical production.

Stone's use of Mezlekia's unpublished work in process marked the most important point at which the man—not even the published author (that matter being under dispute) but the man himself—emerged as actor and as target. Stone was able to smear him by publishing extracts from his letters to her in which he called her a "vulgar slut" and claimed that he would "bury [her] if it [took him] a hundred years" (*National Post,* 4 December 2001, A1). She also felt it wise to hand over these further autobiographical materials by Mezlekia that she was working on because (the text expressing the life) they indicated he could be a very dangerous man. So Mezlekia became not the man who wrote his life story, or the man whose life story won acclaim, but specifically the kind of man who might act in certain ways in the world outside the text. In short, because the autobiographer makes explicit connection between text and life, Stone invited general readers, journalists, and lawyers to read Mezlekia's unpublished text as information about his past and possible actions.

In particular, Stone reopened a bitter dispute that Mezlekia had raised with the Faculty of Civil Engineering at McGill University in 1994 when he alleged that his supervisor had been muscling in on his thesis, that the department was restricting his access to computer software, that various individuals had failed to pay him for photocopying, and so on. McGill set up an independent board of inquiry in January 1995. Mezlekia eventually completed his degree. Officials at McGill refused to comment. But they did apparently ask Stone to hand over the Mezlekia manuscript, suggestively titled "I Can't Recognize Myself Anymore."

This manuscript outlines Mezlekia's concerns during the early 1990s, his growing anger, and his decision, comparing himself to Valeri Fabrikant, to kill several of the McGill faculty and administration, Valeri Fabrikant being the Concordia professor who did indeed shoot and kill four colleagues in 1992.

Extracts and reports of Mezlekia's manuscript that appeared in the press included a trip to Michigan to buy guns and ammunition and an epiphany in a Detroit hotel room in which the narrator heard the Creator tell him to lay these things aside because his life contained greater purposes. In the news at the same time as the Mezlekia story was unfolding, Canadians read of a young boy taken into custody for a class essay in which he described the revenge he would like to take on bullies in his school. Margaret Atwood and Michael Ondaatje were among the writers who wrote and spoke in protest against curtailment of this child's freedom to write.[7] In Mezlekia's case, McGill's legal team used the text to distinguish between the plan of the narrator and the action of the man and to point out that Mezlekia had, indeed, responded to this vision by returning quietly to his studies. They decided not to press charges.

Nevertheless, these associations between text and man, text and action, and text and the law muddy the distinctions we like to make for most literature and have serious difficulty making for autobiography. Mezlekia's tale of revenge includes explicitly literary improvements on Fabrikant's serial murders in that it draws on old gangster movies for its narrative details and form. The *National Post* (12 December 2000, A2) recited the tale of Mezlekia's repeated initiation of lawsuits through the early 1990s in order to demonstrate that the violence imagined in "I Can't Recognize Myself Anymore" was that of a man whose anger had outstripped alternative expression; the tale of his actions in life explained the tale he wrote. Certainly, the media were clear, and McGill's lawyers were clear, and Anne Stone seemed clear, that the tale he wrote said a lot about Mezlekia the man and the shapes his life could take. Even a staunch defender of Mezlekia drew on the life to reinterpret this story. Writing in the *Globe and Mail* (13 December 2000), Karen Connelly, a 1993 winner of the Governor General's Award and a member of the jury that granted Mezlekia his award, noted that Mezlekia was no longer referred to as an author, or an engineer (or indeed a former student), but as a black ex-soldier from Ethiopia. She deplored this rewriting of the man, who had now been separated from his book by the contents of another text and by the threat of legal action. Pointing to the media frenzy, she saw "a lynch mob [gathering] on the not-so-distant edge of our collective memory," reminding her readers that Mezlekia's story was crucial to his recovery from trauma. After all he had been through and all he had lost, he did have and must claim his story. However, personal defence and narrative reconstruction did not stop there. In her passionate defence of the man and his story, Connelly returned to the matter, presumably important to both the book and the man, of Canadian identity. "His aggressiveness ... his anger, his alarming disclosures even in unpublished writing are inexcusable according to our Canadian sensibilities," she wrote. But then, she suggests, perhaps these sensibilities need to be examined along with Mezlekia's past experiences. In other words, an immigrant story may alter Canadian sensibility both because the immigrant experience calls for unexpected response and because the story of that experience now belongs in Canadian literature. Language and story, representing experience, change the world that receives them.

Meanwhile, Mezlekia seems to have written himself into another kind of story as well, specifically the story of place. In "I Can't Recognize Myself Anymore," he writes of crossing the border, planning to buy guns and ammunition (carefully detailed) in Detroit. Presumably, such things are not so readily available in Canada. I do not know. But in Canada we understand from varied story forms that America is the land of the gun. So the border crossing and Detroit as the destination for such purposes, apparently "true to life," are also true to text, as are the hooded overcoat Mezlekia planned to wear and the "Colt handgun fitted with a silencer" that he planned to use (*National Post*, 11 December 2000, A1, with photograph). But if Mezlekia's story, in life and/or in text, includes this specific change of location (and Detroit as the place in which the Creator speaks is surely an original touch), the media, too, made a great deal of fuss about place. The whole of Canada claimed these embattled writers, Stone being at one time a Vancouver writer, at another a Montreal writer, and Mezlekia at one point a Calgary author based in Montreal. Specifying location in repeated adjectival phrases, rather as the media tend to specify age, underscored the Canadian character of this literary dispute. It could also serve to authenticate information (even when, or particularly when, neither location nor information may be accurate). However, changing location also served in Mezlekia's case to free him from the potential honour and then the trap of being a Canadian icon.

Significantly, his story crossed the border once again with a triumphant flourish that cut the Canadian brouhaha down to size. On 21 January 2001, Rob Nixon, Rachel Carson Professor of English at the University of Wisconsin, reviewed *Hyena's Belly* in glowing terms for the *New York Times Book Review*. Nixon's essay, subtitled "Eating Africa's Children," received front-cover attention, and he wrote of *Hyena's Belly* as "the most riveting book about Ethiopia since Ryszard Kapuscinski's literary allegory *The Emperor* and the most distinguished African literary memoir since Soyinka's *Ake* appeared twenty years ago." Recognized so prominently and respectably as among the African greats, armed this time with this top-drawer literary endorsement from the United States, Mezlekia turned to the law for his revenge against the Canadians who had sought to bring him down. He filed a libel suit against Anne Stone; against Insomniac Press, which publishes

Anne Stone and which he claimed was maligning him in order to increase her profits; and against Robert Allen, an English professor at Concordia who had been working on another of his manuscripts. This was not photocopying money he was after now. He was staking his claim as an autobiographer and as a writer and he was operating from a position of power.

If border crossing as part of "I Can't Recognize Myself Anymore" depends on familiar tropes from literature and film, the crossing effected in publication and review conveys power because it means international recognition and a large market for the Canadian writer. The *Globe and Mail* of 6 February 2001 quotes Charles McGrath, editor of the *New York Times Book Review,* as saying he had been unaware of the controversy in Canada. So much for Canadian national glory in the bigger picture. Here are the limits of the Governor General's Award and the presumably public dispute about its winner. According to Sandra Martin in the "Across Canada" section of the *Globe* for 9 February 2001, Nega Mezlekia "ha[d] just sold his first novel to Penguin Canada and Picador in the United States for quadruple the advance he [had] earned for his controversial memoir, *Notes from the Hyena's Belly.*" Would the *New York Times* people have said something if they had known? Charles McGrath is quoted as saying, "I think we would. But at some level, the book is the book. I think we would have reviewed the book anyway, and we would have taken it seriously anyway. Whoever wrote it, it is an achievement" (*Globe and Mail,* 6 February 2001, R2). The "man" who had been impugned in the Canadian media enjoyed sweet revenge in the United States.

Mezlekia seems also to have received no more than a lesson in courtesy in the Canadian courts. In 2003, the *Globe and Mail* ran two items on the court case. The first, on 9 February, seems to have been almost entirely inaccurate in that it had to be "clarified" on 22 March. Whereas the first included Mezlekia's withdrawing his libel action and agreeing to write a letter of apology to Anne Stone and providing some sort of credit for her contributions to *Hyena's Belly,* the second has Mezlekia simply acknowledging her contributions and expressing regret that he had failed to do so publicly before. Stone was to receive neither a written apology nor official credit. "For her part, Stone acknowledged that Mezlekia is, without qualification, the book's sole author, and expressed regret at media reports to the contrary." Presumably, this "ghost," unlike Erdal, had overstated her case. Or she, and those who supported her, had strong personal reasons for challenging this man and his writing. This is not a matter of fiction writing, though Attallah made that too very personal. This case involves opening a gap between life and story, enabling that gap to cast both life and story into doubt, even enabling the story to be read as predictive (or not) of the man's future actions. That wedge of doubt that damages credibility for both text and man may, for all we know, be fully justified (we know nothing of the process from Stone), but the recognition and award then raise further questions about the criteria that publishers, reviewers, and common readers bring to their judgment of autobiographical works. As for Canadian literature, and this particular text as autobiography, we have some rethinking to do both about our conflicted responses to the stranger within our gates and about the unstable relations between a man and his story.

"The man in the ironic mask":[8] (a) the Case of "Andreas Karavis"

Jennie Erdal has no doubt at all that she wrote all the words attributed to Naim Attallah, subsuming her authorial identity in his. Insofar as he enjoyed his literary celebrity, the flamboyant Attallah had a secretly silent identity and had, therefore, good reason to call her "Beloved." However, in Erdal's case, as in Stone's, the difficulty of remaining silent was, in the end, insurmountable. How, for sure, the courts resolved the Mezlekia versus Stone case we may only imagine because the two of them are not telling, but he is now listed on the Web as an engineer and a successful novelist, so he seems to have retained and even developed his identity as an author. However, he has not written himself into the text in any more autobiography. With ghostwriting, as with plagiarism, the man presumably behind the text has evaporated, leaving text as fiction, or as the shame-faced garb, in part or entirely, of another writer—sheep, one might say, in wolves' clothing.

I turn now to two texts presenting rather different problems. In these cases, the autobiographical identity does not in fact exist, though we arrive at this conclusion only after a while because both texts include extensive evidence of a real existence. Nor, when we arrive at the conclusion that no autobiographer stands behind the autobiography, can we simply conclude that these texts should be classified as fictions, because the writer (of the presumed fiction) also seems not to exist, apparently having been subsumed into the apparently autobiographical identity of the text. In short, both wear what I have decided to call an ironic mask. Both, in fact, raise questions of authorship that are reminiscent of problems in the early Church. We are dealing here with faulty attributions, with the merest traces of flesh-and-blood authors to pillory or praise, with texts that claim a man behind them yet seem quite unable to produce him, or that produce a man quite different from the one we might have expected. For these twentieth-century texts, of course, the issue is politics rather than religious faith. However, these politics, which do not concern the evanescent questions of power or wealth, but rather the apparently timeless questions of textual identity, do quite deliberately challenge the faith of the reader. How do we work with questions of source or authenticity or the identity of author or protagonist (or even reader) in cases as slippery as these?

In the case of both Andreas Karavis (in Canada) and Araki Yasusada (in the United States), the text simply is the man, except that no fact about either text is simple. Previously unknown poets of astonishing genius, exotic in the English-speaking world in that one is Greek and the other Japanese, both Karavis and Yasusada are also astonishing and exotic for the more curious reason that both are fictive creations of North American writers. Both creations, furthermore, involve impersonation and imposture, varieties of plagiarism and ghostwriting, processes of translation, and extensive authenticating "research." "Who are these men?" their creators seem to ask. What can we say about their lives? What can we learn from their writings about their personal experiences and their creative processes? Both creators resort to narrative construction of their authors, whose physical reality in time and place they very seriously produce. Furthermore, though both creations are poets, that is, creative artists, their elaborate production sets discussion of "frautobiography" squarely in the academy, the centre of orthodoxy that both of them resist. Karavis and Yasusada keep company with Ern Malley in Australia[9] and the Spectrists in the United States.[10] In each case, a significant part of the point is about academic reception of the work and, therefore, about what fools these mortals be.

David Solway, a Canadian poet, invented a Greek poet, Andreas Karavis, located him precisely in the Aegean Sea, gave him a detailed history, connected him to various people in the real world, living and dead, and produced the poetry from which textual identity, history, geography, and relationships can be deduced, all, of course, supported by detailed notes that enable the reader to co-construct the whole situation. Specifically, after publishing *Saracen Island* by Andreas Karavis and *The Andreas Karavis Companion* by David Solway, Solway explained to Ben Downing of *Lingua Franca* that "Karavis is not a hoax in the usual sense of the term. My intent is not deflationary ... I am not interested in perpetuating a deception but in creating a style" (10).[11] He says that "Karavis" provides him with the "new set of postulates and ... [notably] new quality of experience" that may replace what he feels are his own now exhausted "tone, stance, and poetic attitudes" (9). Elsewhere, in conversation with Carmine Starnino, Solway has complained about poets being trapped in their selves, suffering the gravitational force of their own personality, "obliged to orbit [their] own particular identity" in ways that necessarily limit perspective and understanding (Starnino, "Interview," 149–51). However, engaging his public through imposture ensures wider and more problematic issues and responses than simply re-energized poetry. Just as Bowers complains that his plagiarism case has drawn attention to him in a way that his own poetry never has, so Solway "derives bittersweet irony from the fact that having published a raft of books in both poetry and prose, he has won Canadian fame in the guise of a grizzled Greek sea dog" (Downing 10). In both cases, the man and his situation—albeit created in text—have become more significant than the texts associated with his original or authentic name. The reasons are not far to seek. Not only did Solway create a lively prank in which a number of friends and strangers joined him, but he also trespassed on the fine line of frautobiography, in particular the elaborate mimicry of scholarship that, whatever the reasons he himself may claim, calls conventional scholarship into question—and to account. Like so many other literary hoaxes, this one seems to ask whether indeed we can distinguish fake from authentic. Furthermore, we may ask what kind of authenticity the fake may achieve. Not least, with what purpose or effect does the fake seek to undermine the establishment?

First, however, I want to acknowledge the Karavis situation as sheer fun. It highlights the trickster element inherent in so much fraudulent activity, about which I have from time to time been adopting a more reproving tone. Matthew Hays for the *Globe and Mail* reported on the book launch of *Saracen Island* on 26 October 2000. "A cross-section of Montreal's literary community gathered at a downtown Montreal Greek restaurant on Tuesday night," he reports, wondering whether "the mysterious Greek poet" would turn up. Hays notes that a "man claiming to be Karavis did attend for approximately 20 minutes. However, he did not grant interviews. Wearing a fisherman's cap, he consumed several glasses of wine, spoke only Greek and then left the event." In "Anne Carson and the Solway Hoaxes," Ian Rae suggests that blurry photographs of this bearded man wearing a fisherman's cap that appear in several publications are "actually a bearded Solway" (45). I am impressed by Rae's confident "actually." Of the book launch in the Greek restaurant, Hays takes the sleuth-like trouble to observe that Solway himself was definitely in attendance, in fact appearing "simultaneously with the man who claimed to be Karavis." Expressing relief that Karavis had appeared in person, Solway remarked: "If he did not exist … I would have had to invent him." Solway has been clear about his poetry's need for this man to exist, so the creative fiction evolved seductively into an embodied fact. Suggesting just how little proof imposture truly requires, and how fertile indeterminacy can be, Downing found some "post-party disagreement [despite the well-attested presence of a man in a fisherman's cap speaking Greek] over whether [Karavis] had in fact shown up" (8). Like the original for the photograph, Solway's ability to produce a cliché of a Greek poet seems not to have borne the burden of proof.

Some responses to Karavis may have taken Solway himself by surprise, such as that of Fred Reed in *Books in Canada,* who took issue with Solway's biographical information about Karavis. Reed claimed that one C.D. Candias had shown Karavis to be both a duplicitous character and, possibly, the plagiarist of some early poetry by none other than David Solway (Downing 8–9). Certainly, the Karavis text suggests some sharing of poems, with Solway claiming that page proofs had been lost or that publishers had been careless, so that some poems had suffered inaccurate attribution. The game itself perpetuates questions of authorship and identity. To whom, and under what name, and therefore with what attendant effects, would such poems belong? However, the issue is not really how many people had fun, or even whether or not people believed in the mysterious Greek poet that Solway had created. Known hoaxes are, by nature, ephemeral, and Solway's confession to *Lingua Franca* that he had hoodwinked *Books in Canada* with his creation of Karavis suggests that he himself had no intention of perpetuating the whole charade. So the question, beyond Solway's assertion that he needed a "new set of postulates and … new quality of experience" for his poetry, must address the ramifications and effects of the whole adventure.

Downing concludes his *Lingua Franca* article by suggesting that "to an American audience, all this may look like a big canard in a small pond" (10). I have already observed that the Governor General's Award for *Notes from the Hyena's Belly* did not make news in America even when Mezlekia received his large advance from an American publisher. Almost sadly, Downing notes that "such a national flap is almost inconceivable in the United States." However, a "national flap" in Canada is a more complex matter than Downing may realize, as the case of Nega Mezlekia has already demonstrated. In Solway's case, this "national flap" begins with an Anglo-Canadian Jew in French Canada who has adopted Greece as his second home. Insofar as this whole escapade involves serious cultural critique, and I think it does, Solway is returning to Matthew Arnold's contrast in *Culture and Anarchy* between Hebraism and Hellenism as the twin roots of the Western intellectual tradition. But he also keeps travelling in order to introduce recurring tension in various forms between Greek and Turk (Christianity and Islam). Not only does this poet from the massive northern continent adopt the Greek islands known as the Cyclades, in the Aegean Sea between mainland Greece and Turkey, and create in Karavis a Greek whose family has for generations resisted Turkish occupation, but he also names the collection of poems for the one poem titled "Saracen Island." Solway's notes for Karavis's "Saracen Island" explain that this (the poem / the imaginary place) is where "shipwreck defines our condition" (*Saracen Island* 113). Furthermore, in *An Andreas Karavis Companion,* a magnificent romp of putative notes, diaries, letters, and biography of Karavis, along with Solway's own extensive research and interpretation, Eric Ormsby, who exists in fact as an Ismaili scholar at McGill University in Montreal, is included as claiming that he had seen Karavis, the anti-Turk warrior, in Istanbul, and has reason to suspect a liaison between Karavis and the Turkish poet Nesmine Rifat. (Who other than David Solway would then produce *The Pallikari of Nesmine Rifat,* the grieving poetry of an abandoned lover?) Eric Ormsby not only writes to David Solway with this thrilling gossip but also encloses a Turkish translation by Rifat of a Karavis poem titled "Faith." "There is more here," "Ormsby" concludes with an insider's wink, "than meets the eye" (49).

If Solway is creating "a national flap," then it's surely not on the grounds of Mezlekia's claim to belonging but, rather, as a literary challenge to the very concept of fixed or stable national identity. In Solway's lexicon, Saracen Island, not Canada, defines the nature of his exploration and does so in explicitly literary terms. As an imaginary place embedded in reality, as a poem apparently translated from contemporary Greek literature, and as a book title for Solway's discovery of another man's life and work, Saracen Island brushes with recognizable realities only enough to burgeon as an elaborate metaphor, but not any kind of a metaphor for "Canada." In fact, W.J. Keith attributes Solway's "comparative failure to gain recognition in a period of obsessive Canadian nationalism" to his turning away from Canadian influences, adopting his own equivalent of Rupert Brooke's "foreign field."

Apparently Saracen Island belongs in the northern Sporades archipelago of the Cyclades, near Skyros (and rather nearer to Greece than to Turkey), the island, Solway notes, where Achilles was press-ganged, where Theseus was thrown off a cliff to his death, and where Rupert Brooke (who died on his way to "liberate" Constantinople from the Turks) lies in his corner of a foreign field that is forever England. Solway's pursuit of Karavis, both through his poetry and through his "life," makes inevitable the association between himself and Brooke, poets who have died into new life, transplanted in Greek soil. The *Companion* has Karavis mentioning a visit to Brooke's grave, but not to Saracen Island just nearby. For the Greeks, Brooke joins Byron as a great romancer of Greek history; these two English poets, with their very lives and deaths, turned Greece into a metaphor, just as Solway has done with Saracen Island—a place of the imagination where the poet can conjure up his own heroic reality. This heroic reality, furthermore, is caught in the mythologized movement of the Cyclades, suggesting both a geographical and an ideal impermanence, mirrored in this case in the constant movement of Karavis in his caique.

For all this motion of land and sea and poet in movement, Solway quotes Karavis, who contrasts the poem "Saracen Island" with Seferis's myth of the journey, suggesting that "the predicament we have to work with is precisely that of the arrival or the sojourn … The truth is: there is nowhere left to go" (*Saracen Island* 127). This, it seems to me, is where the critical point of the exercise (beyond the fun) comes into play. Identifying arrival or sojourn as barren belongs to the dark force of Solway's adventure. Interpreting Karavis's poetry in a tight hermeneutic circle, Solway uses his own persona to explain that "Saracen Island is the true reflection of our condition *whether we like it or not*" (*Saracen Island* 128; emphases added). The place of shipwreck, the barren and unmoving self, alarms the poet into becoming his own Pierre Menard, creating the new situation in which plural personae can commune with each other about the relations between poetry and life.

Curiously, these relations confirm poetry as expressive of individual integrity. Karavis emphatically believes in the "single and unified core of our sense of being in this world, the pit at the centre of the cherry." He is convinced that "what we once called the 'self,' the centre of genuine, personal, and reflective response to the grandeur and complexity of existence, is the greatest casualty of the age we live in" because it "has been infiltrated by a political and economic and neoscholastic language that is dangerously abstract." In other words, text has come adrift from life because we think "in terms of slogans, generalities, clichés" (*Companion* 51). The *Companion* includes repeated evidence that Karavis is distressed by the parasites and mountebanks (82) who undermine contemporary literature and culture, but Solway in his own voice is even more vehement and addresses the Canadian academy quite specifically. In a wittily titled article in the *Antigonish Review* in 1989, he deplores the effects of deconstruction, not for the original thinkers with whom it originates, but for the mindless profusion of slogans, generalities, and clichés that have followed. He specifies: "Critical writing in Canada is no exception to this rule. Our journals and reviews bear abundant witness to the spread of deconstruction in an orgy of derivativeness" (58). Surely in the same boat as Sokal, he suggests that we are dealing with "a *collective* phenomenon, a stylistic code which can be learned, deployed and parsed according to a set of complicated instructions" (61). In fact, in this case, "the real victim is literature itself, willy-nilly transformed into a sort of intertextual Rubik's cube which only the virtuoso can satisfactorily manipulate" (63). In contrast, Karavis, or Solway writing as Karavis, is the one who lands on the "bedrock" of personal integrity, excoriating Pound, for example, entirely on "moral considerations which he holds as paramount and non-negotiable" (128). "For Karavis, it seems axiomatic that great art cannot emerge from a questionable moral foundation or from madness and bestiality. Genuine poetry demands not only discipline, thought and talent but," as Touchstone's Audrey would appreciate, "ethical soundness as well" (*Companion* 129). On another occasion, in interview, Karavis says: "Our self is our last resource. Our only resource … the self, the core of wakefulness at the heart of sleep, is the only thing in the world which is not a fiction. And the mother tongue of the self is poetry" (*Companion* 55). From creative whimsy to poetically grounded identity, the wandering caique of Karavis spins home truths out of imposture.

Together, poet and alter ego sound, once again, an Arnoldian note of personal, moral value at the heart of literature as of life. The face behind the ironic mask may, in other words, be less than amused. The identifiable "author" may be using his fiction as a stalking horse not for the freedom to be someone else but to make an entirely different point about the need for man and poet, man and critic, to be authentically and responsibly one and the same. Is that, I wonder, why Solway, who began by duping the editor of *Books in Canada* with his essay introducing Karavis, is now an associate editor of *Books in Canada* on a mast-head that includes his friends Carmine Starnino, W.J. Keith, and Eric Ormsby, among others? Do the letters and interviews and analyses to which these fellow Canadians have put their names extend the Solway/Karavis appeal for serious (Canadian) engagement with serious culture? Or are they further extensions of the elusive fiction of Karavis? Are the Canadian academy and its literary insiders snickering into their ouzo at the rest of us who mistook fiction for autobiography? Given the likelihood that Karavis stays put in no one position but represents all the elements (at least) that I have been attributing to him, he belongs, perhaps, in Jack Lynch's gallery of rogues in eighteenth-century London—another time and place in which another battle of the books challenged scholars to get real.

Another Man in Another Ironic Mask: (b) The Case of "Araki Yasusada"

Like Solway, the American poet Kent Johnson might complain that he is better known for his fictional identity than for work in his own name. Certainly, in both cases, the alias and textual identity that refuse connection with any personal iden-tity provide both discipline and freedom. Solway and Johnson are ghostwriters with a difference in that they have created authors in Karavis and Yasusada who are, themselves, ghostly, unreal. Unlike Erdal or Stone, Solway and Johnson write what they themselves would like to write, and then hide behind their own versions of Martinus Scriblerus, the inscrutable front man. This curious reversal of ghosting plays with traditional notions of authorship, which is why I have referred to these "impostors" as a postmodern phenomenon; but it also puts the reader in an un-enviable position, for while Solway and Johnson disappear in smoke and mirrors, they have invited their readers to look for them and to believe that they, or their "ghosts," are real. They provide clues and connections, histories and relationships. They have made their authors, who are not real (or who could be called fictions) as authentic as possible, producing the right patina, the necessary marks of credible identity. The result, most particularly in the case of the Yasusada poems, is either an extraordinary find (damaged and partial manuscripts rescued from the disaster of Hiroshima) or a challenge to convention in that no author or origin can be found, not even that old standby "Anon." Paradoxically, the Yasusada available in print is a hypertext creation, the tangible body (man or text) etherealized, multiplied, and variable on ethernet.

What do we make of an authorless work? Like Karavis, Yasusada emerged on the scene—in this case in major poetry journals through the early 1990s—as an unknown poet with extravagant claims on our attention. *American Poetry Review* published a special supplement of Yasusada's poetry in June 1996. As with Neal Bowers's plagiarist in hiding, or the possibly unexpected authentication that Solway received, the Yasusada poems were turning up on the desks of American poetry editors from multiple locations—California, Tokyo, Illinois, and London. Nonetheless, in apparent paradox, Emily Nussbaum notes that "messages slowly surfaced on the Internet" (as with James Frey) "warning editors about an ongoing deception" (1). Concerned about rumours of a hoax, Wesleyan University Press refused to go forward with its plans to publish the notebooks, then being translated, "it being out of bounds … for anyone to impersonate a figure as ipso facto tragic as a Hiroshima survivor" (Perloff 149). However, Roof Books stepped into the breach in 1997, so that Yasusada, like Karavis, now appears in book form in heavily annotated translation and with elaborate peritext. Notably, in all these dealings, one Kent Johnson in Illinois gave his name to the copyright and processed the massive literature that Yasusada began to spawn, and received the letters demanding return of the author's payment.

Like Karavis's *Saracen Island,* Yasusada's *Doubled Flowering* contains clues about its own inauthenticity,[12] but for all its playfulness, the Yasusada poet has evoked less humour and significantly more anger than Karavis. Most obviously, Yasusada is a Hiroshima survivor, a witness (like Celan) to atrocity. Emily Nussbaum notes that "many editors who had published the writing—sometimes with poignant footnotes on the death of Yasusada's daughter from radiation poisoning—were furious" (82). Unlike Karavis, and more like Celan, or Mezlekia, or Kosinski, Yasusada wrote not just as a witness but also as a victim. Worse, America had in this instance provided the atrocity rather than the safe haven. Regardless of the merits that individual editors found in the Yasusada materials—and they evidently did find merits (Perloff cites an impressive list of editors and their credentials)—it is really small wonder that they also suffered guilt and anxiety about political correctness.

Furthermore, the whole issue raised questions about Johnson's apparent access to these damaged, partial documents while also exposing a racism of which this readership had not suspected itself. John Solt, a Westerner but also a professor of Japanese culture at Amherst, referred to this poetry as "Japanized crap" (Nussbaum 82), suggesting that what could be palmed off as Japanese in the West was an offence to Japan. Where, Perloff asks, are the experts or authorities in this case, the "bona fide Japanese poets, scholars, or translators?" (164). Why would Western editors think they could distinguish and assess such esoteric materials? Online essays, rants, and dialogues proliferated, many of them engaging Johnson, who remained notably calm and courteous. In Part 5 of his lengthy discussion "On American Poetry Criticism & Other Dastardly-Isms" (28 December 2001), Dan Schneider takes on the APR Hoax as evidence of the more serious fraud of poetry adjudication, including "Kent Johnson Speaks" as an "Addendum" (http://www.cosmoetica .com/D6-DES5.htm). Less abrasively, and more to the point, on 8 January 2005, Roger Pao posted an entry in his Asian-American Poetry Blogspot asking just why

Westerners are so involved in exoticizing the East when the complex work of Asian American poets and poetry seems so totally absent from anthologies and other publications of power. Pao is concerned that "there has NEVER been a book of third-person criticism done on Asian-American poets or poetry," and he suggests "that the absence of scholarship on Asian-Americans is a much more of a racism [sic] than the Yasusada hoax" (http://asianamericanpoetry.blogspot.com/2005/01/my-response-to-yasusada-hoax.html). Ignorance gives rise to stereotyping so that the Japanese survivor, like the Muslim woman, can pass even among those who should know better.

I am engaged by the lively discussion to which these blogs give rise and the reasons they provide for anger, shame, or more thoughtful attention. But for the most part, moved and deluded by an exotic document from an unspeakable past, poetry editors loved what they read and then turned on the "author" when shown they had been deceived. Arthur Vogelsang, editor of *American Poetry Review,* is credited on the back cover of *Doubled Flowering* itself with saying that this hoax is "essentially a criminal act." Whether or not Vogelsang said so, or to whom and in what context, repeated use of this phrase in the peritext of *Doubled Flowering* points both to widespread essentialist criticism, which the whole Yasusada performance critiques, and to the general need for, or assumptions about, an essential being who had committed a crime (or to the hoax creator's desire to create these impressions).

The lively blogging about Yasusada, and the Internet whisper to which Nussbaum refers, point to another significant difference between Karavis and Yasusada. David Solway unambiguously claimed Karavis as his own invention, a created persona that enabled him to resituate himself and renew the possibilities for himself in both language and experience. Kent Johnson, on the other hand, the putative creator of Yasusada, has repeatedly denied that he himself is Yasusada. Rather, he has developed an endless strategy of deferral, suggesting first that "Tosa Motokiyu," whose name appears as a translator, had been his roommate at college and was in fact the author of the Yasusada poems. However, Motokiyu had recently died of cancer, leaving Johnson, and their other roommate Javier Alvarez, as custodians of his work. Just as Motokiyu's suffering and death mirror those of Yasusada, so Motokiyu's name is a pseudonym for an American poet, who shall remain forever nameless. Inevitably, given that the doubt police are looking for the man himself to whom we can attach both the experience and the text, we are lost in a cyberspace for which mortal bodies, personal names, and locatable identities are simply not part of the equation.

On the text itself, Johnson is rather more forthcoming, and for good reason. Clearly, in this instance the text's the thing, not the experience and not the man who lived through the experience and/or wrote about it. For Johnson, the author truly is dead and buried. The question becomes not who is the author but whether, as Mikhail Epstein puts it, "hyper-authorship [may be] dispersed among several virtual personalities which cannot be reduced to a single 'real' personality" (*Doubled Flowering* 134). Put another way, "hyper-authorship is a virtual authorship in which real personalities become almost illusionary, while fictional personalities become almost real" (135). Given the attribution of these observations to a letter from Epstein to Motokiyu in February 1996, and Epstein's apparent explanation that follows as part of the peritext—that he had responded to a letter he had received from Motokiyu and then learned from Johnson that Motokiyu died soon afterwards—I wonder both about Epstein's inclusion of his own name along with Yasusada's as evidence of "the resurrection of authorship after its death" (135) and about his suggestion in his "Commentary and Hypotheses" that follow the letter that "each text is allowed to have as many authors as it needs to have in order to become infinitely meaningful" (145). (Borges, of course, would agree.) Is Epstein part of the shadowy insider's club, passing the ball from hand to hand to avoid being caught when the lights come up? Are these various possible authors dead so as not to be located, or is their biographical death a feature of the death of their authority?

In an article on "Deferral of the Author" in *Poetics Today* in the spring of 2004, Bill Freind suggests that Yasusada illustrates "the potential of heteronyms to satisfy the reader's desire for an author figure behind the text while simultaneously highlighting the fictive status of this figure" (137). Freind's interview with Johnson raises questions about Neoism and multiple-use names (such as Luther Blissett or Karen Eliot) for the "deproduction of subjectivity." I assume this means a more catastrophic exercise than deferral, an actual unmaking. However, Johnson rejects the parallel. Whereas "Blissett" and "Eliot" "are anarcho-deconstructive in intent, [Yasusada] is utopic-constructive … seeking to disseminate identity in fluid configurations" (see Friend, "Hoaxes and Heteronymity"). Johnson imagines "a qualitatively new condition of poesis, one that will unfold beyond the penal, disciplinary rituals of the old order." There's the rub, there's the orthodoxy against which Yasusada emerges. Johnson refers to Yasusada's powerful critique of the present state of poetic affairs as "largely unintended" (I assume this means no specific or deliberate offence was intended, though the critique itself is surely central to the whole affair) but talks also of "the Author Function's contemporary cramp-grip on writing and reading culture [as] in part symptom of a collective, pathological yearning for simulacral states." Recalling Benjamin's distress at the replacement of authenticity with simulacra, and Celan's outrage that his language might be perceived as not his own or not pertaining to his own experience, I read Yasusada as surely representing the liberation, or irresponsibility, of unauthored texts that fly free from their moorings like so many hot-air balloons.

On one hand, Perloff is surely correct to say that editors who found the Yasusada poetry beautiful should not cease to think so merely because Yasusada himself is a fiction (quoted in Nussbaum 83). However, I have repeatedly noted that readers evaluate fiction and fact differently and tend to object when told that their faith has been misplaced. On the other hand, this collection of documents is historical, certainly not of the Hiroshima experience but of an anxiety in the world of American poetry at the end of the twentieth century. Meanwhile, I note the proliferation of the fiction rather than the poetry, which underlines the uncertainty of the whole proceeding. Arthur Vogelsang, for instance, to whom the phrase "an essentially criminal act" has been attributed, began by apologizing to the readers of *American Poetry Review* for publishing work that he had discovered was inauthentic. However, addressing one Professor Cohen in one-sided correspondence in the *Boston Review* in the spring of 1997, he quotes his editorial letter and then continues in another vein. He has realized, as if hit by a thunderbolt, that Marjorie Perloff is the likely source for the Yasusada poems, so he has now suggested to her that they turn to the Holocaust "(the on-going event in the middle of our century in which about six millions civilians were murdered by the German state, if you'll recall)" for a series of texts of a similar spirit and form as the Yasusada materials. Denying that he ever used the phrase "criminal act," he fears that someone is impersonating him in letters to Professor Cohen (http://bostonreview.net/BR22.3/Vogelsang.html). Coming from an editor who has been persuaded of the merits of this poetry and has then apologized, Vogelsang's crude equation between the Hiroshima experience and that of the Holocaust (with its higher body count and longer duration) reiterates Yasusada's grounding in the historical even as Vogelsang himself, drawing the equation, also vanishes, like the good ghost he is, in a puff of smoke.

Imposture in this case, whether a matter of imposing on poetry editors or posing as someone other than one's material self, both eludes all the traditional markers of authenticity and challenges the values that those markers uphold. If the text is to be completely detached from an identifiable author, if it can circulate in what Mason and Roberts have called "a collaborative aesthetic" in which readers are participants, then no meaning or effect can be reliable or even, in the end, communicable. This is surely part of the point that Mason and Roberts are making, and in which they are sensitive and sympathetic to the Yasusada enterprise. However, "Hiroshima" as history and memory and concept cannot escape from meaning. Nor, in the end, can theory and critique; they require some ground from which to spring, some wall to bounce off. For this reason, Johnson's contributions to the paraphernalia surrounding the purported notebooks of Yasusada, and his willingness to discuss the Yasusada creation with so many correspondents online, seem to me to stand in for the old-fashioned author role. He need not be Yasusada, but he is the man who anchors the text and who intervenes to ensure its most useful or effective reception. Johnson has a vision to share, a lesson to teach, and he has remained consistently identifiable as the source or origin for both vision and lesson. He has sought and negotiated the publication of these materials, including Yasusada's history and portrait, not in cyberspace, where engagement with them can detach from specific identity, but between the covers of a book with a copyright (his) and, I hope, royalties (that someone is receiving). I noted in the case of Mezlekia that Charles McGrath concluded that a book is a book and is to be assessed on its own merits separate from the history of its author. Johnson would surely agree, except that he has been involved with a book that he insists has no author and no clear authorial history. No character or identity can be measured against this text. Or, more curiously and precisely, the text originates somewhere but, ironically, the physical death of its author seems to equate not so much with the death of the author as with intense questions about the life of authorship.

Mason and Roberts are surely correct in identifying the Yasusada materials as a set of reading practices. What do we make of an authorless work produced not by "Anon." but by a whole range of heteronyms? However, I am interested that while Johnson supports the "Yasusada collective" to make a number of salient points about authorship in the age of hypertext, "they" are doing so by means of a figure whose specificity in time, place, relationships, and experience they elaborate in detail. Like Celan and Bowers, like Mezlekia and Solway, they work in autobiographical modes in order to suggest to the reader a man in whom we may believe. For me, then, the issue is not only what kinds of ideas they are generating about the sources of language or text or narrative, but, even more so, their explicit grounding of these ideas in autobiography. The author is dead, long may s/he live? We may further wonder whether this elaborate erasure of the human link (despite or because of the human tragedy to which the poetry refers) may not point to a strange future for the autobiographer as the disembodied voice with no apparent referent. We are back with Foucault's rendering of Beckett: "What matter who's speaking?" (138).

The discourses of deception that I have been considering here have all required authors. The name on the cover of the book has not always matched the person who sat at the keyboard, but these deceptions have, nonetheless, depended on traditional book production. Names have been detached from the text, or added to it, or created from whole cloth as part of the production. Work has been purchased or stolen. But in every case, lost, stolen, or strayed, the name of the author has been quite central to the deception, both where the deception was never intended to be discovered and where the deception would have been no fun at all without discovery, for the simple reason that each work has claimed connection to life and experience. Editors, publishers, and critics, coming under fire in some cases for their inability to adjudicate, or the problematic grounds on which they do so, have, in each instance, been given a product they can recognize—a text with a name attached to it. They have been mistaken not necessarily about the value of the product (value judgments being notoriously variable) but about its provenance, so that provenance has, in each instance, become the issue. The question has been not whether this text has an author but just who the author is. Who signs the contract or holds the copyright? Whose work do we criticize or commend? Who claims either the words or the experience, or both? In whom, in the end, do we believe?

6
In Search of the Subject:
The Disappearance of the Jews

On Monday, 25 April 1983, *Stern* magazine in Germany produced 2.25 million copies of a special issue titled "Hitler's Diary Discovered." Robert Harris describes these "diaries," which cost *Stern* some $4 million, as the "the most expensive and far-reaching fraud in publishing history" (25). Too late in the process, even while the presses were rolling, hard evidence began arriving to indicate that this media coup was in hard fact a disaster: the paper on which these diaries were written, the bindings, the thread, the glue were all of postwar manufacture; the typewriter used for the labels on the covers, though a prewar model, showed no sign of wear between 1925 and 1934. The handwriting had been submitted to various experts for analysis but these experts had, in some cases, been matching counterfeit with counterfeit, not with any original of Hitler's hand. Then, finally, the contents were found to be faulty, with Hans Booms of the Bundesarchiv recognizing Max Domarus's *Hitler's Speeches and Proclamations* as the common source. "It became apparent to us that if there was nothing in Domarus for a particular day, then Hitler didn't write anything in his diary that night either. When *Domarus* did include something, then Hitler wrote it down. And when an occasional mistake crept into *Domarus,* Hitler repeated the same error" (Hans Booms quoted in Harris 355.) The media coup, inspired by credulity, opportunism, and greed, collapsed as a disaster once good old-fashioned forensics had been brought to bear on the details.

Innocent as many of the participants were of fraudulent intent, the case of Hitler's diaries carries all the marks of classic fraud. First, these diaries offered a compelling invitation to learn something new about a man whose impact had been so vast. "Only Jesus," Harris writes, "has had more words devoted to him than

Hitler" (19). Then, we have the value of something personal from this man, and the value of the personal is of particular significance in the case of Hitler. J.P. Stern has referred to the difficulty Hitler's followers had at Nuremberg in remembering what the Third Reich had been about when the presence and the voice of their Führer were gone (Harris 51). Then there was the shock value to established orthodoxies, which had, for decades, been correcting and countering Nazi ideology. Russian forces had destroyed Hitler's bunker in 1947, and Allied troops had destroyed his house at Berchtesgaden in 1952, in order to obliterate likely sites for Hitler shrines (49). German schools had suppressed the history of the Third Reich in the curriculum. *Mein Kampf* had been banned. A de-Nazification court in Bavaria had, in 1948, declared Hitler's will illegal, confiscated his personal property, and prevented his former housekeeper from selling her own memorabilia. In fact, public displays of Nazi memorabilia were illegal. In 1985, the same year in which Gerd Heidemann and Konrad Kujau were convicted of fraud in the diary scandal, the German Parliament determined that Holocaust denial was actually illegal.

However, 1973, the fortieth anniversary of the Nazis' rise to power, saw the return of the repressed in a massive production of books, films, and articles. By the time the "diaries" appeared, too many were eager to believe that they might now understand "the truth." Ironically, Henri Nannen, publisher of *Stern,* found these diaries convincing because they were so boring (207), and Hans Booms, President of the Bundesarchiv, did not personally care whether they were true or false because he found them so dull (351). Not least, the detectives themselves were at times deceived. Hugh Trevor-Roper, while doubting Gerd Heidemann himself as implausible, was impressed by the range and size of his archive, which he found too coherent and extensive to be manufactured (297), and trusted to the integrity of the management at *Stern.* He was also persuaded by Hitler's handwriting and by the changes it apparently underwent between 1908 and Hitler's death (302). Truly, we could be back with Baigent's papyrus for all the hard evidence on which Trevor-Roper worked. Sounding rather like Lorenzo Valla or Jean Mabillon, Philip Knightley at the *Sunday Times,* which was involved with subsidiary rights from *Stern,* wrote to his publisher, Rupert Murdoch, to remind him of the Mussolini hoax some fifteen years earlier when the *Sunday Times* had bought Mussolini's diaries written by two Italian women (289). Do not rely on authentication as evidence, Knightley told Murdoch. Do not rely on people close to the subject. Do not rely on legal protection to reclaim money spent on the cause. Beware of secrecy, which works in favour of the con artist.

This memorable case did not involve an impostor in the sense of any man pretending to be Hitler. Rather, it involved exciting but elusive possibilities that a textual Hitler might be available for reading. Journalists and media moguls, forensic scientists and historians, spent many months and tens of thousands of dollars in what proved to be a fruitless search for their subject, whom they could not find because he and his text had not simply come unstuck but had, in fact, never been at one. As I turn from Hitler to his victims, I use the word "subject" to indicate both the subject of discussion and, more significantly, the subject positions (that no one could find, in Hitler's case), which were, for the Jews of Europe, deliberately erased (in law), unvalued (in historiography), and thereby endangered (in autobiography). The consequences of such loss are both tragic and far-reaching and suggest some of the ways in which fraudulent text and identity can be seriously dangerous. Had Hitler's diaries been published, had they evaded the forensic tests that finally arrested their production and ensured their perpetrators were brought to justice, they would have become widely read and would now constitute an important source for biographers of Hitler and for historians of the period. The scandal of the Hitler diaries turns on the magnitude of the lie and on its proximity to respectable procedures in the production of history. As Trevor-Roper himself pointed out: "Both the papers of Bormann and the diaries of Goebbels have come to publication through persons who have never been identified; and no one doubts that they are genuine" (quoted in Harris 261). Having been pressured by secrecy and the speed required for a journalistic scoop, Trevor-Roper, in the end, withdrew his support from the diaries and acknowledged that he had "'to some extent sacrificed'" the usual procedures for "'historical verification'" (322). In short, he had been caught up in the frenzy of the moment and had failed to exercise due rigour.

I have discussed media production of "sensational identities" in Chapter 3, but propose here to consider the ways in which historiography and legal practices operate in relation to autobiography to establish or undermine credible identity. In other words, having explored in Chapter 2 some of the ways in which textual identity is chronically unstable (even though it remains, in the genres of autobiography, one of the pre-eminent modes for relaying personal truths), my questions now include these other means for constructing identity that may be more secure or carry more conviction. Furthermore, my focus on the Holocaust, or Shoah, does far more than limit the time and place of my investigation.[1] Quintessentially, it represents a time when individual identity was in extreme danger, a time about which conflicting stories can raise unacceptable doubts, and a time when law both made and unmade the crises of life and death.

If I am correct in suggesting that impostors emerge in the midst of cultural crises, they insert themselves into these situations—sometimes very successfully—and become part of the legal and cultural components of their time and place, embedded in history. I wonder, therefore, whether elements of their context contribute to their exposure. Could historiography be a more reliable source of information than the personal story even about individual identity? And given the power of law to authenticate or disprove contested information, I wonder whether law might not provide the security that could underwrite historiography. Because each disciplinary context produces specific kinds of knowledge, I propose to consider how each one produces individual identity (the subject of autobiography), specifically of the Jew during the Holocaust, and how it secures its information. Where, in short, does the individual story, the autobiography, stand in relation to the cultural narratives provided by historiography or courts of law, and how can we evaluate the kind of truth that each system produces?

History

Writing about the losses to history and memory that occur when people fail to take responsibility for their past, Susan Sontag suggests that readers today have to think back to "a time when most people accepted that the course of their lives would be determined by history rather than psychology, by public rather than private crises" (13). Saul Friedländer makes this point very particularly about the time of the Holocaust. "Most historians of my generation," he writes, "born on the eve of the Nazi era, recognize either explicitly or implicitly that plowing through the events of those years entails not only excavating and interpreting a collective past like any other, but also recovering and confronting decisive elements of our own lives" (quoted in Young 35). In other words, both Sontag and Friedländer recognize the impact and effects of the historical past on the individual life in its private or psychological present.

Yet to think in terms of history is to recognize just how close we came to having nothing at all about this disaster. After all, I began this whole discussion with reference to Heinrich Himmler speaking to his senior SS officers at Poznan on 4 October 1943 on "the very grave matter [of] the extermination of the Jewish race [as] a page of glory in our history which has never to be written." This page that would have remained a blank if the Nazis had been victorious has been written only in the happenstance of the Allied victory and suffers from all the divisions and relocations and the historical revisionism that followed that victory. What historiography has in common, then, with legislation and court decisions and with autobiography is a fair dose of happenstance, the particular situation in which attention is being paid, and the "moral vigilance"—to borrow Saul Friedländer's term—that particular ingredients impose on the present, or what we might call their forward reach. This "moral vigilance" implies responsibilities in each genre of inquiry to reconstitute several distinct elements or categories of information: facts and events, their effects on the people who lived through them, and their meaning or value both then and now. How, then, does historiography reconstitute experience and meaning?

Traditional historiography depends on archival research, quantitative documentary evidence, and an impersonal, objective, unadorned writing style—the kind of work most notably performed by Raul Hilberg in his monumental work *The Destruction of the European Jews.* Reviewing this work favourably and at length for *Commentary,* Trevor-Roper refers to its "austere style, without literary grace or emotion" (351). For Hilberg, a historian trained in the 1940s, the writing of history is more like a social science than an art, a collection of data that point very clearly to certain very clear conclusions. (To see him in Claude Lanzmann's *Shoah* explaining the intricacies of German railway timetables is to appreciate his passion for documentary sources generated at the time of the events under investigation and prepared with no anticipation of a story. Such information speaks to the head, not the heart, enabling him to account, for instance, for the costs of transporting thousands of Jews from all over Europe to the concentration camps, the structures in place to deal with bulk bookings and border crossings and, central to his thesis, the thorough implication of the whole German bureaucracy and the helpless complicity of the Jewish Councils of Europe in the implementation of the Final Solution.) However, where Hilberg's exhaustive work provides the evidence to support the conclusions he comes to, I am troubled by two of his assumptions: that his own memory is clear and simple, as with his childhood determination, when watching Hitler's troops enter Vienna, that "some day I will write about what I see here" (Hilberg, *The Politics of Memory,* 42); and that unadorned prose, lacking rhetorical flourishes, is necessarily free of rhetorical power. Though he was inspired to keep a diary of his own experience of the war, Hilberg was adamant that he wrote history only as an observer, determined that nothing on the dust jacket of his history should include the personal experiences of the author—a Jewish refugee to the United States.

What is remarkable about an approach like Hilberg's, which is quite brilliant for its logic and for the solidity of its information, is the absence of the human face, the human motive, or the human experience. His autobiography, written to explain just why his major work has not been as influential as he feels it should be, focuses not on his personal experience but on the politics of the reception of his work. Ironically, to my mind, he presents his work as himself. He explains that the new nation of Israel did not welcome his reading of the Jewish councils as complicit in Nazi genocide and therefore denied him access to their archives for further research. Jewish history, as he understands their criticism, needed to focus on victims, not on perpetrators. Indeed, the shapers of Israel wished for the perpetrators, on whom Hilberg had focused, to be erased, like Amalek, from the record. (Notably, when Ben-Gurion's government brought Adolf Eichmann to Jerusalem in 1961, they faced the political issue of Jewish collaboration and then focused not on what Eichmann had done but on what survivors of the Holocaust had to say about their experiences. In other words, the perpetrator, even though present before them in his glass booth, was not the source of the story.) Hilberg is remarkable for writing the history of the losers of the war rather than that of the victors. His process is archival and objective. He worked in the aftermath of the Nuremberg Trials, with much of the archival evidence assembled at Nuremberg, to understand just how this catastrophe could have happened. His explanation of the subject position of Israeli archivists and historians is therefore a curious anomaly, quite unself-reflexive, given the absence of the personal from the rest of his work. The Jews are notably absent from his history of their destruction, except insofar as they were part of the bureaucracy of the Third Reich, and he himself is absent, even though he was a Jewish refugee who had witnessed Hitler's troops entering Vienna.

What is troubling about Hilberg's approach to history is the precedent it sets for historians to reject autobiographical evidence as any kind of fact. James E. Young reiterates a concern repeatedly expressed by Friedländer in his double capacity as both historian and autobiographer about the "near-blanket exclusion of the survivor's memory from normative histories of the Holocaust" ("Between History and Memory" 49). The American historian Jeremy D. Popkin, who has written extensively on the value of autobiographical testimony in history, cites Annette Wievorka as particularly candid but by no means unique when she writes that historians' attempts to use autobiographical information prove it "to be, with metronomic regularity, false" (52).[2] Compared with this approach to historical narrative, autobiography is soft information, inaccurate or unreliable, biased, and limited. The Jewish subject as autobiographer seems not to provide an adequate or acceptable route to understanding what happened during the Holocaust.[3]

Dominick LaCapra comments on a similar absence of the Jewish subject in the Historians' Debate of 1986, in which the popular press in Germany published extensive discussion of the role of the Holocaust in German memory—a debate that became even more complicated with the unification of Germany in 1989 and the need for a unified Germany to make some sense of the very different kinds of archives and histories developed in the East and in the West. LaCapra explains this debate in terms of the interpretive procedures that contextualized Nazi crimes among other instances of genocide, particularly those of Stalin's gulags, in effect "shifting or blurring the focus on the past [in order] to foreground acceptable continuities in German history as a basis for an idealized self-image and an affirmative, pro-Western identity" ("Revisiting" 86). With his own constant focus on distinctions between acting out and working through traumatic memory, LaCapra describes the risks of "harmonizing modes of narration" (86) in such a way that individual or distinct positions all merge and narrative repeats "the processes of avoidance, denial and willed ignorance" that can make history, as a narrative providing access to the past, so problematic. The Historians' Debate, LaCapra further suggests, was distinctive for the absence of Jewish debaters. As with Hilberg's focus on the perpetrators, this debate in some way repeated the "suppression or repression of Jewish voices" (88).

When Raul Hilberg worked as an objective historian, in the 1950s, he was not imagining his interpretation of documents as a form of narrative, and not considering language as any other than a transparent medium onto the reality he discovered in the archives. When the historian Ernst Nolte and the philosopher Jürgen Habermas initiated the Historians' Debate in the 1980s, they seem to have been entirely aware that their methods of reading the past would have specific and extensive effects on national consciousness and the ways in which ordinary Germans received their history. In other words, they understood interpretation as narrative and as therefore powerful. Hayden White's analyses of narrative plot in historiography, and the kinds of assertions that plot can produce, demonstrate persuasively that information is inert until mobilized by narrative purpose. Nonetheless, the Holocaust presents problems whichever way the historian approaches it. Positioning herself as the passionate "heterological historian," Edith Wyschogrod takes issue with narrative as constituting any kind of truth when the cataclysm, as she calls it, makes its victims (potential autobiographers) alien or "other" to the historian. I conclude that even though historiography depends on material evidence, it must always be marked by its time and place, the cultural and political climate in which it is produced.

And the Jews? Can Jewish or Israeli historiography present the subject position missing in these other versions, the position that White has called "the middle voice," neither passive nor active but self-referential, that James E. Young has called "received history" and that Saul Friedländer has called "deep memory," history from within the cataclysm? Curiously, in my experience, the answer is no. For Ben-Gurion, who aligned himself with the new nation of Israel, publishing his autobiography as *Israel: A Personal History,* the four crucial events in Jewish history were the Exodus from Egypt, the assembly of the Children of Israel at Mount Sinai, the conquest of the land of Israel by Joshua, and the establishment of the state of Israel in 1948. Similarly, when Gideon Hausner, Israel's newly appointed attorney general, opened court proceedings against Eichmann in Jerusalem in April 1961, he began with the Biblical stories of Jewish persecution at the hands of Pharoah and Haman. As numerous commentators have suggested, the Eichmann trial saw history, rather than Eichmann, in the dock, a history of thousands of years of persecution.

Yosef Yerushalmi and Amos Funkenstein both address this Biblical frame, or the role of faith, in Jewish history. They explain that Jewish history concluded with the diaspora following the destruction of the Second Temple in 70 CE. Experiencing diaspora in ways that clearly differed with time and place, the Jewish communities of Europe seem not to have made or kept records of particular events but to have accumulated acts of commemoration for entire communities in repeated crisis. They folded distinct events into existing liturgies of mourning and remembrance that absorbed the particular experiences and the particular people involved. So, for example, the fast of Blois, instituted in the twelfth century, and carried to Eastern Europe by waves of Ashkenazic Jews, was still observed with new accretions in the seventeenth century. The Cossack pogroms led by Bogdan Chmielnitzky in Poland in 1648, affecting hundreds of communities and killing thousands of people, were assembled into a fast to be proclaimed for the 20th day of Sivan every year. After decades of expulsion, beginning in England in 1290 and climaxing in Spain in 1492, Western Europe was, in a terrible prequel to the Second World War, effectively emptied of Jews and of any extensive records of Jewish experience. As Ben-Gurion's paradigm makes clear, these hundreds of years of Jewish migration in diaspora can be understood as one continuous experience already recorded.

Only with increasing emancipation in the nineteenth century did modern Jewish historiography come unstuck from ancient patterns of faith. Clusters of enlightened thinkers struggled to create a more fluid and particularized Jewish history, but against considerable odds in that this history necessarily lacked both a national component and a language, Hebrew seeming unlikely as a language for the future. With bitter irony this ambitious "Wissenschaft des Judentums," or science of Jewish studies, finds its archives and its individual voices with the Nazi invasion of Poland. With desperate prescience, the underground archive, led by people like Emmanuel Ringelblum, called on all Jews to provide whatever information they could in order to leave a record of their time. They asked for unadorned information and for personal stories. As Ringelblum put it: "We tried to have the same events described by as many people as possible ... By comparing the different accounts, the historian will not find it difficult to reach the kernel of historical truth, the actual course of an event" (quoted in Roskies 22). In this crisis, Jewish communities of diaspora moved from liturgy and law into the personal history of ordinary lives. Ensuring that "no important fact about Jewish life in wartime shall remain hidden from the world" (23), this project effectively countered the Nazi agenda, which was to overwrite history both by destroying people and by ensuring that these events would never be recorded.

Victims of Nazi persecution in the ghettoes, as in the camps, left fragmentary archival information in which the human presence can be detected both in the individual voice and in the particular archival choices. However, White's recognition of narrative as the shaper of meaning seems to find no resonance in Jewish historiography of the Holocaust itself. On one hand, Saul Friedländer, as both historian and autobiographer, is suspicious of the redemptive quality of narrative of the Holocaust. On the other hand, redemptive narratives that celebrate the nation-state overlook the Holocaust because it belongs in the whole trauma of the diaspora, not the new nation. Whereas historiography may provide a more comprehensive view than the individual narrative because it works with material evidence and provides the checks and balances of comparative objectivity, the historian works with two related limitations. First, of course, s/he can only write from within his or her particular culture, which predetermines the value of certain kinds of knowledge. Second, the historian's presence necessarily—as in Heisenberg's principle—affects the object of study. Working on the Holocaust, the historian may wrestle with the apparent incompatibility of information and experience. Wyschogrod, for example, and Giorgio Agamben, are beset with the problems of the impossibility of their task, their inability to write for and about others who died in such grotesque circumstances. In short, various problems of methodology create lacunae in Holocaust history, in particular those spaces in which the survivor could speak. Whereas survivors suffer from the knowledge that they do not know as much as the dead could tell, they themselves do not get much of a hearing.

Law

History works with hard information but also depends on its narrator in ways that impede or at the very least affect its realization of the subjective elements of its material. I turn, accordingly, to law for access to the human subject that can be so readily discredited as inaccurate or unreliable in history. Like autobiography and like history, law has the power both to bring individual identity into focus and to vitiate the focus, or the identity, or both. However, law presents a different contract between subject and interpretation than autobiography (claiming authentic reference) and history (claiming relative detachment). Law has immediate and real-world consequences because it constitutes the social structure that affirms or denies individual identity. Law represents society in its recognition of individual subjects as valid or not. Working as and for society, law exercises the moral conscience of its constituency. For European Jews of the Third Reich and its occupied territories, law became the primary tool of erasure.

For instance, Trevor-Roper refers to the assimilation of Jews in Western Europe in the century before Hitler as not merely factual but legal. With Hitler's accession to power, he writes, "the German bureaucracy … began a systematic reversal of the law. The first step was to define the Jews" (352). Then came detachment of the persons so identified from the bureaucracy that would be used against them. Then came the expropriation of their goods and possessions to effect systematic impoverishment, then segregation, then concentration camps. Hannah Arendt's treatment of the Eichmann trial follows the same trajectory. Significantly, Jewish communities were also charged to regulate, administer, and enforce their own separate status, a brilliant and cruel detail that Raul Hilberg develops and that Arendt identifies as missing from the Eichmann trial (124–25). This detachment of Jewish people from Aryan people served many political and economic purposes, but the fact that it was legislated rather than the result of simple force necessarily raises the question how the individual can function or even exist outside the law and outside the community for which law speaks with authority. What identity, or rights, or story, or authority does a non-person have? (I have already referred to Paul Celan's sense that he had no place at all to stand except his own text.) "In twentieth-century Germany as in Dreyfus's nineteenth-century France," Shoshana Felman writes, "persecution ratifies itself as persecution in and through civilization—by the civilized means of the law. The Wannsee Conference [of January 1942] legali[zed] genocide" (119). Because law creates the context in which individual people can make their voices heard, or not, and articulates particular information on which historians depend, I propose to look just briefly at some legislation pertaining to Jewish identity under the Vichy regime during the Second World War and at three trials during which law, history, and autobiography converged: the Nuremberg Trials, the Trial of Adolf Eichmann in Jerusalem, and the Klaus Barbie Trial in Lyons. As with my focus on historiography, I fear that the context for what could be more secure information is complex here, too. Law may determine or validate autobiography and create history, but is itself entirely bound by the time and by the people who enact it.

Emphasizing the initiative as German, but far exceeding either the practices or the demands of the occupying forces, the Vichy government in France developed its "Statut des juifs" on 2 June 1941, which it then supplemented with nearly "200 laws, ordinances, decrees and rulings authored by French lawyers and officials" (Weisberg 1376). Richard Weisberg takes issue with the failure of these French lawyers to recognize how their legislation relativized or overrode the constitutional authority of liberty, fraternity, and equality written in French blood some two hundred years earlier. Furthermore, with their hair-splitting determinations about the number of Jewish grandparents required to define a Jew,[4] and the specific dates before or after which the Jew was baptized, or the ability of infants to choose baptism, or circumcision, the lawyers of Vichy raised the problem of burden of proof— which divided them for several years (1380), and on which question of proof "hung careers, fortunes, lives" (1380). The failure of this legal industry to ground itself in history and precedent, and the political authority it wielded in creating nonpersons, speak to the power of law to reflect and determine community and to eliminate those it does not wish to include. As a political weapon, law exercises an apparently absolute authority that is more effective than force precisely because it emerges from and defines the community.

For this reason if no other, the Nuremberg trials of 1945–46 are quite remarkable. With no fixed and universal standards, with no shared purposes, and playing to different home audiences, the legal teams from Britain, the United States, France, and the Soviet Union provided a historically significant alternative to Stalin's 1943 suggestion that 50,000 German war criminals should be summarily shot. Seeking to give international law the kind of vitality that it can have only if it is a real expression of moral judgment, Robert H. Jackson, lead prosecutor for the United States, reported on 6 June 1945: "We must establish incredible events by credible evidence" (Marrus 42). For Jackson and his colleagues, however, credible evidence was essentially the massive documentation maintained by the SS themselves. The Jewish victim, like the Roma and the Sinti, is almost entirely missing from this substantial process. Telford Taylor from the American team, reading passages on the war crimes trials forty years later, recognizes "a jarring omission of reference to Jews and the Holocaust" (296). Finding the films of camps and of the Warsaw Ghetto "terrible and convincing," Judge Norman Birkett noted in his diary that this human and personalized picture is "a complete waste of valuable time. The case has been proved over and over again" (Marrus 164). Recognizing psychological rather than practical reasons for rejecting such images, Agamben describes the English film shot at Bergen-Belsen after liberation in 1945, in which the camera rests on piles of emaciated bodies (evidence of genocide) but turns quickly away from the *Muselmänner,* or living dead, the invisibles, what Young has called the inaudibles of history (to whom only survivors defer) (Agamben 69; Young, "Towards a Received History," 42). The court worked like the historian Raul Hilberg, with the documents of the oppressors; it also seemed unwilling to address the legal and moral creation of non-persons that preceded the mass killings, the very different kinds of evidence that these non-persons might have provided, or the authority that the creation of non-persons might have suggested should be ascribed to personal testimony. However, Birkett's revulsion at the films, given that he felt "the case" (against the Nazi regime but not for the victim) had been sufficiently proven, is impressive when we consider the later marketing of "the Holocaust" and the "the victim" as a form of righteous voyeurism. Better, perhaps, not to ask who these desperate figures are than to exploit their suffering as such marketing has since done.

In addition to providing evidentiary overload, personal evidence threatened political complications. So François de Menthon, conscious of his French audience divided by collaboration and anti-Semitism, managed to discuss crimes against *la condition humaine* with only one fairly innocuous sentence on damage to Jewish rights and personal dignities. Briefed by Jewish organizations, Robert Jackson proposed to bring in Chaim Weizman, president of the World Zionist Organization, as a witness for the prosecution. However, this move was blocked by Great Britain, which was concerned that any particular sympathy for Jews might have negative repercussions for the British as the ruling authority in Palestine (Marrus 192). These trials therefore included minimal personal narrative. When the

Resistance fighter Marie-Claude Vaillant-Couturier gave witness to the gassing at Auschwitz, the *New York Herald Tribune* reported that her testimony was so overwhelming that some of the defendants removed their headphones (Marrus 157). The Russians were the exception. Anxious to represent the nightmare of suffering in the Soviet Union, they called on Abram Suzkever to talk about the persecution of the Jews of Vilna. From him we get the same kind of personal information that Ringelblum had required from his archivists:

> "When I arrived at the ghetto I saw the following scene: Martin Weiss came in with a young Jewish girl. When we went in farther, he took out his revolver and shot her on the spot. The girl's name was Gitele Tarlo.
> "Tell us, how old was this girl?
> "Eleven." (Marrus 200)

What is missing even here, of course, is the experience of the child, not only because she is dead but also because she was, even at the time, observed rather than recording her own experience. In a trial that needed both to determine the relative guilt of numerous Nazi officials involved in murdering millions, establish the righteousness of the Allied cause despite its own atrocities, and clean up the German image for the Cold War already on its way, the death of the one child Gitele Tarlo invokes a momentary presence only to reinforce its absence.

Overcoming political obstacles to judicial proceedings, coordinating an unlikely team of lawyers and judges, the Nuremberg trials judged the guilt of particular war criminals, effectively separating them from German people at large, and brought legislative closure to European trauma. However, what this trial highlights for my present purposes is the limitation of judicial narrative as a mode of access to what Deborah Britzman has called "difficult knowledge" (2). That this limitation may be part not just of this most difficult trial but in fact also a common feature of trials pertaining to the Holocaust is born out by my understanding of the Eichmann trial in Jerusalem and the Barbie trial in Lyons. In both cases, the involvement or responsibility of the accused was not in question. As at Nuremberg, evidence was massive and clear. As at Nuremberg, on trial were not just the perpetrators but also the community in which they acted as well as the community bringing them to judgment. So, for example, the Israeli government, which had dragged its feet for several years over bringing Eichmann to trial, until threatened with the possibility that Germany would call for his extradition from Argentina, was more concerned to avoid questions of Jewish collaboration than to deal with the high-profile criminal that might open such a Pandora's Box.

The Eichmann trial, attended by several hundred journalists from fifty countries, followed too close for comfort on the heels of the trial of the Hungarian Jew

Rudolf Kasztner, charged more than once during the 1950s with Nazi collaboration. Kasztner, however, was not a former member of the SS but an Israeli, a member of the ruling Mapai Party in Israel, as well as a spokesperson for the Minister of Trade and Industry, and therefore in a position to raise questions about Mapai's role, and Ben-Gurion's role, during the war. Despite its extensive, historic use of Jewish witnesses, the Eichmann trial needed, therefore, to control such political issues as Israeli unity, public recognition of Nazi (and, by quite clear extension, Arab) hostility to the Jewish peoples, and the history of the Holocaust—becoming, in effect, a call for international support for the peoples of such a diaspora. The Israeli prosecutor, Gideon Hausner, was determined that the Eichmann trial should succeed where the Nuremberg trials had failed in impressing "on the hearts of men" some experience of the disaster. "In order merely to secure a conviction," he wrote, "it was obviously enough to let the archives speak, [but they] needed more than a conviction; [they] needed a living record of a gigantic human and national disaster" (quoted in Felman 133). Personal testimony accordingly overwhelmed the political difficulties attending this trial and the archival evidence against Eichmann, establishing the experience of the Holocaust as important to the history of the Jews, the history of Israel, and the history of Israel in relation to other nations. To Hannah Arendt's dismay (she felt very strongly that this trial too should focus on the criminal and not on his victims), personal testimony became central, to powerful effect. In fact, the complete collapse of one witness, involving, in one sense, a failure of testimony and a breakdown in legal proceedings, effectively expressed to the court and to the worldwide television audience the necessity and the impossibility of the personal story (Arendt 223–24, Felman 134–37).

The trial of Klaus Barbie in Lyons (11 May–4 July 1987) faced political complications not unlike those at Nuremberg and Jerusalem. It involved an illegal kidnapping as in the case of Eichmann. Indeed, it made clear that the Americans had seen Barbie as useful for their Cold War interests and had used what they called the "Rat Line" to get him out of Europe. It brought the brutal French repression of the Algerians into the context of Barbie's treatment of French Jews. It opened up not, as many French had hoped, the heroism of the Resistance, but rather the extensive involvement of French collaborators in the deaths and deportations of hundreds of French Jews, including the children in hiding in the secluded community of Izieu. French Jews had not returned to France after the war as heroes but as reminders of French complicity during the German Occupation; anti-Semitism was still very much an issue. Furthermore, this trial coincided with increasing anti-Arab feeling, with Le Pen generating political energy on the far right. As with the Eichmann trial, the Barbie trial could be read as a reminder of national values (two years before the bicentennial of the French Revolution), but national values included national shame and the confusions attendant on finger pointing of any kind.[5] In this context of the court case implicating the community that had brought the accused to trial, I note Helmut Kohl's public acknowledgement of history and historically informed use of law: in 1985, as the first German chancellor to visit the site of a Nazi concentration camp, he spoke of "shame" and "historical responsibility" and legislated that revisionist history was to be an offence in Germany" (Paris 228–29).

Writing about the monologic nature of judicial opinion, Robert A. Ferguson suggests that the "goal of judgment is to subsume difference in an act of explanation and a moment of decision" (205). Such an achievement should be satisfying and most likely often is. However, I am concerned that these particular attempts at decision in court achieved only the obvious and that efforts at explanation, even as they succeeded in bringing the past into the present, did so in ways that sidestepped all sorts of explanation and accounting. In Agamben's words, "it has taken almost half a century to understand that law did not exhaust the problem, but rather that the very problem was so enormous as to call into question law itself, dragging it to its own ruin" (20). I am persuaded, therefore, that the justice system is also a time-bound, history-bound, complex, and therefore prejudiced mode of access to this particular past. The very repetition of legal cases against war criminals speaks less to the numbers of war criminals not yet brought to trial than to the need for different communities to study the implications of this history for themselves (as readers of and participants in problematic text), and what decisions they need to make about their attitude to it. In short, law in these cases speaks for and to its community more clearly than for the "inaudible" subject.

Echoing Ferguson's point about legal judgment as monologic, Felman distinguishes quite explicitly between legal action and historical or personal text:

> A trial and a literary text do not aim at the same kind of conclusion, nor do they strive toward the same kind of effect. A trial is presumed to be a search for truth, but, technically, it is a search for a decision, and thus, in essence, it seeks not simply truth but a finality: a force of resolution. A literary text is, on the other hand, a search for meaning, for expression, for heightened significance, and for symbolic understanding. (54–55)

Ironically, "heightened significance" and "symbolic understanding" can lose their moorings in the survivor's experience. Seeming also to echo Ferguson's point about the monologism of the judiciary, Dori Laub writes of the monologism of the Nazi system that could convince "its victims, the potential witnesses from the inside, that what was affirmed about their 'otherness' and their inhumanity was correct and that their experiences were no longer communicable even to themselves, and therefore perhaps never took place" ("An Event" 82). How, then, can the personal text ground itself in personal experience and memory in order to assert any kind of meaning?

Autobiography

When the lawyers assembled at Nuremberg heard of the death of eleven-year-old Gitele Tarlo, they received a clue, a mere trace of the life of this child. In the very fact of being named, she steps out of statistics and so, briefly, into life. She is not a survivor who wrote or told of her ordeal after the event. She walks to her death in the borderland between those who maybe *would* have written, those whom Agamben describes as lacking all agency, part of the production of death (71–72), and those from whom we have vivid, because very personal, glimpses: the little boy, for example, who did not even know his own name, so described himself simply as "Pierre's brother" (Paris 70), or the other small child on whom Emmanuel Ringelblum reports in his *Notes from the Warsaw Ghetto,* who went mad and began shouting: "'I want to steal, I want to rob, I want to eat, I want to be a German'" (39). In each case, the little knowledge we have of these lives depends on the witness of another. Even so, that knowledge is more personal and more subjective than the Nazi documentation on which both Raul Hilberg and the Nuremberg trials so largely depended. Curiously, the impressionistic glimpses we get of such children are likely more vivid for their suggestion of felt experience than the official documents that serve as finite evidence in history and law.[6]

As Debórah Dwork observes, she herself could only reconstruct the lives of hundreds of thousands of children who had died "through those who had lived" (xi). By way of contrast, the editors of the *Death Books from Auschwitz,* who appear anonymously on the title page as "State Museum of Auschwitz-Birkenau," describe their documents as not only impersonal but also as doctored and "incomplete" (18). "The documentation of the crimes," they write, "which the SS kept meticulously and supervised with a huge bureaucratic effort, has been preserved only fragmentarily." Furthermore, "more than a million Jews deported to Auschwitz in mass transport from all the Nazi-occupied countries of Europe were not registered by name, alive or dead" (18). In other words, these official documents, the ones that remain, that were not lost or destroyed, cannot tell a fuller or more accurate story than autobiographical traces. Their contribution to knowledge is also limited.

The best we can say is that official registers and personal documents provide very different kinds of access to the past.[7] Retrospective autobiographies, for example, may include items of personal significance but little evidentiary value. I think of Elisabeth Raab's photograph of her "recipes of nameless women—whoever happened to pass by," which she recorded with a "stump of a pencil" on "scrap paper found in trash cans in the factory—taken, stolen." These scraps, she writes, were "covered in pencilled recordings of German workers' wages, but I overlooked the words underneath" (81). Creating a palimpsest of what may have been drafts for official documents, Raab retains her entirely personal record of hunger and community, of her desperate retention of the world from before the concentration camps. Similarly, Leon Kahn dedicates *No Time to Mourn* to "all the 'lost souls' including [his] own" (see figure 1). His list of twenty-nine names is distinct from all official lists (see figure 2) not only because he names individuals but also because he identifies each name in relation to himself. His memory and his record situate their lives in particular value and meaning.

Figure 1 Leon Kahn's dedication page

I dedicate this book to all the "lost souls" including my own:—

Shael Kaganowicz	Father
Miriam Kaganowicz	Mother
Benjamin Kaganowicz	Brother
Freida Kaganowicz	Sister
Liebe Gitl Rudzian	Grandmother
Alter Kaganowicz	Uncle
Basha Kaganowicz	Aunt
Mote Kaganowicz	Cousin
Moshe Kaganowicz	Cousin
Mashe Kaganowicz	Cousin
Gneise Kaganowicz	Cousin
Samuel Bastunski	Uncle
Rebecah Bastunski	Aunt
Leib Bastunski	First Cousin
Sarah Bastunski	First Cousin
Moshe Bastunski	First Cousin
Elijah Bastunski	Uncle
Ethel Bastunski	Aunt
Motl Bastunski	Uncle
Chana Bastunski	Aunt
Meier Bastunski	Cousin
Jankel Bastunski	Cousin
Abraham Kaplan	Uncle
Alta Kaplan	Uncle
Moshe Kaplan	First Cousin
Rachele Kaplan	First Cousin
Abraham Mordecai Pacianko	Uncle
Sarah Pacianko	Aunt
Ita-Malka Pacianko	First Cousin

Source: Leon Kahn, *No Time to Mourn: The True Story of a Jewish Partisan Fighter* (Vancouver, BC: Ronsdale P & the Vancouver Holocaust Education Centre, 1978), 2004.

Figure 2 Page from *Death Books from Auschwitz*

Date	Origin	Total	F	M	Notes
13.4.1942	Krakau	60		60	a
14.4.1942	Sammeltransport	3		3	a
14.4.1942	Krakau	57		57	a
15.4.1942	Kattowitz	2		2	a
15.4.1942	Krakau	30		30	a
16.4.1942	Kattowitz	1		1	a
16.4.1942	Kattowitz	1		1	a,b
16.4.1942	Krakau	58		58	a
17.4.1942	Oppelin	2	2		a
17.4.1942.	Krakau	58		58	a
17.4.1942	Kattowitz	1		1	a
17.4.1942	Sammeltransport	25		25	a
17.4.1942	RSHA Slowakei	1000	27	973	a
17.4.1942	Lublin	132		132	a
18.4.1942	Warschau	461		461	a
18.4.1942	Krakau	20		20	a
19.4.1942	RSHA Slowakei	1000	536	464	a
21.4.1942	Warschau	50		50	a
21.4.1942	Sammeltransport	10		10	a
23.4.1942	RSHA Slowakei	1000	457	543	a
24.4.1942	Kattowitz	4		4	a
24.4.1942	Krakau	98		98	a
24.4.1942	Sammeltransport	62		62	a
24.4.1942	RSHA Slowakei	1000	558	442	a
25.4.1942 ·	Krakau	100		100	a
27.4.1942	Krakau	127	127		a
27.4.1942	Kattowitz	14		14	a
28.4.1942	Kattowitz	24		24	a
28.4.1942	Krakau	31		31	a
29.4.1942	Sammeltransport	26		26	a
29.4.1942	RSHA Slowakei	723	300	423	a
29.4.1942	Prag	287		287	a
29.4.1942	RSHA Prag	497	497		a
30.4.1942	Radom	606		606	a
April 1942		369		369	r
1.5.1942	Sammeltransport	100		100	a
1.5.1942	Krakau	24.	24		a
					[...]

Source: *Death Books from Auschwitz: Remnants*, Volume 1, ed. State Museum of Auschwitz-Birkenau, trans. Michael Jacobs, Georg Mayer, Jacek Plesiarowicz (Munich & New Providence: K.G. Saur, 1995), 175.

Given the effective erasure of both victims and survivors from history and law, I suspect that the autobiographical practices embedded in massive historical processes resist the closure that history and law achieve. Instead, they activate memory and attention. Maybe they can produce some new meaning in a future tense. I am not referring to the "comic plot" of testimony written by survivors who have created new lives in the New World, or to hope that springs eternal—next year in Jerusalem—or even to the commonly expressed sense of obligation to children and grandchildren, but rather to the cultural usefulness of the autobiographical endeavour. These writers have for decades been creating what Stanley Fish would call their interpretive community, the readership that can begin to recognize and respond to their work. Depending on when and where they write, they express the recurring nightmare of camp inmates: that no one would ever listen to or believe their stories. Curiously, sympathetic to this scenario, the historian Michael Marrus explains the absence of survivor testimony from historiography, not on the common grounds that history requires solid information and testimony is unreliable but rather on the grounds that their world is "so horrifying and bizarre, and the cultural landmarks so unintelligible that customary historical methods may simply fail" (129). Indeed, when the camps were first liberated and survivors wandered across war-torn Europe or sat in Displaced Persons camps waiting, hoping, to emigrate, they discovered that their stories really were unwelcome, embarrassing, or inaudible. (At the Eichmann trial in Jerusalem, members of the audience sobbed, but they also fainted, rendering them quite unable to hear more [Felman 222n46].) Whereas history, law, and autobiography all make whatever sense is possible in terms of their orientation toward the future, autobiography seems to me to provide the most radical means for clutching the arm of the wedding guest and forcing attention. If I try, then, to think at the intersection of these three modes of inquiry into the past, I am looking not for completeness but for connections and for what will surely be continuous processes of interpretation.

So I return to my original questions. How can Holocaust autobiographies establish (or undermine) credible identity? Can they be any more secure or carry any more conviction than historiography or legal evidence and practice? The major works in this genre tend to be self-reflexive, raising their own questions about memory and knowledge. At their best as literature, they tell profoundly disturbing stories. As contributions to hard knowledge, they accumulate corroboration of detail. Despite their subjective and necessarily limited approach to historical events, these autobiographies are read as authoritative and do not seem to attract impostors. So I set aside the works of Paul Celan, Saul Friedländer, Primo Levi, Elie Wiesel, and their peers, whose contributions are well recognized, and focus instead on the traces left by children. Gitele Tarlo was not alone. The children hiding at Izieu have many counterparts. Most important, given the risk of sentimentalizing the experience (readers surely begin with the premise that children were entirely innocent and entirely helpless victims), the great impostors of Holocaust autobiography—Misha Defonseca, Binjamin Wilkomirski, and Jerzy Kosinski—attracted first fame and then infamy precisely for their focus on childhood. (Kosinski was in fact a Polish Jew who, with his family, survived the German occupation of Poland during the war. His claim to Jewish and survivor identity is therefore authentic. However, his distortion of his history in text and in life created the new identity of the solitary child survivor of appalling atrocities and belongs, accordingly, among the impostors.)

So astonishing is the very concept that this girl and these two small boys had survived on their own—walking across Europe in Misha's case, in the death camps in Wilkomirski's case, in hiding in Kosinski's—that their accounts seem like a bizarre response to Himmler; these children were not intended or expected to live.[8] Their intense and episodic narratives read like eruptions of memory that can be neither verified nor doubted, indicating horrors that lay outside the resources of history or law. Seeming to treat of terrible flashbacks beyond the child's control or understanding, Kosinski and Wilkomirski in particular set themselves apart from most autobiographers who remember childhood experience later in life and bring even to inexplicable disaster the order of narrative. They provide bleak and alarming episodes rather than stories. They require the reader to make sense of what the child found incomprehensible. Their work is shocking precisely because it does not wear the interpretive or narrative clothing of autobiography and therefore seems to claim unmediated access to unprocessed memories. Furthermore, and in the end more problematically, the intensity of *The Painted Bird* and of *Fragments* was persuasive because it matched readers' expectations of what childhood horror must be like. These, we might be tempted to say, are the kinds of records we might expect from children, and therefore the kinds of records we can surely trust. Defonseca's text, by contrast, offers a retrospect that is both vague and sentimental and is therefore more interesting for being believed in the first place than for any insight it suggests into a child's manner of processing trauma. In each case, the experience of the child, apparently captured by adult flashbacks to trauma, lends itself to forms of modernist fiction, in particular, dodging the doubt police where memories of adult experience might be suspect. Ironically, the child who apparently lived through the Holocaust represents both the most vulnerable subject and the narrator through whom the genres of Holocaust autobiography become suspect and therefore vulnerable.

However, the capacity for autobiography to shock and therefore convince raises another problem for the reception of autobiography as authentic record. Holocaust writing receives its rhetorical power directly from its subject matter; aesthetic questions about the quality of writing or narrative form miss the mark entirely. As Daniel Ganzfried put it indignantly with reference to Binjamin Wilkomirski's story: "When an author writes about Auschwitz, people don't question the quality of his work" (quoted in Lappin 22). We have seen in other cases of trauma, too, that the tension between fact and its representation, between life and narrative, resolves in favour of the life—with direct benefit for the reception of the work. Even a poorly written story makes its mark for the significance of the experience it struggles to represent. This common reception of Holocaust writing supports in practice Theodor Adorno's concern about art or aesthetic effects after Auschwitz; experience of suffering provides the moral authority for autobiography—beyond aesthetic judgment. That moral authority includes representation of the horrors that remain suspended in time and experience, not moving to redemption; and of course, that moral authority both creates and commands its readership. So, for example, Elie Wiesel, who approved Defonseca's book, apparently found Kosinski's work quite unpalatable and was reluctant to review it until he was given to understand that it was not fiction but was based on life experience (Sloan, *Jerzy Kosinski,* 223). Wiesel's endorsement, appearing as a review at the end of October 1965, emphasizes the moral value of a true story: "Written with deep sincerity and sensitivity," he writes of *The Painted Bird,* "this poignant first-person account transcends confession and attains in parts the haunting quality and the tone of a quasi-surrealistic tale. One cannot read it without fear, shame and sadness" (47). Implicitly acknowledging the judicial inquiry that followed the Holocaust, Wiesel calls Kosinski's "little boy" a "witness for the prosecution" (47). Philip Gourevitch refers to Wiesel as "hoodwinked" by an impostor (67). Wiesel did not know, and so was unequivocal in his moral support for a work that "transcends confession."

But what about this "tone of a quasi-surrealistic tale"? How can we balance the needs of fact and of fiction, the moral value and the elements needed to communicate it? The honourable autobiographer writes from his personal perspective but remains onside for historical truth. Yet these truths certainly invite the language of fiction. Wiesel himself has written novels based on personal experience, presumably because fiction served him better in these cases than autobiography. Treading this fine line between the literal and the figurative, Chaim Kaplan expresses concern both that his diary be "source material for the future historian" (104) and that this experience—his own and that of his community—was not open to figurative language. To say that the sun was darkened at noon, he writes, would not be a mere metaphor; experience of literal horror requires figurative language to carry literal meaning. So I set aside concerns about figurative language or fictional situations. If the literal is worse than we can imagine, then language must be bent to serve the occasion even if acceptance of some fiction blurs the distinction I would like to make between impostor and survivor. Both at times resort to the language of fiction.

In his seminal work *The Holocaust and the Literary Imagination* (1975), Lawrence L. Langer discusses *The Painted Bird* at some length, clearly as an archetypal fiction with ties to Conrad and Camus, to Dante and Shakespeare. Relatively early, then, Kosinski's dance of self and text, autobiography and fiction, had moved from Wiesel's court to that of the literary critic. By the end of the century, in *Imagining the Holocaust,* Daniel R. Schwarz is concerned with the quality of the narrative, with the ethics of such narrative, and with Kosinski's self-invention. Dealing explicitly with fiction in 2000, Sue Vice discusses therapeutic narration (79), "generic ambiguity" (80), and, like Schwarz before her, the ethical question of making the Holocaust a vehicle or symbol for other issues. The distinction between memoir and fiction, as Aharon Appelfeld, another child survivor, told Gourevitch, is that "in memoir, you just write what you write because it happened, which is not up to you. But fiction must have a reason" (Gourevitch 63). Appelfeld writes fiction himself because he remembers "almost nothing" of his childhood, but can be truthful to "the world of his memory" if he is not factual (62). Robert Krell reminds me that child survivors do not remember their experiences in full, clear, or narratable order;[9] a child's trauma does not lend itself to narrative—a point on which Wilkomirski relies.

What about the starting point of personal experience? How reliable is that? That too, for the child in particular, lends itself to the forms of fiction for which no coherent explanation is required. "While I can retrieve no clear memory of them," writes Dori Laub, "in some way I am certain that I watched a public hanging, and this occasionally occurs in my dreams" (Glassner and Krell 51). "Memory," Krell comments, "may precede by years the ability to describe that memory with words" (Glassner and Krell 105). So Wilkomirski remembers babies who had chewed their fingers to the bone, or rats emerging from a dead woman's body. Kosinski describes bestiality and the gouging out of a young man's eyes. Both insist on their memories, and all we know for sure is that such things certainly did happen. Since Krell also describes the difficulties with which he himself and other child survivors have had to fight for their memories, insisting on them in the face of adult resistance (as in "you could not possibly remember"), those of us who were not there may simply have to accept their appalling and bizarre information as, indeed, information.

When in doubt, however, we may ask: "Whose information is this? To whom do these stories belong?" The impostor can only impose when his audience believes that he owns his own story, that he is the one who remembers. The child survivor has a unique opportunity for imposture not only because his adult readers are predisposed to respond, and not only because his memories themselves may seem like surreal fiction, appalling and without explanation, but also because his story does not require corroboration to be plausible. Kosinski, writing in 1965, produced the kind of history to which few in the West had had prior access.

When questioned, he acknowledged that he had supported his own memories with some European texts, including the 1946 Polish publication of children's stories that did not appear in English until 1996 as *The Children Accuse*. Writing very much later, Wilkomirski had access to massive archives that were accessible to his readers as well as to himself. However, the child's story remained a relatively rare phenomenon, and Wilkomirski was convincing for his remarkable and highly specific information and for the impression that he was recalling unexpected details. Both men assumed—and likely believed in—identities shaped for and by their publications. In his documentary video *Who was Jerzy Kosinski?* Jack Kuper, whose childhood experience paralleled so many aspects of *The Painted Bird*, finds himself asking whose story this was ("Who Was Jerzy Kosinski?"). Had Kosinski stolen Kuper's story or had he himself been the thief? Authentic and inauthentic blurred through narrative.

Furthermore, verifiable identify shifts both mirrored and exaggerated the Holocaust child's confusions about identity. Kosinski's father had already changed the family name from Lewinkopf to evade identification as a Jew, and Kosinski fluctuated between roundly denying he was a Jew and jovially agreeing that of course he was a Jew. Wilkomirski had been known before the saga of his erupting memories as Bruno Dösseker, a Swiss Gentile, and adopted his distinctly Jewish names in response to particular external suggestion (Gourevitch 59). Both men faced their public with curious claims on a survivor identity—Kosinski with the justification that he had indeed grown up as a Jew in disguise in wartime Poland, Wilkomirski refashioning his entire personal history to claim he was a child survivor and a Latvian Jew. In both cases, the stories they tell likely deserve some psychological explanation as responses to some trauma other than those they relate. One key difference between the two men and their texts is surely Wilkomirski's adamant insistence on his own version of his life regardless of disproofs and Kosinski's more variable theorizing about fiction and truth.

As with all fraud, the central problem with imposture is the writer's claim. What does he want his reader to believe? What, in the case of autobiography, is the proportion of fiction to fact? Or, maybe more precisely, what are the uses of fiction in the presentation of fact? Kosinski's biographer, James Park Sloan, has identified the few pieces of known information from Kosinski's childhood that contribute to the otherwise fantastic tale of *The Painted Bird:* the family did indeed spend the German occupation of Poland in small communities where they passed as Christians; the child did indeed have to hide and deny the fact that he was Jewish; not he but his brother Henryk was indeed adopted as a mascot by Russian soldiers near the end of the war, before their father's return to successful business under Russian occupation. However, the small child was not separated from his parents and did not wander among superstitious and sadistic villagers on his own. Kosinski interested Dorothy de Santillana of Houghton Mifflin in stories of his childhood that he recounted over dinner in Boston. He had told many of these stories to Mira Michalowska, an early friend and translator in the United States, and even earlier to his high school friend "Stash" Pomorski, who has suggested three stages for a Kosinski storytelling process that may well apply to Wilkomirski as well: first, something or other happened; second, something or other happened in which Kosinski was involved; finally, Kosinski himself was the main character in whatever had happened (Sloan 190). When de Santillana found that a couple of editorial reports referred to Kosinski's work as fiction, she wrote for clarification: "It is my understanding that fictional as the material may sound, it is straight autobiography" (quoted in Sloan 207). Perhaps Pomorski's explanation makes sense. Perhaps Kosinski needed to believe in his final version in order to tell a compelling story. Perhaps dinner table stories offered as personal could not, without shame, be later acknowledged as fiction.

Kosinski seems to have prevaricated, referring both to fiction and to frozen memories and repeatedly reinventing himself to meet the question of the moment. His disclaimer in "Notes of the Author on *The Painted Bird*," first appended to the German edition for European readers, is evasive and disingenuous: "to say that *The Painted Bird* is nonfiction," he writes, "may be convenient for classification, but it is not easily justified." Given that I am not at all concerned with the role of fiction either in autobiography or in treatment of the Holocaust, but only with the author's claims to be telling his personal truth, Kosinski's "convenience" is not persuasive. The man was ensuring by this point that he was closely aligned with his text. Also, as we have seen in other contexts, life stories sell more readily than fiction, which must be judged on its aesthetic merits, and Kosinski sold.

Published in 1965 and reviewed as an "account," a "confession," a "document," and a "testimony," *The Painted Bird* rapidly became a key text for courses and reading lists on the Holocaust (Sloan 223). The German edition, which came out at the same time as the American, was "an out and out hit," with *Der bemalte Vogel* on bestseller lists (234). In France, *L'Oiseau bariole* won the Prix du Meilleur Livre Étranger. Wilkomirski, too, won numerous prizes before being exposed, including the Prix de Mémoire de la Shoah in Paris and the National Jewish Book Award in New York in competition with autobiographies by Alfred Kazin and Elie Wiesel—the fraud, in other words, being more impressive than the true stories. *The Painted Bird* was not published in Polish but was reviewed in Polish as a libel on the Polish nation and as evidence of Western propaganda. Certainly, Houghton Mifflin's marketing of the work as memoir handicapped Polish reviewers even when they had access to alternative versions of Kosinski's stories. Homegrown critics behind the Iron Curtain were helpless; readers in the West simply saw Kosinski as a martyr to ideological criticism.

Kosinski played into this reading with his extraordinary preface to the second edition of *The Painted Bird* in 1976. Here he recounts the birth and growth of his idea for what he here calls "a novel," in which he intended to deal with particular archetypes. "Man would be portrayed in his most vulnerable state, as a child" (xii) and would exist in "a mythic domain, in the timeless fictive present, unrestrained by geography or history" (xiii). In this preface, Kosinski blames readers for ascribing autobiographical elements to the work, paints a grim picture of Soviet hostility to him because of his defection to the West, and then tells the strange story of his being threatened by some Poles, who forced entry to his apartment. With their "rural dialect that I recalled so well ... their broad peasant faces, their stocky bodies, the poorly fitting raincoats ... They seemed to have stepped out of the pages of *The Painted Bird,* and for a moment I felt very possessive of the pair. If indeed they were my characters, it was only natural that they should come to visit me" (xviii). As, later, with Hitler's diaries, the text that would have made no impact if it had been presented as fiction fed the tensions of East–West relations. When Pocket Books adopted *The Painted Bird* in 1966, they worked on its value as sensational literature, printing 300,000 copies in their first run and marketing it with a detail from *The Last Judgment* by Hieronymous Bosch on the front cover (Sloan 239).

The moral value of autobiography depends less, for sure, on the scrupulous morality of its author than on the truthfulness of his tale. However, in Kosinski's case, the tale itself also came unravelled in two stages of investigation and exposure—first the text and then the man. The story of the text became as sensational as the childhood experience that readers had been asked to believe. In May 1982, Geoffrey Stokes and Eliot Fremont-Smith (who had listed *The Painted Bird* among the best books of the year in 1965 [226]) exposed Kosinski's dishonesty and pretensions in an article in *The Village Voice* titled "Jerzy Kosinski's Tainted Words." Kosinski responded with passion about every comma, every word, every draft, and every proof being his alone. However, as so commonly in cases of imposture, fame and success bring out both the doubt police and, quite often, those who identify themselves as silenced, manipulated, or hurt by their own involvement in the imposture. In the process of their own righteous indignation, these accusers raise the terrible possibility that their impostor has not led the life he claims to have lived and that he has not even written the book about that life that he claims to have written.

As Philip Knightley pointed out to Rupert Murdoch in the case of Hitler's diaries, secrecy serves the impostor. So when Kosinski advertised for a translator in 1964, he was clear that he did not intend to acknowledge the translator. When he asked for sample work from Steven Krause, whom he did not hire, he used the sample work for which he had not paid (199). Aleksandr Lutoslawski worked on sections of the text and was happy not to have his name attached; he found the work pornographic and lacking in literary merit. Later, he seems to have noticed his missed opportunity and claimed, along with others, that he had written *The Painted Bird* (200). When Peter Skinner wanted to identify his work for Kosinsky in his own curriculum vitae, Kosinski had him sign a document about "secretarial services" rendered to himself and his late wife (278). Kosinski seems to have worked with a number of accomplices, all drawn into collaboration by the extraordinary circumstances of a charismatic man with an incredible history. Stanley Corngold, who had compared the mute child at the end of *The Painted Bird* with Stephen Dedalus's discovery of his voice at the end of Joyce's *Portrait of the Artist as a Young Man,* was as dismayed by the poor quality of the writing that Kosinski later wanted him to work on as by his own sense of being manipulated and exploited. George Reavey protested Kosinski's nomination as president of the American Center for PEN, writing to Thomas Fleming: "He didn't write *The Painted Bird*. I did" (315). Kosinski, he added, "gave me an illiterate manuscript … part English, part Polish, and part Russian. I put it into prose, added details, and got five hundred dollars" (316). These kinds of quarrels, which may, of course, have as much to do with professional jealousy as with a working relationship, sound remarkably like the strange case of Nega Mezlekia, who won the Governor General's Award for non-fiction in Canada. Common to both are the remarkable problems of writing in another language than one's own and therefore needing help with translation and editing. However, Kosinski, like Mezlekia in his turn, entered a curious double bind: on one hand, his story succeeded because it was apparently a personal account; on the other, he had literary aspirations. He wanted recognition on both moral and aesthetic grounds. Where the autobiographer could accept and acknowledge help, the artist could not. The autobiographer owns his experience, but the artist owns his text.

Unleashed on the case of *The Painted Bird,* the doubt police were able, over the years, to demonstrate that Kosinski's sense of ownership both of this and of other works had all along been rather less than scrupulous and to suggest, accordingly, that his life as well was therefore open to question. Critics identified one successful novel, *Being There,* with *The Career of Nikodem Dyzma* by Dolega Mostowicz, published in Polish in 1932, and learned that *The Devil Tree* drew extensively on the journals Kosinski had stolen from his lover, Jean Kilbourne. As in a political thriller, questions arose about Kosinski's pseudonym, Joseph Novak, providing a front for CIA anti-communist propaganda. Raiding the lives and the stories of others, Kosinski had fabricated a world for himself that raised suspicion and that could not stand the test of verification. For the man who had built his celebrity on a Holocaust childhood, questions also arose about *The Painted Bird* being drawn from Roman Polanski's experiences, or Jack Kuper's, but not likely from his own.

In 1994, Joanna Siedlecka published a book in Poland called *Czarny ptasior* ("Black Bird"), which described Kosinski as never separated from his parents, enjoying such goods as sausages and cocoa that were unavailable to his neighbours, and later distorting experiences that other people remembered (Sloan, "Kosinski's War"). Siedlecka's "black bird" taunts the "painted bird" of Kosinski's title and of his metaphor for the cruelty of humankind. Where her angry exposure of factual shortfall would not matter in the slightest for fiction, it created a crisis for Kosinski precisely because he claimed to be telling both fiction, sometimes, and always the truth. In a *New Yorker* article that responds to this crisis and that preceded his biography, Sloan describes his own visit to Poland and his own interviews with people who had known Kosinski's family and who also knew the literary world of the 1990s. Sloan spoke with Tad Krauze, once a close friend of Kosinski's, who described him now as betraying an ideal, "a man recklessly in pursuit of literary fame and fortune" (Sloan, "Kosinski's War"). Similarly, Kuper met the farmer from Dombrowa who had sheltered the Kosinski family and who felt betrayed by this "fabrication" ("Who Was Jerzy Kosinski?"). This theme of betrayal recurs in autobiographical imposture; because these texts claim to draw on life, they belong in the moral realm in which other people get hurt.

However, we return from expressions of hurt to what Primo Levi so famously calls "the grey zone" with Kosinski's apparent raid on one of the very earliest studies of children's experience of the Holocaust, *The Children Accuse,* which was not published in English until 1996 (see under Hochberg-Marianiska). The question here is not about direct plagiarism but about the ways in which common experiences can become embedded in one another, indistinguishable from one another, but not therefore untrue. Like Jack Kuper's story, or like the stories collected by Shia Moser in the Peterswald Children's Home in Lower Silesia in 1945, *The Children Accuse* presents a bleak litany of terror: children see their parents and other people beaten and shot; they hide in cramped and dark places, not daring to move; they see other children, often their siblings, being drowned or thrown into the snow to freeze to death; a mother gives birth in the snow and is too weak to walk; children live on stolen potatoes, beetroot, and cabbage; they die of hunger, or wounds, or illness; they regain consciousness among a heap of corpses; repeatedly, they are harried and tormented by other children who know they are Jews; they survive in rags, often completely alone, exhausted, and traumatized by violence and fear.

If *The Children Accuse* is any kind of source for Kosinski, he can certainly claim gross and continuous sexual violence as completely his own. He has also failed to mention the numerous courageous individuals identified in *The Children Accuse,* who sheltered and protected Jewish families in hiding. Kosinski, who always claimed the child narrator of *The Painted Bird* and the child's most appalling experiences as his own, perhaps overstated his case. The audience, on whom he depended for recognition, began to doubt.

By way of immediate comparison, Kuper's *Child of the Holocaust,* which came out just after *The Painted Bird,* cannot bear the burden of proof any more than *The Painted Bird,* but its claims on credulity are less frantic, less extreme. *Child of the Holocaust* echoes the desperate wanderings of Kosinski's child and of so many other children, and claims Kuper's own childhood with first-person narrative. Disguising his Jewish identity, pretending to be Christian, Kuper's child, too,. is confused about who he is, what language he speaks, what god he prays to, and is terrified of betrayal. He lies and steals and pretends. He starves and he runs, but he concludes by staking a single and clear identity when he leaves his message, "Jankele Kuperblum is alive," on the wall of the semi-destroyed Jewish registry in the hope that his family will find him (283). Kuper's claim is more modest than Kosinski's: not that the world was relentlessly evil but that he himself was alone in desperate trouble. Perhaps, too, Kuper persuades because he does not, as an adult, perform a survivor identity. Unlike Kuper, Kosinski required attention for a performance that astonished but did not, in the end, convince. When factual information can be neither proven nor disproven and can be found in a number of different places that may corroborate one another or suggest that one has borrowed another's story, this performance, this play's the thing in which to catch the conscience of the impostor.

Binjamin Wilkomirski's *Fragments* falls apart on many of the same grounds. A much finer literary performance than Kosinski's, lacking Kosinski's voyeuristic journey through sexual deviance and random sadism, and lacking, too, the archetypal dimensions that signal fiction in Kosinski's work, *Fragments* disconnects from its author along similar fault lines. Life, in both cases, seems to betray the text because both men have created histories and identities that they cannot perform persuasively. Their adult lives do not cooperate, do not carry conviction, in relation to the stories they have created for themselves. Wilkomirski (or Bruno Dösseker) presented in *Fragments* not simply a false autobiography about his Latvian Jewish descent and his time at Majdanek and Auschwitz as a very small child but also a fictional identity for the grown man and author. Arthur H. Samuelson of Schocken Books, for example, was disturbed by Wilkomirski's continuous weeping on his reading tour. Either because he was emotionally overwrought or because he made assumptions about how a survivor would behave, Wilkomirski overplayed his hand. "He cried everywhere we brought him," Samuelson has said. "I told him if he didn't stop crying I'd send him home. That shocked his publicist, who wasn't Jewish. Maybe it was insensitive of me, but I've published Primo Levi, Elie Wiesel, Aharon Appelfeld—I know a lot of survivors—and one thing they have in common is they don't cry. This guy couldn't stop" (quoted in Gourevitch 51). If, on one hand,

Kosinski and Wilkomirski understood the mode in which their shocking stories could seem credible, Wilkomirski rather more than Kosinski seemed in person, in himself, untrue to the situation and the story as these have become recognized over the past fifty years. His "corpus delicti" lost touch with the reality of his text.

Levi's "grey zone" in these cases may have something to do with the neuroses of two very troubled men, it may have to do with the impossibility of knowing, in Leopold von Ranke's words, "wie es eigentlich war"—how it really was. Certainly, as with history and as with law, uncertainty with autobiography rests on the documents and evidence that underpin any particular account. In autobiography as in law, precedent educates reader and writer alike about what can be imagined or written and what can be read or, in the end, received. Young has referred to some survivors with stories polished and slick from many tellings where others are raw and hard to receive ("Towards a Received History" 41). Responding to Primo Levi's version of him as "Henri" in *If This Is a Man,* Paul Steinberg, under a title he deliberately steals from Celan, says he is unsure whether Levi is right or whether he himself is right. Like Kuper with Kosinski, he is not sure what he has read and what he thinks of as his own experience. When Wilkomirski is exposed by the incompatibility of DNA evidence, the literary critic of my generation may cry foul, this is evidence from way outside the text. For autobiography, however, where man and text must match, perhaps only this kind of external "proof" can carry the burden of making the match or the mismatch. For most Holocaust narrative, however, such proofs are neither meaningful nor possible. I must conclude that the childhood autobiography that is subject to imposture is no more adequate than history or law for producing the identity or the narrative that convinces beyond a shadow of a doubt.

Levi's "grey zone" is not morally ambiguous, it does not confuse clear distinctions between good and evil, right or wrong. Rather, the grey zone recognizes the forces for good and evil, right and wrong, in every human being. It invites very humble self-reflection in place of finger pointing. So Levi would perhaps sympathize with the emotional confusions of both Kosinski and Wilkomirski. However, I suspect he would also be angered by the invitation they provide for Holocaust denial. By their fruits shall you know them. If I have seen imposture as partly whimsical (as in the case of "Andreas Karavis"), or somewhere on a spectrum between harmless and beneficial (as in the case of "Grey Owl"), I deplore the potential damage that the opportunistic impostures of Kosinski and Dösseker create, using the lives, the suffering, and the deaths of others to their own advantage and giving rise to any doubt at all that others lived, and suffered, and most abominably died. For these reasons I have been calling on the "moral authority" of law and Friedländer's "moral vigilance" in history so that readers of the future may not doubt but may have faith in the personal stories they receive of atrocity.

In Conclusion
Textual Identities at Work in the World

One of my favourite stories, which has stayed with me since childhood, is that of "Little Lady Margaret." Timid and plain, Lady Margaret grows up the only child of a grim duke (who had wanted sons) and is to be given in marriage to his former enemy, an elderly and very nasty earl, thus proving herself useful for the only time in her young life. However, Lady Margaret's one great talent lying in embroidery, she creates for herself a magnificent tapestry, a garden full of beautiful plants and animals, a veritable Eden. She discovers the power of her work when her hound disappears from her room—because she has embroidered him into the garden. So, of course, and triumphantly, she escapes her marriage by embroidering herself into the tapestry as well. I am sure this story provided me with an early dose of a kind of feminism; but far more significantly, even at first reading, it suggested the power of "text" to supersede life. "You embroider too well," her hound tells her when she first steps into her tapestry world. "You made me too life-like. I cannot be in two places at once" (Picard 78). Of course it matters that Little Lady Margaret escape the oppression of her real world. Perhaps it matters, too, that she creates an Adamless Eden. Most of all, it matters now, as it did in my childhood, that she does not simply escape from her ugly world but that she actually (with precision and great skill) creates her own world as she would like it to be. For her, far more completely than for any autobiographer, her text defaces her life. Her story celebrates textual identity (and happy endings) even as it engages with power politics. In fact, even as a fairy tale, "Little Lady Margaret" suggests textual identity at work to change its world.

Here, I suspect, is the baseline. I have referred throughout this discussion to the specific political and cultural situations in which specific textual identities have become opportune if not, in fact, inevitable. At this baseline, the creation even of the impostor serves his public well. After all, the forms of fraud and imposture that pertain to textual identity present a paradox: on one hand, they consist, without doubt, of theft and deceit and impersonation; on the other, they clarify what exactly their reading communities accept as true. Not least, imposture presupposes posture, or the positions we adopt because we are interpellated into them, or because they make sense to us, or because we choose them, or because that is how others recognize us. Such minimalist determinants affect the everyday living of entirely honest people, with the result that most of us, most of the time, believe that we are who we say we are and that our real presence in the real world is entirely credible, that we are the personal origins for any textual life in which we may put or find ourselves. The impostor depends upon but also supports this common faith. The ghost presumes an original and substantial body, emphasizing by her very invisibility the physical presence with which "the author" lives in the world, that physical presence also providing the ultimate connection between lived and textual identity. Plagiarism, which I have noted implies kidnapping, certainly suggests an original author; either the plagiarist is pretending to be that original author, or the plagiarist exposed reveals the original author. Either way, the author (however we want to read that term) becomes significant as the origin of the text. Similarly, ethnic or racial imposture, like strategic identity, depends on essentialist notions of ontology, the skin colour or the cultural community determining personhood. This kind of imposture shows up more than the binaries of self and other because it exposes and challenges the felt politics of specific communities. For each kind of imposture that I have discussed, the effects or repercussions derive from autobiographical practice, that is, from productions of self that claim to be authentic and that readers tend to believe in. The impostor, in other words, even with deliberate deceit, depends on and confirms that in which "we" believe, the orthodox (as in correct teaching or opinion), that which is commonly held to be true.

Furthermore, faith in whatever may be true seems very frequently to emerge from confusion and doubt or, at least, to require articulation, which then convinces. If truth depends on community agreement, however temporary that may be, then the detection and exposure of imposture are important for defining orthodoxy; for determining, for the community at large at a given time, what in the end is acceptable, or how one acts to eject the "foreign" from what Eakin has identified as the normative body politic. My study has been historical and political not only because textual manipulation is surely as old as textuality itself, but also, significantly, because the identities produced in text spring from and address their own times and places. Fraud and imposture therefore provide a touchstone for faith and doubt in quite varied conditions. For me, the difficulties facing Jerome and Erasmus and Psalmanazar resonate through Mezlekia or Yasusada or Grey Owl, not generalizing the phenomenon of textual shenanigans but in fact *particularizing* each specific situation, which is necessarily distinct in its own historical and cultural context. Each situation is a product of history and of specific external forces (often legal or economic) to which each case responds. In each case, too, it seems to me, the fraud or imposture shows us why and how we believe what we believe in any given time and place. I suspect that imposture is in fact (most often unintentionally, no doubt) a political weapon; it operates within susceptible communities and forces them to recognize themselves. How do Americans read their own needs or desires after the successes of Jumana Hanna, Norma Khouri, or James Frey? How do the British read a history of empire that includes the defection of Archibald Belaney? Because of the choices these impostors have made, and because they have fooled their audiences, they reflect their audience back to itself.

If faith tends to emerge from doubt, so discovery may come from knowledge or from what we think we understand. Kelly Oliver suggests that we tend to discover what is new only in terms of what we already know. She develops her paradox in original and important ways, but I propose to stay right here with her opening gambit. To make the point quite crudely, identification of lies and outrage at the detection of lies bring us back to shared assumptions about what we constitute as truth. Binjamin Wilkomirski may claim to be a Latvian Jew and a child survivor of the concentration camps of the Second World War, but the shared and certain knowledge that he was none of these things establishes, by its solid negativity, some things we know for sure—about him, about his story, about his identity, and about what we consider "true." His case also raises the question of unwanted identities. Griffin's choice to be black, like Belaney's choice to be "Indian," has also clarified for me some of the power dynamics, the stereotyping, and the exclusionary practices that I, as a well-meaning white woman, have not learned from honest-to-goodness black and Native people. Performing what I have called an "encumbered" identity, racial and ethnic imposture puts into play, realizes, or makes real the numerous components of particularized identity—not necessarily to the communities being personified, but to their "readers," the communities who may not have recognized their own participation in this phenomenon. To what "self" can this identity be "true"?

As if these subjects were not difficult enough, they also keep changing. When Polonius told Laertes, "This above all, to thine own self be true, / And it must follow, as the night the day, / Thou canst not then be false to any man" (*Hamlet* I.iii), he really could assume that Laertes would understand him, and in a general way, surely Laertes did. Unlike many of the impostors I have been considering, Laertes knew something about his "self" and something about "truth." He understood what his father meant because he was able to accept his father's wise saws as relevant to his own identity as a scholar and a gentleman. However, contemporary autobiographers and impostors alike lead more complicated lives; either they do not understand Polonius at all or they refuse to obey him, insisting that they have no single selves or identifiable truths. (Frey may claim to be a reformed character, but I have serious doubts that Khouri is, or that Kosinski could have been, and Solway and Johnson are surely lost causes.) Nonetheless, I suspect that most of my rogues' gallery, not being blessed with a strong sense of irony or with any particular theories of self, have by their very indirections been finding directions out, maybe not for themselves, but for us, their readers. Paradoxically, I suspect their impostures may provide some useful approaches to post-Polonian self and truth.

These post-Polonian selves tend to be both ephemeral and plural, Protean rather than Polonian. So Kent Johnson makes a solid and very courteous front man for Yasusada. He, too, seems to be both a gentleman and a scholar, and to appreciate what these terms mean. However, the cyberspace in which Yasusada has been seeded to increase and multiply, even depending as it fairly significantly does on the bound and published text, defies familiar or agreed understanding of reality or truth. Yasusada does not simply ignore such icons of certainty; Yasusada plays games with the very notion that they might exist anywhere at all or for any identity, textual or lived. In this sense, the Internet functions as an instrument for the cultural post-humanities, challenging long-accepted notions of what "identity," personal or textual, could even begin to mean. Identity becomes speculative, shifts perspectives, responds to other players in a game of multidimensional tic-tac-toe. Such concepts as faith or doubt or identity itself lose their meaning and value. The impostor could thrive but has no fixed point of origin or departure. Shakespeare may have imagined such a world, but Polonius could not. Post-humanist culture will surely affect the wisdom we can confer on our children as well as the confidence we place in distinctions between falsehood and truth, or kinds of truth, or truth for the moment. Curiously, the processes of autobiography itself lead to the same kinds of uncertainty—about the text, for sure, but also about identity in text. Mezlekia, for instance, apparently titled his second, unpublished, autobiographical work in these terms, which suggests that he did not know himself any more. The process, one might say, had unmanned him. So I wonder what Yasusada's heirs may have to tell us about self-production, camouflage, vulnerable identities, or communities of faith and of doubt.

My own earliest work on autobiography, born in a graduate seminar on fiction, began with questions about truth in autobiography, the genre that so pre-eminently claims access to self and to truth. Returning to these questions more than thirty years later may suggest stupidity or, perhaps, a core self to whom the same concerns remain important, but also an alternative approach. For one thing, I continue to agree with myself that truth (whatever it may be) is both desirable and impossible. Furthermore, I do not object when you use all your skills as a storyteller to create a textual identity in which I can believe, but I object very strenuously when you hurt someone else by doing so. And I recognize myself not in the impostors or the doubt police who have exposed the impostors but in the reader who is by turns astonished, fascinated, voyeuristic, gossipy, and, in the end, disillusioned. Each time, I feel I know myself better than before, and each time I swear never to be so caught out again. We, their readers, are the ones sporting fraught identities; we think we know what we value, or believe, and why, but we receive our most useful or effective education by means of the doubts they raise.

Notes

Notes to Chapter 1

1 E-mail received March 5, 2008.
2 For work on eighteenth-century autobiography, see in particular Felicity A. Nussbaum, Patricia Meyer Spacks, Eugene L. Stelzig, and James Treadwell. English usage of the term "autobiography" is attributed to an article by Robert Southey in *The Quarterly Review* in 1809. I note that these scholars associate autobiography in the decades before 1809 with the novel and with nascent Romanticism.
3 E-mail dated 12 November 2005.
4 See, for example, H. Porter Abbott, Francis R. Hart, William L. Howarth, Stephen A. Shapiro, and Jean Starobinski.
5 I think with particular gratitude of Mary Mason's article "The Other Voice," with its clear articulation of different experience necessitating different constructions of the female self, surely providing the groundwork for what Eakin has since described as "the relational self." Sidonie Smith's work on women's writing and on autobiography as performative, and the numerous Smith and Watson collections of essays, have transformed autobiography studies with their careful attention to the implications of women's lives for the production of women's narratives and texts.
6 For the ethical turn in autobiography studies, see, in particular, Couser, Eakin, Freadman, and Parker.
7 See Schaffer and Smith, *Human Rights and Narrated Lives;* Gillian Whitlock, "Autographics" and *Soft Weapons;* and Judith Lütge Coullie, ed., *Selves in Question.*

Notes to Chapter 2

1 *Vancouver Sun*, April 8, 2006, A17.
2 Sarah James, The Mystery of "The Jesus Papers," MSNBC, April 2, 2006, http://www.msnbc.msn.com/id/12084683/page/3.

3 For much of the discussion that follows I am indebted to Courtney Booker, who suggested and provided numerous readings and who then responded to an early draft with emendations and yet further readings.

4 The illustration appears in a manuscript c. 830. See Gombrich, *The Story of Art*, 120.

5 Clark's argument, based on her observation that the death of the author parallels the death of history, is that we need to develop an intellectual history rather than a history of fact, to study the construction of meaning and observe how texts "work."

6 Courtney Booker has referred me to the work of Karl Hulley, with his discussion of Jerome's higher and lower criticism as Foucault's point of departure for work on "the author-function," as well as to E.P. Goldschmidt for medieval authorship. Discussing the reasons why various works appear under "obviously false names" (86), Goldschmidt includes the problem of bibliographical entries for collections of texts alphabetized under the name of the first author, who therefore becomes, by default, author of the other works in the same collection (116–17). Medieval books were sources of wisdom and knowledge rather than expressions of particular authors.

7 David Wootton suggests rich possibilities for atheism in the language and thought of the early modern period. However, actual documentation has been lost or destroyed, so that the clearest surviving evidence takes the form of some poems and songs and the records of trials and judicial inquiries. Wootton also discusses evidence of private convictions masked or coded in public presentations of texts, as well as the emerging role of science in establishing methods for determining what might be doubted or believed.

8 See both Peter Burke and Giles Constable on the concept of anachronism as itself an anachronism in the medieval world view. Burke, for example, refers to the humanists' sense "of 'nostalgic distance'" from the past, "an awareness of difference joined with admiration and a desire to annihilate that difference" (158). Burke notes that the term "anachronism" "began to come into use in Latin, Italian, French and English" around 1650 (173). Constable refers to anachronism as sometimes a "form of simultaneity, where events that took place at different times are shown or described together (as in charters, where it has led to many mistaken charges of forgery)" (62).

9 Jack Lynch, "Pyrrhonism and Paranoia: Recognizing a Fake When You See One," delivered at the Princeton Eighteenth-Century Conference, 18 March 2000, http://andromeda.rutgers.edu/~jlynch/Papers/pyrrho.html.

10 Anna Wierzbicka suggests that particular patterns of speech relating to faith and doubt emerged in England in this period. She cites, for instance, the frequent use of "I think," "I suppose," and "probably," "possibly," "clearly," "obviously," "presumably," "evidently," "apparently," and so on. She also notes that the phrase "I believe" comes into frequent use to refer not to faith but to reason. See Jonathan Hope's review of Wierzbicka's *English: Meaning and Culture*, titled "Probably, Possibly, Perhaps" in *The Times Literary Supplement*, 16 March 2007.

Notes to Chapter 3

1 See Gillian Whitlock, *Soft Weapons: Autobiography in Transit*, 131–60, for a very interesting treatment of the American media in wartime Iraq.

2 Kay Schaffer and Sidonie Smith, in *Human Rights and Narrated Lives,* discuss both the venues and the occasions for storytelling and the political effects of traumatic stories on history, redress, and national identity. Bina Toledo Friewald has been an early exponent of the relations between minority or disadvantaged stories and national identity. See "Gender, Nation, and Self-Narration" and "Nation and Self-Narration."

3 Addiction as a hot topic surfaces again in discussion of Roberto Bolano's *2666,* which appeared on many bestseller lists in 2008. Bolano's widow claims that his story of addiction in an earlier collection was just that—a story and not a fragment of autobiography. The distinction she wants to make has not protected his memory from fierce speculation. See Larry Rohter, "A Chilean Writer's Fictions Might Include His Own Colorful Past," *The New York Times* January 28, 2009: C1.

4 E-mail dated 1 October 2006. See Hamilton, "Mixing Memoir and Desire," published after that e-mail exchange.

5 Subsequent events have proved me wrong about Frey's having shot his bolt. On Saturday, 12 April 2008, I received an e-mail addressed to me quite personally, giving me James Frey's telephone number, inviting me to leave him a message, inviting me also to preorder his new book, *Bright.Shiny Morning* (surely a wholesome title), to be published by HarperCollins on 13 May 2008 (also available on audio CD, audio cassette, and CD-ROM), and providing advance notice of his book tour. While I, along with many millions of others, know something about James Frey, I am concerned to know how James Frey has identified *me.*

6 This double approach to the text and to evidence outside the text is not uncommon in verification of autobiography. In the case of Olaudah Equiano, for instance, to whom I return in Chapter 4, S.E. Ogude found that the text itself raised his doubts; whereas Vincent Carretta is quoted as saying, "I, having a mind of concrete, said, 'He gives me a date, he gives me a place, he gives me a name, it should be verifiable.'" See Jennifer Howard, "Unraveling the Narrative."

7 "Truth-Proof Pages," *The Australian,* 28 July 2004, http://www.theaustralian.news .com.au/printpage/0,5942,10264337,00.html.

8 As with autobiography, a journalist's fine story must stand the test of verification. Consider, as just a few recent examples, the exposure of fraudulent journalism in the cases of Jayson Blair, exposed in an article on the front page of *The New York Times* on 11 May 2003, headlined "Times Reporter Who Resigned Leaves Long Trail of Deception"; Stephen Glass of the *New Republic,* exposed on CBS's *60 Minutes,* 11 May 2003; Ruth Shalit of *The New Republic,* accused of extensive plagiarism in 1995; and CBS in its reporting on President Bush's National Guard record (September 2004).

9 G. Thomas Couser, citing a conversation he enjoyed with a colleague in Turkey, draws my attention to the possible benefits of ethnic imposture in that, perversely, it draws attention to the problematics of ethnic distinctiveness as one of the major causes of strife and violence in the world today. Undated letter.

Notes to Chapter 4

1 John Howard Griffin's infiltration of the black community in the Deep South took place from 1 November to 15 December 1959 and was written up first for *Sepia Magazine*. Though Griffin thought of his research as sociological, he found it, in the end, so profoundly personal that he wrote of his experience autobiographically in the first person. See "Journey into Shame," *Sepia* 12, nos. 4–9 (April to September 1960); and the first edition of *Black Like Me* that followed in 1961. See also Grace Halsell's *Soul Sister*, a report on Halsell's similar infiltration, which took her through some northern states as well. See also Eddie Murphy's wonderful spoof of racial stereotyping, in which he prepares to infiltrate the white community by watching a lot of *Dynasty* and reading Hallmark cards (http://www.youtube.com/watch?v=oXCv_OQw46Q).

2 In practice, white was pure and all other possibilities were collapsed into "coloured" and segregated from the whites. Certainly, white supremacists made no distinctions among them. Donald B. Smith lists thirty-eight blacks lynched in the United States in 1917, the same year that Sylvester Long as Long Lance was hailed as a "Full-Blooded Cherokee ... First Lieutenant of Princess Pat's Crack Canadian Regiment" when he was wounded at Vimy Ridge. Fifty-eight blacks were hanged in 1918. Seventy were lynched in 1919, the year of the "red summer," when twenty-five race riots broke out in American cities. This was the year that Long Lance first left the United States for Canada (Smith, *Long Lance*, 43–44).

3 See Paige Raibmon for the significance of who defines authenticity for "the Indian." She opens her book with the case of the Makah whaling controversy in 1999, when the Makah claimed they were fulfilling their traditional practices in the whale hunt, even while non-Aboriginal communities complained that use of speedboats and 50-calibre rifles could not be understood as traditional practices. "According to prevailing notions of authenticity," Raibmon concludes, "Aboriginal people could not be 'Aboriginal' and 'modern' at the same time. These were mutually exclusive categories" (201). Both Raibmon and Francis describe stereotypes of Native authenticity as trapped in the past.

4 For all their manipulations of public perception, Aboriginal status for Grey Owl and for Chief Buffalo Child Long Lance depended not on such claims as they could make, or such acceptance as they could and did gain in various Native communities, but on governments that quantified and controlled the Native populations of Canada and the United States. Long Lance was in fact exposed not because he had no Cherokee blood in his ancestry but because Chauncey Yellow Robe among others made inquiries at the Bureau of Indian Affairs in Washington (Smith, *Long Lance*, 191). Similarly, Grey Owl was subjected to an investigation at the Department of Indian Affairs in Ottawa, though this was not the actual source of his exposure (Smith, *From the Land of the Shadows*, 1990, 213).

5 As prime minister in 1982, Pierre Elliott Trudeau was responsible for "patriating" the British North America Act in order to create a Canadian-controlled constitution, into which he then inserted the Canadian Charter of Rights and Freedoms.

6 John Diefenbaker was listed as counsel for Yvonne Perrier (Grey Owl's last "wife") and his daughter Shirley Dawn, when Angle [sic] Belaney contested his will on the grounds that she was his first and in fact his only legal wife; she therefore sought one-third of his estate under Section 10 of the Widows' Relief Act. Her claim was disputed on the ground that she may have had a relationship with one Charlie Potts during Grey Owl's extended absence. However, the court found in her favour. P.M. Anderson appended his name to the report, which is dated Regina, 24 November 1939. Perhaps Anderson is therefore the one to take credit for the romantic language on which this court record depends. It notes, for instance, Archibald Belaney's two-year courtship of Angele Eguana: "she taught him her Indian language and schooled him in the quaint lore and beautiful traditions of the Indian race. No doubt this had a marked effect on his future writings … Though his absence was more prolonged as the years passed by, he always found his way back eventually to their home, receiving a welcome from his patient, docile, waiting wife." This document also refers to Grey Owl as "somewhat of a fascinating masquerader … not essentially a charlatan, but with an instinctively histrionic bent and vision." These documents also include various correspondence and photographs that clarify that Archibald Belaney, Archie McNeil, and Grey Owl are all one and the same man. (H.J. Fraser Papers, Saskatoon Office, Saskatchewan Archives Board.)

Notes to Chapter 5

1 See Chapter 3, note 8, for the scandal that attends dishonest journalism.
2 Naim Attallah was the force behind Quartet Books and The Women's Press; chief executive of Asprey's, the luxury store on Bond Street in London; and an ambitious impresario, admired and respected for his major funding of *The Literary Review* and *The Oldie*. He was also known in London literary circles for hiring only beautiful women from eminent social circles.
3 The *Independent*, 12 November 2000, http://findarticles.com/p/articles/mi_qn4158/is_20001112/ai_n14345074.
4 Celia Brayfield, "Emperor's New Clothes." *New Statesman*, 1 November 2004, http://www.newstatesman.com/200411010045.
5 Mezlekia has since published two books: *The God Who Begat a Jackal* (Toronto: Penguin, 2001), and *The Unfortunate Marriage of Azeb Yitades* (Toronto: Penguin, 2006). Both are set in Ethiopia, but neither claims to be autobiographical. *Notes from the Hyena's Belly* was also published by Picador in 2002.
6 The Governor General's Literary Awards were inaugurated in 1937, when the Governor General of Canada, John Buchan, Lord Tweedsmuir—no mean literary figure himself—honoured the best books published in Canada in 1936. A prize of $250 was introduced in 1951, and had risen to $15,000 by 2000. Publishers of winning books also receive $3,000 for promotion.
7 See Jonathan Kay, "Twisted Furor over Schoolboy Essay," *National Post*, 27 January 2001.

8 I owe this wonderful phrase to Robert Douglas-Fairhurst, who uses it of A.E. Housman in the *Times Literary Supplement*, 22 June 2007, 5.

9 Ern Malley was the brainchild of James McAuley and Harold Stewart, who submitted "his" poetry to Max Harris, editor of a modernist magazine called *Angry Penguins* in 1943. The scandal, which lasted for many weeks in the Australian media, and had repercussions throughout the Australian literary world, centred effectively on the inability of a reputable literary critic to distinguish between junk and genius. See Peter Carey, *My Life as a Fake*.

10 A parody of modernism, and modernism's own uses of parody, *Spectra: A Book of Poetic Experiments* was the creation of "Emanuel Morgan" and "Anne Knish" in the United States in 1916. *Spectra* was followed by poems to leading journals and by a manifesto deriding the pretensions of the Imagists, the Vorticists, the Futurists, and so on. Like the creator of Yasusada rather than the creator of Karavis, the Spectrists managed for a couple of years to keep themselves spectral.

11 True to its name, which suggests a shared linguistic, cultural, and commercial ground, and its subtitle, *The Review of Academic Life*, *Lingua Franca* was also the coming-out site for Alan Sokal in 1996, when he published his paper, titled "Transgressing the Boundaries: Towards a Transformative Hermeneutics of Quantum Gravity," in *SocialText*. Sokal used no pseudonym and lost no time at all in explaining that his paper was nonsense and that the editors of *SocialText* had been gullible and foolish.

12 Marjorie Perloff, in an essay that now forms an appendix item in the Roof publication of *Doubled Flowering*, lists seven specific incongruities and anachronisms that ought to have alerted poetry editors if not the reading public. Among these are Yasusada's indebtedness in the 1930s to the poetry of Paul Celan, who did not start publishing until 1952, and then in German, which Yasusada did not read (150–51).

Notes to Chapter 6

1 Elie Wiesel is credited with first using the term "Holocaust" to describe the Nazi genocide of European Jews. He almost immediately regretted doing so because the term connotes sacrifice, suggesting some religious value in this mass slaughter. Unfortunately, the Hebrew term "Shoah," or catastrophe, has never replaced "Holocaust" in general parlance.

2 Jeremy Popkin's work on Holocaust survivors as historians examines their pre-Holocaust history, their treatment of the problematics of Jewish identity, and their sense of themselves, by virtue of their training as historians, as "products of history" (64). He identifies Saul Friedländer as the only one to conclude that history should be done differently (67). For the most part, "the historian-memoirist's first-person narrative is relativized; what it gains in perspective it loses in dramatic force" (68). Referring both to Peter Gay and to Hans Schmitt, Popkin writes that autobiography is "not merely source material for history [but] an alternative way of narrating the past, capable of teaching historians some important lessons" (78). Martin Gilbert's histories are unusual for their reliance on memoirs.

3 Dori Laub tells the story of the woman interviewed for the Yale Archives who vividly recalled four crematorium chimneys going up in flames during the uprising at Auschwitz in the fall of 1944, whereas historians knew that only one had been destroyed (Felman and Laub, *Testimony*, 59–63). See also Kelly Oliver, who builds her theories of subjectivity and identity in part on this situation. See also Martin Gilbert *Never Again*, 126.

4 I have discussed Sylvester Long's problems with essentialist identification in Chapter 4. Elaine K. Ginsberg refers to the *Plessy v. Ferguson* decision in the United States in 1896, in which the Supreme Court "confirmed that a person with one-eighth Negro ancestry could be legally defined as Negro under Louisiana law, even though, as in the case of Plessy, that ancestry was not physically visible" (7). In the case of European Jews as of American Negroes, identity was determined by notions of racial purity that establish difference and preclude assimilation.

5 Barbie's attorney, Jacques Vergès, who later defended Saddam Hussein, has been distinguished for turning defence into attack, ensuring that the criminal issues that have brought the accused to court play out as political issues and are so perceived by the media.

6 Marlene Kadar, in her work on the absence of the Roma from traditional narratives of the Holocaust, which the Roma knew as the *Porrajmos*, or "Devouring," suggests that "traces and fragments must stand in for autobiographical telling." She therefore proposes "the fragment and trace as member-genres in the taxonomy of auto/biographical practices" (223). Into this category fall the fragments of *Muselman* testimony with which Agamben ends his work, giving them the last voice, or of men like Zelman Lewenthal, whom Agamben also cites, a member of the Sonderkommando, who buried a few sheets of paper under crematorium III at Auschwitz. In Yiddish, Lewenthal writes: "Just as the events that took place there cannot be imagined by any human being, so is it unimaginable that anyone could exactly recount how our experiences took place … We, the small group of obscure people who will not give historians much work to do" (12). Philip Müller also refers to contemporaries writing and hiding their fragments of testimony.

7 The many, many hours of audio-visual recordings of individual interviews with survivors that are extant in various Holocaust archives contradict my present findings, which are based on historical, legal, and faulty autobiographical texts. Thanks to David Boder, Shia Moser, and the psychologists who followed them, and to the men and women who have done their best honestly to record their experience, we do in fact have access to personal stories. This note serves as a reminder that I am describing a problem rather than any kind of absolute fact. For David Boder's work, see http://voices.iit.edu/about.html. For Shia Moser, see http://www.virtualmuseum.ca/Exhibitions/orphans/english/themes/pdf.

8 Robert Krell notes that children who survived did not think of themselves as a special category of survivors. Only in the early 1980s did they begin to organize a federation for mutual support. Whereas the original Polish version of *The Children Accuse* was published by the Jewish Historical Commission in Cracow in 1946 (see Hochberg-

Marianska and Grüss), the rush of literature by and about children from the 1990s supports Krell's observation. This delayed outpouring and collecting of children's narratives is hardly surprising, given that the children who suffered are now elderly men and women who value the contributions they can make to this history.

9 Private conversation in Vancouver, 11 April 2007.

Works Cited

Abbott, H. Porter. "Autobiography, Autography, Fiction: Groundwork for a Taxonomy of Textual Categories." *New Literary History* 19 (1988): 597–615.

Adams, Timothy Dow. *Telling Lies in Modern American Autobiography.* Chapel Hill: University of North Carolina Press, 1990.

——— . "The Mock-Biography of Edwin Mullhouse." *Biography* 5 (1982): 205–14.

Adorno, Theodor W. *Notes to Literature.* Edited by Rolf Tiedeman. Translated by Sherry Weber Nicholsen. New York: Columbia University Press, [1998] 1999.

Agamben, Giorgio. *Remnants of Auschwitz: The Witness and the Archive.* Translated by Daniel Heller-Roazen. New York: Zone Books, 1999.

Anahereo. *Devil in Deerskins: My Life with Grey Owl.* Toronto: New Press, 1972.

Arendt, Hanna. *Eichmann in Jerusalem: A Report on the Banality of Evil.* Revised and enlarged ed. New York: Penguin Books, [1963] 1992.

Atwood, Margaret. "The Grey Owl Syndrome." In *Strange Things: The Malevolent North in Canadian Literature.* Oxford: Clarendon Press, 1995. 35–61.

Ben-Gurion, David. *Israel: A Personal History.* Translated by Nechemia Meyers and Uzy Nystar. London: New English Library, 1972.

Benjamin, Walter. "The Work of Art in the Age of Mechanical Reproduction." In *Illuminations.* Edited by Hannah Arendt. Translated by Harry Zon. New York: Schocken Books, 1969. 217–51.

Berton, Pierre. *Hollywood's Canada: The Americanization of Our National Image.* Toronto: McClelland and Stewart, 1975.

Billinghurst, Jane. *Grey Owl: The Many Faces of Archie Belaney.* Vancouver: Greystone Books, 1999.

Blaise, Clark, and Bharati Mukherjee. *Days and Nights in Calcutta.* St. Paul: Hungry Mind Press, 1995.

Boese, Alex. *The Museum of Hoaxes.* New York: Dutton, 2002.

Bonazzi, Robert. *Man in the Mirror: John Howard Griffin and the Story of* Black Like Me. Maryknoll: Orbis Books, 1997.

Booth, Wayne C. *The Company We Keep: An Ethics of Fiction.* University of California Press, 1988.

Borges, Jorge Luis. "Pierre Menard, Author of Don Quixote." Translated by Anthony Bonner. In *Ficciones.* New York: Alfred A. Knopf, [1962] 1993. 29–38.

Bowers, Neal. *Words for the Taking: The Hunt for a Plagiarist.* New York: W.W. Norton, 1997.

Boyle, Leonard E. "Diplomatics." In *Medieval Studies: An Introduction.* Edited by James M. Powell. Syracuse: Syracuse University Press, 1992. 82–113.

Braz, Albert. "The Modern Hiawatha: Grey Owl's Construction of His Aboriginal Self." In *Auto/biography in Canada: Critical Directions.* Edited by Julie Rak. Waterloo: Wilfrid Laurier University Press, 2005. 53–68.

——. "The White Indian: Armand Garnet Ruffo's Grey Owl and the Spectre of Authenticity." *Journal of Canadian Studies / Revue d'études canadiennes* 36, no. 4 (Winter 2002): 171–87.

Britzman, Deborah P. *Lost Subjects, Contested Objects: Toward a Psychoanalytic Inquiry of Learning.* Albany: SUNY Press, 1998.

Browder, Laura. *Slippery Characters: Ethnic Impersonators and American Identities.* Chapel Hill: University of North Carolina Press, 2000.

Bruss, Elizabeth. "Eye for I: Making and Unmaking Autobiography in Film." In *Autobiography: Essays Theoretical and Critical.* Edited by James Olney. Princeton: Princeton University Press, 1980. 296–320.

——. *Autobiographical Acts: The Changing Situation of a Literary Genre.* Baltimore: Johns Hopkins University Press, 1976.

Burke, Peter. "The Sense of Anachronism from Petrarch to Poussin." In *Time in the Medieval World.* Edited by Chris Humphrey and W.M. Ormrod. York: York Medieval Press with Boydell and Brewer, 2001. 157–73.

Burr, Anna Robeson. *The Autobiography: A Critical and Comparative Study.* New York: Houghton Mifflin, 1909.

Butler, Sandra, and Barbara Rosenblum. *Cancer in Two Voices.* 2nd ed. Duluth: Spinsters Ink, 1996.

Callaghan, Dympna. "The Vicar and Virago: Feminism and the Problem of Identity." In *Who Can Speak? Authority and Critical Identity.* Edited by Judith Roof and Robyn Wiegman. Urbana: University of Illinois Press, 1995. 195–207.

Cantwell, R. "Grey Owl: Mysterious Genius of Nature Lore." *Sports Illustrated,* April 8, 1963.

Carey, Peter. *My Life as a Fake.* New York: Alfred A. Knopf, 2003.

Carr, Emily. *Klee Wyck.* Toronto: Oxford University Press, 1942.

Carretta, Vincent. *Equiano, the African: Biography of a Self Made Man.* Athens: University of Georgia Press, 2005.

———, ed. *Olaudah Equiano: The Interesting Narrative and Other Writings.* Harmondsworth: Penguin, 2003.

Carter, Dan T. "The Transformation of a Klansman." Letter. *New York Times,* October 4, 1991, A31.

Chartier, Roger. *The Order of Books: Readers, Authors, and Libraries in Europe between the Fourteenth and Eighteenth Centuries.* Translated by Lydia G. Cochrane. Stanford: Stanford University Press, 1994.

Clanchy, M.T. *From Memory to Written Record: England 1066–1307.* Oxford: Blackwell, [1979] 1993.

Clark, Elizabeth A. *History, Theory, Text: Historians and the Linguistic Turn.* Cambridge, MA: Harvard University Press, 2004.

Cohen, Boaz. "The Children's Voice: Postwar Collection of Testimonies from Child Survivors of the Holocaust." *Holocaust and Genocide Studies* 21, no. 1 (Spring 2007): 73–95.

Constable, Giles. "A Living Past: The Historical Environment of the Middle Ages." *Harvard Library Bulletin* 1, no. 3 (Fall 1990): 49–70.

Coullie, Judith Lütge, et al., eds. *Selves in Question: Interviews on Southern African Autobiography.* Honolulu: University of Hawai'i Press, 2006.

Couser, G. Thomas. *Altered Egos: Authority in American Autobiography.* New York: Oxford University Press, 1989.

———. "Disability as Metaphor: What's Wrong with Lying." *Prose Studies,* special double issue on disability, 27, nos. 1–2 (April–August 2005): 141–54.

———. *Vulnerable Subjects: Ethics and Life Writing.* Ithaca: Cornell University Press, 2004.

———. "Making, Taking, and Faking Lives: Ethical Problems in Collaborative Life Writing." In *Mapping the Ethical Turn: A Reader in Ethics, Culture, and Literary Theory.* Edited by Todd E. Davis and Kenneth Womack. Charlottesville: University Press of Virginia, 2001. 209–226.

D'Amico, John F. *Theory and Practice in Renaissance Textual Criticism: Beatus Rhenanus between Conjecture and History.* Berkeley: University of California Press, 1988.

Davis, Natalie Zemon. *The Return of Martin Guerre.* Cambridge, MA: Harvard University Press, 1983.

Davis, Rocio G. *Begin Here: Reading Asian North American Autobiographies of Childhood.* Honolulu: University of Hawai'i Press, 2007.

Dawson, Carrie. "Never Cry Fraud: Remembering Grey Owl, Rethinking Imposture." *Essays on Canadian Writing* 65 (1998): 120–40.

Death Books from Auschwitz: Remnants. 3 vols. Edited by the State Museum of Auschwitz-Birkenau. Translated by Michael Jacobs, Georg Mayer, Jacek Plesnĭarowicz. Munich and New Providence: K.G. Saur, 1995.

Defonseca, Misha. *Misha: A Mémoire of the Holocaust Years*. Bluebell, MA: Mt. Ivy Press, 1997.

Deloria, Philip J. *Playing Indian*. New Haven: Yale University Press, 1998.

De Man, Paul. "Autobiography as De-defacement." *Modern Language Notes* 94–5 (1979): 919–30.

Dickson, Lovat. *Wilderness Man: The Strange Story of Grey Owl*. Toronto: Macmillan of Canada, 1973.

——, ed. *The Green Leaf: A Tribute to Grey Owl*. London: Lovat Dickson, 1938.

Downing, Ben. "The Phantom Fisherman." *Lingua Franca: The Review of Academic Life* 11, no. 2 (March 2001): 8–10.

Dwork, Debórah. *Children with a Star: Jewish Youth in Nazi Europe*. New Haven: Yale University Press, 1991.

Eakin, Paul John. "Breaking Rules: The Consequences of Self-Narration." *Biography* 24, no. 1 (Winter 2001): 113–27.

——, ed. *The Ethics of Life Writing*. Ithaca: Cornell University Press, 2004.

——. *How Our Lives Become Stories*. Ithaca: Cornell University Press, 1999.

Egan, Susanna. *Mirror Talk: Genres of Crisis in Contemporary Autobiography*. Chapel Hill: University of North Carolina Press, 1999.

——. *Patterns of Experience in Autobiography*. Chapel Hill: University of North Carolina Press, 1984.

Equiano, Olaudah. *The Interesting Narrative of the Life of Olaudah Equiano, or Gustavus Vassa, the African, Written by Himself*. Edited by Robert J. Allison. Boston: Bedford/St. Martin's, [1789] 2007.

Erdal, Jennie. *Ghosting: A Memoir*. Toronto: Doubleday Canada, 2004.

Felman, Shoshana. *The Juridical Unconscious: Trials and Traumas in the Twentieth Century*. Cambridge, MA: Harvard University Press, 2002.

Felman, Shoshana, and Dori Laub. *Testimony: Crises of Witnessing in Literature, Psychoanalysis, and History*. New York: Routledge, 1992.

Ferguson, Robert A. "The Judicial Opinion as Literary Genre." *Yale Journal of Law and the Humanities* 2 (1990): 201–19.

Foucault, Michel. "What Is an Author?" In *Language, Counter-Memory, Practice: Selected Essays and Interviews*. Edited by Donald F. Bouchard. Translated by Donald F. Bouchard and Sherry Simon. Ithaca: Cornell University Press, 1977. 113–38.

Francis, Daniel. *The Imaginary Indian: The Image of the Indian in Canadian Culture*. Vancouver: Arsenal Pulp Press, 1992.

Freadman, Richard. *The Threads of Life: Autobiography and the Will*. Chicago: University of Chicago Press, 2001.

Freind, Bill. "Deferral of the Author: Impossible Witness and the Yasusada Poems." *Poetics Today* 25, no. 1 (Spring 2004): 137–58.

———. "Hoaxes and Heteronymity: An Interview with Kent Johnson." http://www .litvert.com/KJ_Interview.html.

Freiwald, Bina Toledo. "Gender, Nation, and Self-Narration: Three Generations of Dayan Women in Palestine/Israel." In *Tracing the Autobiographical.* Edited by Marlene Kadar, Linda Warley, Jeanne Perreault, and Susanna Egan. Waterloo: Wilfrid Laurier University Press, 2005. 165–88.

———. "Nation and Self-Narration: A View from Québec/Quebec." *Canadian Literature* 172 (Spring 2002): 17–38.

Frey, James. *A Million Little Pieces.* New York: Doubleday, 2003; Random House, 2004.

Friedländer, Saul. "Afterword: The Shoah between Memory and History." In *Breaking Crystal: Writing and Memory after Auschwitz.* Edited by Efraim Sicher. Chicago: University of Illinois Press, 1998. 345–57.

Funkenstein, Amos. "Collective Memory and Historical Consciousness." *History and Memory* 1, no. 1 (1989): 5–26.

Gates, Henry Louis Jr. "'Authenticity,' or the Lesson of Little Tree." *New York Times Book Review,* November 24, 1991, 26.

———, ed. *The Classic Slave Narratives.* New York: Signet, 2002.

Gilbert of Nogent. *Medieval Sourcebook: Autobiography.* http://www.fordham.edu/ halsall/basis.guibert-vita.html#bk1ch9.

Gilbert, Martin. *Never Again: A History of the Holocaust.* London: HarperCollins, 2000.

Gill, W.A. "The Nude in Autobiography." *Atlantic Monthly* 99 (1907): 71–79.

Gilmore, Leigh. *Autobiographics: A Feminist Theory of Women's Self-Representation.* Ithaca: Cornell University Press, 1994.

———. *The Limits of Autobiography: Trauma and Testimony.* Ithaca: Cornell University Press, 2001.

Ginsberg, Elaine K., ed. *Passing and the Fictions of Identity.* Durham: Duke University Press, 1996.

Ginzburg, Carlo. *History, Rhetoric, and Proof.* Lebanon: University Press of New England, 1999.

Glassner, Martin Ira, and Robert Krell, eds. *And Life Is Changed Forever: Holocaust Childhoods Remembered.* Detroit: Wayne State University Press, 2006.

Goldschmidt, E.P. *Medieval Texts and Their First Appearance in Print.* London: Bibliographical Society at the University Press, Oxford, 1943.

Gombrich, E.H. *The Story of Art.* London: Phaidon, [1950] 1972.

Gourevitch, Philip. "The Memory Thief." *The New Yorker,* June 14, 1999. 48–68.

Grafton, Anthony. *The Footnote: A Curious History.* Cambridge, MA: Harvard University Press, 1999.

———. *Forgers and Critics: Creativity and Duplicity in Western Scholarship.* Princeton: Princeton University Press, 1990.

Grey Owl. *Men of the Last Frontier.* Toronto: Macmillan, 1932.

———. *Pilgrims of the Wild.* London: Lovat Dickson and Thompson, 1935.

———. *Tales of an Empty Cabin.* London: Lovat Dickson, 1936.

Griffin, John Howard. *Black Like Me.* Boston: Houghton Mifflin, 1961.

Groom, Nick. *The Forger's Shadow: How Forgery Changed the Course of Literature.* London: Picador, 2002.

Gusdorf, Georges. "Conditions and Limits of Autobiography" [1956]. In *Autobiography: Essays Theoretical and Critical.* Edited by James Olney. Princeton: Princeton University Press, 1980. 28–48.

Halsell, Grace. *Soul Sister.* Washington: Crossroads International Publishing, 1999.

Hamilton, Geoff. "Mixing Memoir and Desire: James Frey, Wound Culture, and the 'Essential American Soul.'" *Journal of American Culture* 30, no. 3 (September 2007): 324–33.

Harris, Mark Jonathan, and Deborah Oppenheimer. *Into the Arms of Strangers: Stories of the Kindertransport.* London: Bloomsbury, 2000.

Harris, Robert. *Selling Hitler: The Story of the Hitler Diaries.* London: Faber and Faber, 1986.

Hart, Francis R. "Notes for an Anatomy of Modern Autobiography." *New Literary History* 1, no. 3 (1970): 485–511.

Hiatt, Alfred. *The Making of Medieval Forgeries: False Documents in Fifteenth-Century England.* London/Toronto: British Library/University of Toronto Press, 2004.

Hilberg, Raul. *The Destruction of the European Jews.* New Haven: Yale University Press, [1961] 2003.

———. *The Politics of Memory: The Journey of a Holocaust Historian.* Chicago: Ivan R. Dee, 1996.

Hochberg-Marianska, Maria, and Noe Grüss, eds. *The Children Accuse.* Translated by Bill Johnston. London: Vallentine Mitchell, 1996.

Howard, Jennifer. "Unraveling the Narrative." *Chronicle of Higher Education* 52, no. 3 (2005): A11.

Howarth, William L. "Some Principles of Autobiography." *New Literary History* 5, no. 2 (1974): 363–81.

Huhndorf, Shari M. *Going Native: Indians in the American Cultural Imagination.* Ithaca: Cornell University Press, 2001.

Hulley, Karl Kelchner. "Principles of Textual Criticism Known to St. Jerome." *Harvard Studies in Classical Philology* 55 (1944): 87–109.

Irmscher, Christopher. "Nature Writing." In *The Cambridge Companion to Canadian Literature.* Edited by Eva-Marie Kröller. Cambridge: Cambridge University Press, 2004. 94–114.

Johnson, Kent, with Jack Spicer and Mikhail Epstein. *Doubled Flowering: From the Notebooks of Araki Yasusada.* Edited and translated by Tosa Motokiyu, Ojiu Norinaga, and Okura Kyojin. New York: Roof Books, 1997.

Kadar, Marlene. "The Devouring: Traces of Roma in the Holocaust: No Tattoo, Sterilized Body, Gypsy Girl." In *Tracing the Autobiographical.* Edited by Marlene Kadar, Linda Warley, Jeanne Perreault, and Susanna Egan. Waterloo: Wilfrid Laurier University Press, 2005. 223–46.

Kahn, Leon. *No Time to Mourn: The True Story of a Jewish Partisan Fighter.* Vancouver: Ronsdale Press and Vancouver Holocaust Education Centre, [1978] 2004. 5–38.

Kaplan, Caren. "Resisting Autobiography: Out-Law Genres and Transnational Feminist Subjects." In *De-Colonizing the Subject: The Politics of Gender in Women's Autobiography.* Edited by Sidonie Smith and Julia Watson. Minneapolis: University of Minnesota Press, 1992. 115–38.

Kaplan, Chaim. *Scroll of Agony: The Warsaw Diary of Chaim A. Kaplan.* Edited and translated by Abraham A. Katsh. New York: Macmillan, 1965.

Keith, W.J. "David Solway's Islands." *Antigonish Review* 138 (Summer 2004): 125–37.

———. "'A Prosodic Itch': Notes on David Solway's Development as a Poet." In *David Solway: Essays on His Works.* Edited by Carmine Starnino. Toronto: Guernica Editions, 2001. 39–68.

Kelley, Donald R. *Foundations of Modern Historical Scholarship: Language, Law, and History in the French Renaissance.* New York: Columbia University Press, 1970.

Kenner, Hugh. *The Counterfeiters: An Historical Comedy.* Baltimore: Johns Hopkins University Press, 1985.

Kernan, Alvin. *Samuel Johnson and the Impact of Print.* Princeton: Princeton University Press, [1987] 1989.

Klinkowitz, Jerome. "Betrayed by Jerzy Kosinski." In *Critical Essays on Jerzy Kosinski.* Edited by Barbara Tepa Lupack. New York: G.K. Hall, 1998. 194–207.

———. "Jerzy Kosinski: An Interview." In *Conversations with Jerzy Kosinski.* Edited by Tom Teichol. Jackson: University Press of Mississippi, 1993. 37–59.

Kortenaar, Neil ten. "Nega Mezlekia Outside the Hyena's Belly." *Canadian Literature* 172 (Spring 2002): 41–68.

Kosinski, Jerzy. *The Painted Bird.* 2nd ed. Boston: Houghton Mifflin, [1965] 1976.

———. *Notes of the Author on "The Painted Bird."* New York: Scientia-Factum, 1965.

Krell, Robert. "Psychological Reverberations of the Holocaust in the Lives of Child Survivors." Monna and Otto Weinmann Lecture Series, United States Holocaust Memorial Museum, Washington, 5 June 1997.

———, ed. *Messages and Memories: Reflections on Child Survivors of the Holocaust.* 2nd ed. Vancouver: Memory Press, 2001.

Kuper, Jack. *Child of the Holocaust.* Toronto: General, 1967.

——. "Who Was Jerzy Kosinski?" Kuper Productions Ltd., in association with Vision TV, 1995.

LaCapra, Dominick. *History and Criticism*. Ithaca: Cornell University Press, 1985.

——. *History and Memory After Auschwitz*. Ithaca: Cornell University Press, 1998.

——. *History in Transit: Experience, Identity, Critical Theory*. Ithaca: Cornell University Press, 2004.

——. *Writing History, Writing Trauma*. Baltimore: Johns Hopkins University Press, 2001.

——. "Revisiting the Historians' Debate." *History and Memory* 9, no. 1 (1997): 80–112.

Langer, Lawrence L. *The Holocaust and the Literary Imagination*. New Haven: Yale University Press, 1975.

Lappin, Elena. "The Man with Two Heads." *Granta* 66 (Summer 1999): 7–65.

Laub, Dori. "An Event Without a Witness: Truth, Testimony, and Survival." In *Testimony: Crises of Witnessing in Literature, Psychoanalysis, and History*. Edited by Shoshana Felman and Dori Laub. New York: Routledge, 1992. 75–92.

——. "Sparkling Jewels in a Sea of Terror." In *And Life Is Changed Forever*. Edited by Martin Ira Glassner and Robert Krell. Detroit: Wayne State University Press, 2006. 45–57.

Lawrence, Bonita. *"Real" Indians and Others; Mixed-Blood Urban Native Peoples and Indigenous Nationhood*. Vancouver: UBC Press, 2004.

Lejeune, Philippe. *On Autobiography*. Edited by Paul John Eakin. Translated by Katherine Leary. Minneapolis: University of Minnesota Press, 1989.

Levi, Primo. *If This Is a Man*. Translated by Stuart Woolf. London: Abacus, 1979.

Lupack, Barbara Tepa, ed. *Critical Essays on Jerzy Kosinski*. New York: G.K. Hall, 1998.

Lynch, Jack. *Deception and Detection in Eighteenth-Century Britain*. Aldershot: Ashgate, 2008.

Mallon, Thomas. *Stolen Words: Forays into the Origins and Ravages of Plagiarism*. New York: Ticknor and Fields, 1989.

Mandell, Barrett J. "Full of Life Now." In *Autobiography: Essays Theoretical and Critical*. Edited by James Olney. Princeton: Princeton University Press, 1980. 49–72.

Manne, Robert. *The Culture of Forgetting: Helen Demidenko and the Holocaust*. Melbourne: Text, 1996.

Marcus, Laura. *Auto/biographical Discourses: Theory, Criticism, Practice*. Manchester: Manchester University Press, 1994.

Marrus, Michael R. *The Nuremberg War Crimes Trial 1945–46: A Documentary History*. Boston: Bedford Books, 1997.

Mason, Mary. "The Other Voice: Autobiographies of Women Writers." In *Autobiography: Essays Theoretical and Critical*. Edited by James Olney. Princeton: Princeton University Press, 1980. 207–35.

McCourt, Frank. *Angela's Ashes: A Memoir.* New York: Scribner, 1996.

Meltzer, Françoise. *Hot Property: The Stakes and Claims of Literary Originality.* Chicago: University of Chicago Press, 1994.

Menchú, Rigoberta. *I, Rigoberta Menchú: An Indian Woman in Guatemala.* Edited by Elisabeth Burgos-Debray. Translated by Ann Wright. London: Verso, 1984.

Mezlekia, Nega. *Notes from the Hyena's Belly: Memories of My Ethiopian Boyhood.* Toronto: Penguin, 2000.

Misch, Georg. *A History of Autobiography in Antiquity.* Translated by E.W. Dickes. 2 vols. Westport: Greenwood Press, [1950] 1973.

Mitcham, Allison. *Grey Owl's Favourite Wilderness Revisited: Drawings and Photographs by Peter Mitcham.* Manotick: Penumbra Press, 1991.

Momaday, N. Scott. "The Man Made of Words." In *Indian Voices: The First Convocation of American Indian Scholars.* San Francisco: Indian Historian Press, 1970.

Morton, A.Q. *Literary Detection: How to Prove Authorship and Fraud in Literature and Documents.* New York: Scribner, 1978.

Mota, Miguel. "What's in a Name? The Case of Jeanettewinterson.Com." *Twentieth Century Literature* 50 (2004): 192–206.

Müller, Filip. *Eyewitness Auschwitz: Three Years in the Gas Chambers.* Chicago: Ivan R. Dee with the U.S. Holocaust Memorial Museum, 1975.

Nelson, J.L. "Dispute Settlement in Carolingian West Francia." In *The Settlement of Disputes in Early Medieval Europe.* Edited by W. Davies and P. Fouracre. Cambridge: Cambridge University Press, 1986. 57–58.

Neuman, Shirley. "The Observer Observed: Distancing the Self in Autobiography." *Prose Studies* 4 (1981): 317–36.

Nolan, Maggie, and Carrie Dawson, eds. *Who's Who? Hoaxes, Imposture, and Identity Crises in Australian Literature.* Special issue of *Australian Literary Studies* 21, no. 4 (2004).

Nussbaum, Emily. "Turning Japanese: The Hiroshima Poetry Hoax." *Lingua Franca: The Review of Academic Life* 6, no. 7 (November 1996): 82–84.

Nussbaum, Felicity A. *The Autobiographical Subject: Gender and Ideology in Eighteenth-Century England.* Baltimore: Johns Hopkins University Press, 1989.

——— . *The Limits of the Human: Fictions of Anomaly, Race, and Gender in the Long Eighteenth Century.* Cambridge: Cambridge University Press, 2003.

Oliver, Kelly. "Witnessing and Testimony." Parallax: A Journal of Metadiscursive Theory and Cultural Practices 10, no. 1 (2004): 79–88.

——— . *Witnessing: Beyond Recognition.* Minneapolis: University of Minnesota Press, 2001.

Olney, James. "Autobiography and the Cultural Moment: A Thematic, Historical, and Bibliographic Introduction." In *Autobiography: Essays Theoretical and Critical.* Edited by James Olney. Princeton: Princeton University Press, 1980. 3–27.

—— . *Metaphors of Self: The Meaning of Autobiography.* Princeton: Princeton University Press, 1972.

Paris, Erna. *Unhealed Wounds: France and the Klaus Barbie Affair.* Toronto: Methuen, 1985.

Parker, David. *The Self in Moral Space: Life Narrative and the Good.* Ithaca: Cornell University Press, 2007.

Pascal, Roy. *Design and Truth in Autobiography.* Cambridge, MA: Harvard University Press, 1960.

Perelman, Chaim. "'The New Rhetoric': A Theory of Practical Reasoning." In *The Rhetorical Tradition.* Edited by P. Bizzell and B. Herzberg. 2nd ed. New York: Bedford/St. Martin's, 2002. 1384–409.

Perloff, Marjorie. "In Search of the Authentic Other: The Poetry of Araki Yasusada." In *Doubled Flowering: From the Notebooks of Araki Yasusada.* Edited and translated by Tosa Motokiyu, Ojiu Norinaga, and Okura Kyojin. New York: Roof Books, 1997. 148–68.

Picard, Barbara Leonie. "Little Lady Margaret." In *The Mermaid and the Simpleton.* London: Oxford University Press, 1949. 71–83.

Polk, James. *Wilderness Writers.* Toronto and Vancouver: Clarke, Irwin, 1972.

Popkin, Jeremy D. "Holocaust Memories, Historians' Memoirs: First-Person Narrative and the Memoir of the Holocaust." *History and Memory* 9, no. 1 (1997): 49–84.

Raab, Elisabeth M. *And Peace Never Came.* Waterloo: Wilfrid Laurier University Press, 1997.

Rae, Ian. "Anne Carson and the Solway Hoaxes." *Canadian Literature* 176 (Spring 2003): 45–65.

Raibmon, Paige. *Authentic Indians: Episodes of Encounter from the Late Nineteenth-Century Northwest Coast.* Durham: Duke University Press, 2005.

Randall, Marilyn. *Pragmatic Plagiarism: Authorship, Profit, and Power.* Toronto: University of Toronto Press, 2001.

Ringelblum, Emmanuel. *Notes from the Warsaw Ghetto.* Edited and translated by Jacob Sloan. New York: Schocken Books, 1974.

Roskies, David G. *The Jewish Search for a Usable Past.* Bloomington: Indiana University Press, 1999.

Rubenstein, Jay. "Biography and Autobiography in the Middle Ages." In *Writing Medieval History.* Edited by Nancy Partner. London: Hodder Arnold, 2005. 22–41.

Ruffo, Armand Garnet. *Grey Owl: The Mystery of Archie Belaney.* Regina: Coteau Books, 1996.

Rugg, Linda Haverty. "'Carefully I Touched the Faces of My Parents': Bergman's Autobiographical Image." *Biography* 24, no. 1 (Winter 2001: 72–84.

Schaffer, Kay, and Sidonie Smith. *Human Rights and Narrated Lives: The Ethics of Recognition.* New York: Palgrave Macmillan, 2004.

Schwarz, Daniel R. *Imagining the Holocaust.* New York: St. Martin's Press, 1999.

Shapiro, Stephen A. "The Dark Continent of Literature: Autobiography." *Comparative Literature Studies* 5, no. 4 (1968): 421–54.

Sicher, Ephriam, ed. *Breaking Crystal: Writing and Memory after Auschwitz.* Urbana: University of Illinois Press, 1998.

Siedlecka, Joanna. *Czarny ptasior.* Gdańsk-Warszawa: Wydawn, 1994.

Skarstedt, Sonja A. "Interview with David Solway." In *David Solway: Essays on His Works.* Edited by Carmine Starnino. Toronto: Guernica Editions, 2001. 16–38.

Sliwowska, Wiktoria, ed. *The Last Eyewitnesses: Children of the Holocaust Speak.* Translated by Fay and Julian Bussgang. Chicago: Northwestern University Press, 1998.

Sloan, James Park. *Jerzy Kosinski.* New York: Dutton, 1996.

——— . "Kosinski's War." In *Critical Essays on Jerzy Kosinski.* Edited by Barbara Tepa Lupack. New York: G.K. Hall, 1998. 236-46. Reprinted from *The New Yorker,* October 10, 1994.

Slotkin, Richard. *Regeneration through Violence: The Mythology of the American Frontier, 1600–1860.* Norman: University of Oklahoma Press, 1973.

Smith, Donald B. *From the Land of Shadows: The Making of Grey Owl.* Saskatoon: Western Producer Prairie Books, 1990.

——— . *Long Lance: The True Story of an Impostor.* Toronto: Macmillan of Canada, 1982.

Smith, Sidonie, and Julia Watson. *Reading Autobiography: A Guide for Interpreting Life Narratives.* Minneapolis: University of Minnesota Press, 2001.

——— . "The Rumpled Bed of Autobiography: Extravagant Lives, Extravagant Questions." *Biography* 24, no. 1 (Winter 2001): 1–14.

——— . "The Trouble with Autobiography: Cautionary Notes for Narrative Theorists." In *A Companion to Narrative Theory.* Edited by James Phelan and Peter J. Rabinowitz. Oxford: Blackwell, 2005.

Solovitch, Sara. "The American Dream." *Esquire,* January 2005, 88–93, 114–18.

Solway, David. *An Andreas Karavis Companion.* Montreal: Véhicule Press, 2000.

——— . *Bedrock.* Montreal: Véhicule Press, 1993.

——— . *The Pallikari of Nesmine Rifat.* Fredericton: Goose Lane Editions, 2004.

——— . "The Pursuit of Absence, or Culling and Dereading." *Antigonish Review* 77–78 (Spring–Summer 1989): 57–67.

——— . *Saracen Island: The Poems of Andreas Karavis.* Montreal: Véhicule Press, 2000.

Sontag, Susan. "Cases of the Comrades: Why Victor Serge Should Be as Famous as Koestler and Orwell." *Times Literary Supplement,* April 9, 2004. 12–15.

Spacks, Patricia Meyer. *Imagining a Self: Autobiography and Novel in Eighteenth-Century England.* Cambridge, MA: Harvard University Press, 1976.

Spalding, J.M. "Interview." *Cortland Review* 5 (November 1998). http://www
.cortlandreview.com/issuefive/interview5.htm

Starnino, Carmine, ed. *David Solway: Essays on His Works.* Toronto: Guernica
Editions, 2001.

———. "Interview with David Solway." In *David Solway: Essays on His Works.* Edited
by Carmine Starnino. Toronto: Guernica Editions, 2001. 148–56.

Starobinski, Jean. "The Style of Autobiography" [1971]. In *Autobiography: Essays
Theoretical and Critical.* Edited by James Olney. Princeton: Princeton University
Press, 1980. 73–83.

Steinberg, Paul. *Speak You Also: A Survivor's Reckoning.* Translated by Linda
Coverdale with Bill Ford. New York: Henry Holt, [1996] 2000.

Stelzig, Eugene L. *The Romantic Subject in Autobiography: Rousseau and Goethe.*
Charlottesville: University Press of Virginia, 2000.

Stern, J.P. *Hitler: The Führer and the People.* Brighton: Harvester Press, 1975.

Stewart, Susan. *Crimes of Writing: Problems in the Containment of Representation.*
Oxford: Oxford University Press, 1991.

Stier, Oren Baruch. *Committed to Memory: Cultural Mediations of the Holocaust.*
Amherst: University of Massachussetts Press, 2003.

Stillinger, Jack. *Multiple Authorship and the Myth of Solitary Genius.* New York:
Oxford University Press, 1991.

Stoll, David. *Rigoberta Menchú and the Story of All Poor Guatemalans.* Boulder:
Westview Press, 1998.

Stone, Albert E. "Modern American Autobiography: Texts and Transactions." In
American Autobiography: Retrospect and Prospect. Edited by Paul John Eakin.
Madison: University of Wisconsin Press, 1991. 95–120.

Sturrock, John. "The New Model Autobiographer." *New Literary History* 9, no. 1
(1977): 51–63.

Swiderski, Richard M. *The False Formosan: George Psalmanazar and the
Eighteenth-Century Experiment of Identity.* San Francisco: Mellen Research
University Press, 1991.

Taylor, Drew Hayden. "James Owl or Grey Bond." In *Further Adventures of a Blue-
Eyed Ojibway: Funny, You Don't Look Like One.* Penticton: Theytus Books,
1999. 119–21.

Taylor, Telford. *The Anatomy of the Nuremberg Trials: A Personal Memoir.* New York:
Alfred A. Knopf, 1992.

Treadwell, James. *Autobiographical Writing and British Literature, 1783–1834.*
Oxford: Oxford University Press, 2005.

Trevor-Roper, Hugh. "Nazi Bureaucrats and Jewish Leaders." *Commentary* 33, no. 4
(April 1962): 351–56.

Van Toorn, Penny. "Aboriginal Writing." In *The Cambridge Companion to Canadian Literature*. Edited by Eva-Marie Kröller. Cambridge: Cambridge University Press, 2004. 22–48.

Vessey, Mark. *Latin Christian Writers in Late Antiquity and Their Texts*. Aldershot: Ashgate, 2005.

Vice, Sue. *Holocaust Fiction*. London: Routledge, 2000.

Weales, Gerald. "Jerzy Kosinski: The Painted Bird and Other Disguises." In *Critical Essays on Jerzy Kosinski*. Edited by Barbara Tepa Lupack. New York: G.K. Hall, 1998. 142–52.

Weisberg, Richard. "Legal Rhetoric Under Stress: The Example of Vichy." *Cardoza Law Review* 12 (1991): 1371–415.

White, Hayden. *The Content of the Form: Narrative Discourse and Historical Representation*. Baltimore: Johns Hopkins University Press, 1987.

——. *Figural Realism: Studies in the Mimesis Effect*. Baltimore: Johns Hopkins University Press, 1999.

——. *Metahistory: The Historical Imagination in Nineteenth-Century Europe*. Baltimore: Johns Hopkins University Press, 1973.

Whitlock, Gillian. "Autographics: The Seeing 'I' of the Comics." *Modern Fiction Studies* 52, no. 4 (Winter 2006): 956–79.

——. *Soft Weapons: Autobiography in Transit*. Chicago: University of Chicago Press, 2007.

Wierzbicka, Anna. *English: Meaning and Culture*. Oxford: Oxford University Press, 2006.

Wiesel, Elie. "The Painted Bird: Everybody's Victim." In *Critical Essays on Jerzy Kosinski*. Edited by Barbara Tepa Lupack. New York: G.K. Hall, [1965] 1998.

Wilkomirski, Binjamin. *Fragments: Memories of a Wartime Childhood*. Translated by Carol Brown Janeway. New York: Schocken Books, 1996.

Wimsatt, W.K., and Monroe Beardsley. *The Verbal Icon: Studies in the Meaning of Poetry*. Lexington: University of Kentucky Press, 1954.

Wootton, David. "Lucien Febvre and the Problem of Unbelief in the Early Modern Period." *Journal of Modern History* 60, no. 4 (1988): 695–730.

Wyschogrod, Edith. *An Ethics of Remembering: History, Heterology, and the Nameless Others*. Chicago: University of Chicago Press, 1998.

Yamamoto, Traise. *Masking Selves, Making Subjects: Japanese Women, Identity, and the Body*. Berkeley: University of California Press, 1999.

Yerushalmi, Yosef Hayim. *Zakhor: Jewish History and Jewish Memory*. Seattle: University of Washington Press, 1982.

Young, James E. "Between History and Memory: The Uncanny Voices of Historian and Survivor." *History and Memory* 9, no. 1 (1997): 47–58.

———. "Towards a Received History of the Holocaust." *History and Theory* 36, no. 4 (1997): 21–43.

Zinsser, William K. *On Writing Well: The Classic Guide to Writing Nonfiction*. New York: HarperPerennial, 1998.

Index

Books in the Life Writing Series
Published by Wilfrid Laurier University Press

The Water Lily Pond by Han Z. Li • 2004 / x + 254 pp. / ISBN 0-88920-431-4

The Life Writings of Mary Baker McQuesten: Victorian Matriarch edited by Mary J. Anderson • 2004 / xxii + 338 pp. / ISBN 0-88920-437-3

Seven Eggs Today: The Diaries of Mary Armstrong, 1859 and 1869 edited by Jackson W. Armstrong • 2004 / xvi + 228 pp. / ISBN 0-88920-440-3

Love and War in London: A Woman's Diary 1939–1942 by Olivia Cockett; edited by Robert W. Malcolmson • 2005 / xvi + 208 pp. / ISBN 0-88920-458-6

Incorrigible by Velma Demerson • 2004 / vi + 178 pp. / ISBN 0-88920-444-6

Auto/biography in Canada: Critical Directions edited by Julie Rak • 2005 / viii + 264 pp. / ISBN 0-88920-478-0

Tracing the Autobiographical edited by Marlene Kadar, Linda Warley, Jeanne Perreault, and Susanna Egan • 2005 / viii + 280 pp. / ISBN 0-88920-476-4

Must Write: Edna Staebler's Diaries edited by Christl Verduyn • 2005 / viii + 304 pp. / ISBN 0-88920-481-0

Food That Really Schmecks by Edna Staebler • 2007 / xxiv + 334 pp. / ISBN 978-0-88920-521-5

163256: A Memoir of Resistance by Michael Englishman • 2007 / xvi + 112 pp. (14 b&w photos) / ISBN 978-1-55458-009-5

The Wartime Letters of Leslie and Cecil Frost, 1915–1919 edited by R.B. Fleming • 2007 / xxxvi + 384 pp. (49 b&w photos, 5 maps) / ISBN 978-1-55458-000-2

Johanna Krause Twice Persecuted: Surviving in Nazi Germany and Communist East Germany by Carolyn Gammon and Christiane Hemker • 2007 / x + 170 pp. (58 b&w photos, 2 maps) / ISBN 978-1-55458-006-4

Watermelon Syrup: A Novel by Annie Jacobsen with Jane Finlay-Young and Di Brandt • 2007 / x + 268 pp. / ISBN 978-1-55458-005-7

Broad Is the Way: Stories from Mayerthorpe by Margaret Norquay • 2008 / x + 106 pp. (6 b&w photos) / ISBN 978-1-55458-020-0

Becoming My Mother's Daughter: A Story of Survival and Renewal by Erika Gottlieb • 2008 / x + 178 pp. (36 b&w illus., 17 colour) / ISBN 978-1-55458-030-9

Leaving Fundamentalism: Personal Stories edited by G. Elijah Dann • 2008 / xii + 234 pp. / ISBN 978-1-55458-026-2

Bearing Witness: Living with Ovarian Cancer edited by Kathryn Carter and Lauri Elit • 2009 / viii + 94 pp. / ISBN 978-1-55458-055-2

Dead Woman Pickney: A Memoir of Childhood in Jamaica by Yvonne Shorter Brown • 2010 / viii + 202 pp. / ISBN 978-1-55458-189-4

I Have a Story to Tell You by Seemah C. Berson • 2010 / xx + 288 pp. (24 b&w photos) / ISBN 978-1-55458-219-8

We All Giggled: A Bourgeois Family Memoir by Thomas O. Hueglin • 2010 / xiv + 232 pp. (20 b&w photos) / ISBN 978-1-55458-262-4

Burdens of Proof: Faith, Doubt, and Identity in Autobiography by Susanna Egan • 2011 / x + 200 pp. / ISBN 978-1-55458-332-4